Commitment, Value,
and Moral Realism

Despite the importance of commitment in moral and political philosophy, there has hitherto been little extended analysis of it. Marcel Lieberman examines the conditions under which commitment is possible, and offers at the same time an indirect argument for moral realism. He argues that realist evaluative beliefs are functionally required for commitment – especially regarding its role in self-understanding – and since it is only within a realist framework that such beliefs make sense, realism about values is a condition for the possibility of commitment itself. His ambitious study addresses questions that are of great interest to analytic philosophers but also makes many connections with continental philosophy and with folk psychology, sociology, and cognitive science, and will be seen as a novel and distinctive intervention in the debate about moral realism.

MARCEL LIEBERMAN has held research fellowships at Stanford University, the Université Catholique de Louvain, and the Centre de Recherche en Epistémologie Appliquée (CREA), Paris.

CAMBRIDGE STUDIES IN PHILOSOPHY

General editor ERNEST SOSA

RECENT TITLES

WILLIAM G. LYCAN   *Judgement and justification*
GERALD DWORKIN   *The theory and practice of autonomy*
MICHAEL TYE   *The metaphysics of mind*
DAVID O. BRINK   *Moral realism and the foundations of ethics*
W. D. HART   *Engines of the soul*
PAUL K. MOSER   *Knowledge and evidence*
D. M. ARMSTRONG   *A combinatorial theory of possibility*
JOHN BISHOP   *Natural agency*
CHRISTOPHER J. MALONEY   *The mundane matter of the mental language*
MARK RICHARD   *Propositional attitudes*
GERALD E. GAUS   *Value and justification*
MARK HELLER   *The ontology of physical objects*
JOHN BIGELOW & ROBERT PARGETTER   *Science and necessity*
FRANCIS SNARE   *Morals, motivation and convention*
CHRISTOPHER S. HILL   *Sensations*
JOHN HEIL   *The nature of true minds*
CARL GINET   *On action*
CONRAD JOHNSON   *Moral legislation*
DAVID OWENS   *Causes and coincidences*
ANDREW NEWMAN   *The physical basis of predication*
MICHAEL JUBIEN   *Ontology, modality and the fallacy of reference*
WARREN QUINN   *Morality and action*
JOHN W. CARROLL   *Laws of nature*
M. J. CRESSWELL   *Language in the world*
JOSHUA HOFFMAN & GARY S. ROSENKRANTZ   *Substance among other categories*
PAUL HELM   *Belief policies*
NOAH LEMOS   *Intrinsic value*
LYNNE RUDDER BAKER   *Explaining attitudes*
HENRY S. RICHARDSON   *Practical reasoning about final ends*
ROBERT A. WILSON   *Cartesian psychology and physical minds*
BARRY MAUND   *Colours*
MICHAEL DEVITT   *Coming to our senses*
SYDNEY SHOEMAKER   *The first-person perspective and other essays*
MICHAEL STOCKER   *Valuing emotions*
ARDA DENKEL   *Object and property*
E. J. LOWE   *Subjects of experience*
NORTON NELKIN   *Consciousness and the origins of thought*
PIERRE JACOB   *What minds can do*
ANDRE GALLOIS   *The world without, the mind within*
D. M. ARMSTRONG   *A world of states of affairs*
DAVID COCKBURN   *Other times*
MARK LANCE & JOHN O'LEARY-HAWTHORNE   *The grammar of meaning*
ANNETTE BARNES   *Seeing through self-deception*

Commitment, Value, and Moral Realism

Marcel S. Lieberman

CAMBRIDGE
UNIVERSITY PRESS

PUBLISHED BY THE PRESS SYNDICATE OF THE UNIVERSITY OF CAMBRIDGE
The Pitt Building, Trumpington Street, Cambridge CB2 1RP, United Kingdom

CAMBRIDGE UNIVERSITY PRESS
The Edinburgh Building, Cambridge CB2 2RU, United Kingdom
40 West 20th Street, New York, NY 10011-4211, USA
10 Stamford Road, Oakleigh, Melbourne 3166, Australia

First published 1998

Printed in the United Kingdom at the University Press, Cambridge

Typeset in 10.5/12pt Bembo   [SE]

A catalogue record for this book is available from the British Library

Library of Congress cataloguing in publication data

Lieberman, Marcel S.
Commitment, Value, and Moral Realism/Marcel S. Lieberman.
p.   cm. – (Cambridge Studies in Philosophy)
Includes bibliographical references and index.
ISBN 0 521 63111 4 (hardback)
1. Ethics.   2. Realism.   3. Commitment (Psychology)   I. Title.
II. Series.
BJ1012.L49   1998   170–dc21   97-41740 CIP

ISBN 0 521 63111 4 hardback

To my father

Contents

Acknowledgments		*page* xi
1	Introduction	1
2	The challengers: Allan Gibbard and Richard Rorty	6
3	Commitment and intention	57
4	Commitment and belief	88
5	Self-conception and substantive commitments	134
6	Conclusion	183
Bibliography		199
Index		208

Acknowledgments

A number of people have played an important role in the writing of this book, and without their help and support it might never have been completed. Rachel Cohon, Michael Bratman, and Timothy Jackson all read (and reread) early versions of the text in one form or another, and patiently provided comments and criticisms.

Most of the revisions of the material took place while I was a Chateaubriand Fellow at the Centre de Recherche en Epistémologie Appliquée, at the Ecole Polytechnique. I wish to thank Jean-Pierre Dupuy for kindly welcoming me to CREA and making its resources available to me, as well as the Services Culturels Français who made possible my stay in Paris. The researchers and graduate students at CREA are a dynamic mix of philosophers, anthropologists, economists, and cognitive scientists, among others, who show the immense value of not respecting disciplinary boundaries.

For their friendship, patience, and indulgence in listening to my philosophical worries and questions over the years – questions I think we all have, but about which few philosophers venture to write – I am grateful to Shirley Collins, David Porter, and Tom Andersson. But had it not been for P. J. Ivanhoe's continued encouragement, enthusiasm, and support, both intellectual and moral, from the very beginning of this project, I have no doubt that it would not have been realized.

Finally, there are two very special and very extraordinary people for whom a simple "thank you" is grossly insufficient, but I find myself at a loss to say in a few words how much they have helped me, not just in writing this book, but in the bigger scheme of things. To my brother, Erik Gregory, and to Alberta Milone, thanks.

1

Introduction

I.I COMMITMENT, VALUE, AND MORAL REALISM

In recent years the debates in metaethics over moral realism have been dominated by arguments from the philosophy of science, epistemology, and the philosophy of language.[1] The goal of the present book is to introduce a new voice into the debate as well as a new approach. Rather than directly addressing the question of whether or not moral realism is true, that is, whether moral judgments do indeed represent subject-independent facts, I propose to ask a question which has been forgotten in these discussions, namely, what is at stake in the truth of moral realism? and in doing so to bring in action theory as an active participant in the debate.[2] I examine whether the truth of moral realism makes what one might call a "practical" difference, that is, a difference not just in our ability to explain, but also to retain certain ordinary, moral *experiences*. To this end, I focus on commitment.

1.1.1 The hypothesis

The central claim is the following: in order to explain commitment and in order for an individual's commitment to remain stable over

[1] In the philosophy of science the question includes whether moral facts figure in our best *causal* explanations (Gilbert Harman and Nicholas Sturgeon) and whether they are more like secondary qualities (John McDowell); in epistemology the problem is to explain how moral knowledge is possible (David Brink); and in the philosophy of language the classical question has been whether moral judgments are the kinds of judgments capable of expressing truth or falsity (R. M. Hare, C. S. Stevenson, Mary Forrester, Mark Platts).

[2] Nicholas Sturgeon is the most recent philosopher to pose a similar question. He focuses, however, on the question of whether the truth of moral realism makes a difference in explanations of the possibility of amoral agents, moral disagreement, and moral fallibility. See "What Difference Does it Make Whether Moral Realism is True?" *Southern Journal of Philosophy*, Supplement 24 (1986): 115–42.

time and to fulfill its roles in the governance of action, enhancement of self-understanding, and constitution of identity, one must assume the truth of moral realism and so make room for the possibility of moral facts. I thus seek to provide an analysis of commitment and the conditions under which it is possible, and in so doing to offer at the same time an *indirect* argument for moral realism – the view that moral judgments represent subject-independent facts. For I argue that realist evaluative beliefs are functionally required for commitment, and since it is only within a realist framework that such beliefs make sense, realism about values is a condition for the possibility of commitment itself. Thus, rather than seeking to defend moral realism, as others have done, on epistemological, metaphysical, or linguistic grounds, I seek to show how one very important feature of our experience can only be explained and retained on the assumption of moral realism. Although it is still possible for others to reject realism in ethics, one cannot do so and retain commitment at the same time. In other words, the price one pays for being an antirealist in ethics is the value we place on commitment.

1.1.2 Moral realism defined

The realism underlying the position I defend is intended to be a very modest one. The temptation to interpret the claims of moral realism in strong ontological or metaphysical terms needs to be avoided, since this leads to precisely the wrong set of questions that are repeatedly posed by noncognitivists and antirealists regarding, for example, the "queerness" of moral facts and properties,[3] how or where we find them, and the causal connection between the observation of such facts and moral judgments.

The position I defend is both cognitivist and realist. When one says, "Doing X is wrong," one is expressing a belief one takes to be true in virtue of a certain objective matter of fact. Now this fact is "objective" to the extent that it is independent of any particular standpoint, that is, independent of the speaker's particular desires, attitudes, and beliefs.[4] These facts will concern the way the world is and the way

---

[3] Ever since Mackie's charge of queerness, moral realists have felt compelled, unfortunately, to follow his strong metaphysical reading of realism.

[4] It is important to see that this is not a strong ontological claim. The kind of realism I propose is best described as a realism about truth which grants independent authority

human beings are. As Peter Railton states, the moral facts at issue "need be grounded in nothing more transcendental than facts about man and his environment, facts about what sorts of things matter to us, and how the ways we live affect these things."[5] Rather than examining the standard metaphysical or epistemological issues, I want to focus on a more practical, and what I take to be a prior, question regarding what is at stake in the acceptance or rejection of realism in ethics.

I.2 WHY COMMITMENT?

Our commitments to certain principles, persons, or ideals, or one's solidarity to certain groups and communities, are widely thought to be an important part of our ordinary experience as individuals. The importance of commitment to our self-conceptions as moral agents seems to be shared by moral realists and antirealists alike: from writers such as Gabriel Marcel and Charles Taylor, to J. L. Mackie, Richard Rorty, and Allan Gibbard. Despite this agreement over the importance of commitment, there is sharp disagreement over what commitment requires. While Marcel and Taylor claim that commitments are ultimately grounded in universal and transcendent values,[6] antirealists and noncognitivists clearly disagree. They assert, as J. L. Mackie does, that a person "could hold strong moral views . . . while believing that they were simply attitudes and policies with regard to conduct that he and other people held."[7] Some go on to suggest, like Richard Rorty, that one can fully accept that the grounds of one's values are purely "subjective," or even that all of one's moral beliefs are false (since they fail to represent anything), and still remain committed to these values

to our moral judgments. Tim Jackson calls this "alethiological" realism. See "The Theory and Practice of Discomfort: Richard Rorty and Pragmatism," *The Thomist* 51(1987): 270–98. On the nonmysterious, nonmetaphysical basis of moral realism, see Stuart Hampshire, *Innocence and Experience* (Cambridge, MA: Harvard University Press, 1989), p. 90.

[5] P. Railton, "Moral Realism," *The Philosophical Review* 95 (1986):163–207.

[6] See Gabriel Marcel, *Homo Viator* (Paris: Aubier, 1945), pp. 34, 197–8 (henceforth, *HV*); Charles Taylor, *Sources of the Self* (Cambridge, MA: Harvard University Press, 1989), pp. 27, 99, 507. (henceforth, *SS*).

[7] J. L. Mackie, *Ethics: Inventing Right and Wrong* (New York, Penguin Books, 1977), p. 16.

and beliefs, and be willing to act on them.[8] Yet these assertions on the part of both realists and antirealists remain just that – assertions with little or no argument to support them.[9]

If, however, by examining the structure of commitment and its requirements one were able to show that moral realism was the only metaethical position compatible with commitment and the only one capable of explaining its possibility, this would force its opponents either to concede the untenability of antirealism in ethics, or to relinquish the importance they place on commitment.

I.3 COMMITMENT AND ITS FEATURES

The term "commitment" is used in a variety of ways and contexts. The kind of commitment I am ultimately interested in examining, however, is the commitment one has to political causes, for example, or to moral principles, ideals, and even other persons.

Within this general category of commitment there is obviously a great deal of variation: from the very ordinary, like being committed to carrying out a certain plan, to the more complex such as a commit-

---

[8] Rorty actually says: "a belief can still regulate action, can still be thought worth dying for, among people who are quite aware that this belief is caused by nothing deeper than contingent historical circumstance": R. Rorty, *Contingency, Irony and Solidarity* (Cambridge: Cambridge University Press, 1989), p. 189 (henceforth, *CIS*). There are two ways of reading this: in the first case, one can admit a belief is caused by "contingent historical circumstance" and still assert it is true – true beliefs can have contingent origins; the second reading falls prey to the genetic fallacy and denies truth to any such beliefs. My criticism is directed toward the second stronger claim Rorty seems to be making that no truth attaches to these beliefs, that we recognize this, *and still find them worth dying for.*

[9] Although my interest in commitment is related primarily to moral realism, the importance of the topic extends beyond the limits of metaethics and moral philosophy. Importantly, the analysis of commitment in these other fields is just as undeveloped as in ethics. For discussions in political philosophy, see Charles Taylor, "Atomism," in *Philosophy and the Human Sciences: Philosophical Papers*, vol. II (Cambridge: Cambridge University Press, 1985), pp. 185–210 (henceforth, *PHS*), and Allen Buchanan, "Assessing the Communitarian Critique of Liberalism" *Ethics* 99 (1989): 866–7. In action theory, see S. I. Benn and G. F. Gaus, "Practical Rationality and Commitment," *American Philosophical Quarterly* 23 (1986): 256. For discussions on commitment in sociology, see Howard S. Becker, "Notes on the Concept of Commitment," *American Journal of Sociology* 64 (1960): 32; James V. Downton, Jr., "The Determinants of Commitment," *Humanitas* 8 (1972); and Sidney M. Jouard, "Some Notes on the Experience of Commitment," *Humanitas* 8 (1972).

ment to becoming a doctor, or a commitment to moral and political ideals. The first kind of commitment, which might be thought of as a steadfast determination in the sense that one has settled upon one course of action and is determined to see it through, belongs to what I will call the "intention-like" commitments. The other type of commitment I shall label "substantive" commitments. It is to these two subgroups of commitments – the substantive and the intention-like – that the arguments and focus of the subsequent chapters will turn.[10]

Drawing on our own common-sense understanding of commitment, as well as some of the literature in psychology and philosophy, we can define three central features of commitment:

1. its stability over time and its capacity to be revised and reconsidered;[11]
2. its action-guiding force;[12]
3. its relation to self-understanding and identity.[13]

I will argue that if one accepts this description of commitment and its roles, then one must also accept the theory that best explains how commitment functions the way it does. And if it turns out that the best explanation incorporates moral realism, then one must either accept moral realism (as a condition for the possibility of commitment), or reject commitment altogether.

---

[10] I leave aside what one might call the promissory commitments, i.e., commitments which can be viewed as obligations.

[11] See Jill Novacek and Richard S. Lazarus, "The Structure of Personal Commitments" *Journal of Personality* 58 (1990): 695–6; Gabriel Marcel, *Etre et Avoir* (Paris: Aubier, 1935), pp. 56–7 (henceforth *EA*); *Du Refus à l'Invocation* (Paris: Gallimard, 1940), p. 211 (henceforth *RI*); *HV*, p. 34; *Présence et Immortalité* (Paris: Flammarion, 1959). (henceforth *PI*) See also Peter Kemp, *Théorie de l'Engagement: Pathétique de l'Engagement* (Paris: Seuil, 1972).

[12] See Stan Van Hooft, "Obligation, Character, and Commitment," *Philosophy* 63 (1988): 345–62; Roger Trigg, *Reason and Commitment* (Cambridge: Cambridge University Press, 1973), p. 44; and Bruce Buchanan II, "Building Organizational Commitment: The Socialization of Managers in Work Organizations," *Administrative Science Quarterly* (1974): 533. See also Novacek and Lazarus, "The Structure,", 695–6.

[13] See Charles Taylor, *SS*, pp. 19, 27; Gabriel Marcel, *EA* p.74; *RI*, p.154; *HV*, pp. 197–8, 217; Peter Kemp, *Théorie*, p. 171; Charles O'Reilly III and Jennifer Chatman, "Organizational Commitment and Psychological Attachment: The Effects of Compliance, Identification, and Internalization on Prosocial Behavior," *Journal of Applied Psychology* 71 (1986): 492–9.

2

The challengers: Allan Gibbard and Richard Rorty

2.1 INTRODUCTION

The position I want to defend is (a) cognitivist since it takes moral beliefs to be part of our commitments and so views them as being more than mere expressions of sentiments or feelings, and (b) (moderately) realist since these beliefs purport to represent facts of the matter, and are viewed by the agent as doing so. Clearly, my position could be challenged in two ways: either by denying that commitments incorporate beliefs, and so by implication that moral judgments involve beliefs (since such commitments, I say, include judgments regarding what is right, valuable, or good) – the noncognitivist challenge; or by denying that commitments involve these kinds of beliefs since there are no moral facts for them to represent, i.e., not only are such beliefs unnecessary for commitment, but they lack any content – the challenge from antirealism. Allan Gibbard[1] poses the first challenge with his noncognitivist theory of rationality and normative judgments, while Richard Rorty[2] poses the second in his notion of "irony" which forms part of his more general neopragmatist (and what he calls "antirepresentationalist") position.

Although Gibbard and Rorty approach the question of moral realism from two radically different orientations – the former stays and operates within the standard philosophical categories and methods, while the latter seeks to overcome these – they share an assumption common to all noncognitivists and irrealists in ethics, namely, the separability of theory from practice. One has the impression that the theories they propose are only (potentially) successful at giving an alternative explanation of our moral practices on condition that these theories either do not become common knowledge or are

---

[1] A. Gibbard, *Wise Choices, Apt Feeling: A Theory of Normative Judgment* (Cambridge, MA: Harvard University Press, 1990).   [2] *CIS.*

6

forgotten as they are developed. The problem they face, I suggest, is to explain and retain our ordinary moral experience *in light of the theoretical principles* they propose: to combine theory and practice by offering a complete explanation of what it is we do and how within the context of the theory *and with a shared knowledge of it*. There is the suspicion that the plausibility of their theories rests on what has variously been described as "theoretical akrasia," "intellectual schizophrenia," and "two-level thinking":[3] they allow and participate in, as Hilary Putnam says, "first-level" realist talk about, for example, the wrongness of slavery, but then deny "the objectivity of [their] own first-level talk when [they come] to comment philosophically on this talk" (Putnam, *Realism*, p. 147).[4] Although the typical response of noncognitivists and irrealists to this "practical" inconsistency is to distinguish the logical from the psychological possibility of their position, invoking the former as the only constraint they need to respect, I want to see if the latter can be used as a limit to theory formation as well by more carefully examining the structure and dynamics of such psychological states as commitment.[5] Such a test is not, in fact, so foreign to the discipline; both Allan Gibbard and Richard Rorty accept it as a real challenge to their positions. Rorty recognizes that one of the main objections to his theory is that "it is psychologically impossible to be a liberal ironist – to be someone for whom 'cruelty is the worst thing we do,' and to have no metaphysical beliefs about what all human beings have in common" (*CIS*, p. 85), and goes on, unsuccessfully I argue, to dispel that worry. Allan

---

[3] Renford Bambrough, *Moral Scepticism and Moral Knowledge* (New Jersey: Humanities Press, 1979); Hillary Putnam, *Realism with a Human Face* (Cambridge, MA: Harvard University Press, 1990), p. 147.

[4] David McNaughton also notes a similar split. "Non-cognitivism," he says, "invites us to stand outside our own evaluative commitments and recognize that, from this external standpoint, nothing is intrinsically valuable, for values are no part of the real world but are created or invented by us." Yet, noncognitivists and irrealists still claim to be able to make sense, and maintain the possibility, of commitments to moral ideals. D. McNaughton, *Moral Vision: An Introduction to Ethics*, (New York: Basil Blackwell, 1988), p. 12.

[5] Compare this with Owen Flanagan's thesis of minimal psychological realism in *Varieties of Moral Personality: Ethics and Psychological Realism* (Cambridge, MA: Harvard University Press, 1991). The principle states: "Make sure when constructing a moral theory or projecting a moral ideal that the character, decision processing, and behavior prescribed are possible, or are perceived to be possible, for creatures like us" (p. 32).

Gibbard spends considerable time trying to give a negative answer to the question of whether his theory of norm-expressivism does in fact miss something in ordinary normative talk (Gibbard, *Wise Choices*, p. 154). While this is a different question from the one regarding psychological possibility, Gibbard extends it in that direction by claiming that his noncognitivist theory, i.e., norm-expressivism, also adequately explains and describes our ordinary, normative practices.

In the sections that follow I shall examine some of the arguments of Rorty and Gibbard against moral realism and cognitivism using the following questions as a guide: (1) do they offer a psychologically plausible story (given the dynamic of certain mental states such as commitment)? and (2) do they miss something in ordinary normative talk and practice? The goal is both to underscore, once again, the centrality of the question of commitment in the debates on moral realism, and to locate the main points of contention regarding commitment in order to foreshadow the direction of the arguments in subsequent chapters.

Before beginning the main arguments of this chapter, I want first to turn to an actual example to help put in context the arguments that follow. This will, I expect, provide an intuitive test by which one can assess the plausibility of Rorty's and Gibbard's theories. The example is taken from the biography of Eugene Debs.

2.1.1 Eugene V. Debs

The son of French immigrants, Eugene V. Debs was born in Kansas in 1855. A bright student, he left school at the age of thirteen to help support his family, first working as a paint scraper and later as a railway worker, where he saw first hand the toll that late nineteenth-century industrial capitalism exacted from wage laborers, who worked in dangerous conditions, with no benefits, for wages well below what was needed to live. It was this early exposure to their hardships that served as a catalyst for his later embrace of socialism and activism on behalf of workers' rights.

Debs's legacy to the American labor movement is remarkable. He secured the right to organize and strike, seeing this as the only effective tool against the much more powerful corporations. He obtained safer working conditions, higher wages, and welfare benefits, and fought fiercely for a minimum wage. Debs also came to the defense of women's rights, supported the equal treatment of blacks, denounced the Ku Klux Klan, white supremacy, and the sexual exploitation of black women by white men, all at a time when having such views was not only highly unpopular, but also potentially life threatening. He was a man of great charisma – a highly motivating speaker who drew people by the tens of thousands to hear his simple messages of harmony, justice, and equality.

Eugene Debs, however, was also a man of his times and a product of his culture. He was known to criticize immigrant Italians as the "dagos [who] work for small pay, and live far more like a savage or a wild beast, than the Chinese."[6] He could be "vain and egocentric," and was often "impressed with his prominence": traits which could at times cloud his judgment (Salvatore, *Eugene V. Debs*, p. 95). Though married, he spent little time with his wife and preferred the company of his mistress. In short, Eugene Debs was a very human hero: while progressive and clearly ahead of his times in some areas, he was obviously short-sighted in others. But, unlike other characters often used as examples of people of conviction and dedication, who made great sacrifices for a principle – Mother Theresa and Mahatma Gandhi are usually mentioned – Eugene Debs is accessible. Moreover, he was not a zealot who sought to realize some religious utopic ideal on earth. In fact, he had a powerful distaste for organized religion; whatever else his motivations were, they were not religious fervor.[7] While he was no saint, he was certainly an extraordinary individual, but one who is within reach of the understanding of flawed, worldly, less-than-saintly readers. For this reason, the life of Eugene Debs provides useful material for the study of commitment.

I mentioned briefly above some of the contributions Debs made in the American labor movement and toward the recognition of the rights of women and blacks. It is important to note that these contributions were bought at a high personal cost, and with the threat of considerable personal risk. Indeed, it is through such risk that we can describe him as being committed to the principles he advocated.

Although initially critical of immigrant labor, he later came to see

---

[6] Quoted in Nick Salvatore, *Eugene V. Debs: Citizen and Socialist* (Chicago: University of Illinois Press, 1982), p. 104.

[7] From an early age and throughout his adult life, Debs opposed organized religion. See Bernard J. Brommel, *Eugene V. Debs: Spokesman for Labor and Socialism* (Chicago: Charles H. Kerr Publishing Co., 1978), pp. 14, 15; and Salvatore, *Eugene V. Debs*, p. 103.

the "hue and cry against the 'foreign pauper immigrants' . . . as the work of the same capitalists who enticed them to America in the first place" (Salvatore, *Eugene V. Debs*, p. 105), and wrote against immigrant restrictions and discrimination, saying that such disputes only divided labor's ranks, to the benefit of business. As a result, he was "threatened with assassination, and accused of pro-Catholic sympathies" (*ibid.*, p. 106). In an era of "mad, patriotic conformity" (*ibid.*, p. 292) in which the "press . . . supported management and inflamed public opinion against leaders of strikes . . . [and] anti-war speakers" (Brommel, *Eugene V. Debs*, p. 210), Debs remained undeterred in speaking out against America's involvement in Cuba, the Philippines, and W.W.I, as well as organized labor's treatment of immigrant workers. Even after the passage of the Espionage Act of 1917 which made speaking out against America's war effort punishable by imprisonment, Debs continued to do so (Salvatore, *Eugene V. Debs*, p. 291).

The risks he and others faced, however, were more than loss of freedom, but also loss of life. Salvatore describes the range of risks individuals took for the right to organize and strike:

> With a thoroughness [Debs] never anticipated, federal marshals corralled radicals of every nationality, faction, and ideological persuasion, and US district attorneys freely interpreted a vague Espionage Act, passed in 1917, to win indictments and convictions on charges of treason and antiwar activity. Not to be outdone, local patriots in the Arizona mining community of Bisbee . . . "captured" over 1200 IWW copper miners, the majority of whom were American-born citizens, loaded them into cattle cars with minimal provisions, and deported them into the New Mexico desert. In Butte, Montana, during the same summer of 1917, Frank Little, an antiwar IWW organizer, was dragged from his bed, tortured, and then lynched by local vigilantes . . . Closer to [Debs's] home, the Vigo County Council for Defense caused the discharge of a Terre Haute schoolteacher for her Socialist party membership, attacked German-Americans on the streets of Debs's "beloved little community," and invaded private homes to commandeer and then burn publicly all German language books. In that community where "all were neighbors and all friends," a Socialist coal miner was lynched for refusing to buy a Liberty Bond (*ibid.*, p. 288).

Real people took on real risks. There should be no question of Debs's commitment to his political causes. What we want to know is in what this commitment consisted.

2.1.2 Irony, norm-expressivism, and the possibility of commitment

On a first examination of Debs's understanding of his commitments, and the description of how he came to have them, we see a disconcerting fit with what Rorty will define as the liberal ironist, and his nonessentialist neopragmatism. Like the liberal ironist who avoids theory-building, Debs "was not a theoretician. He was innocent of subtlety, and ignorant of logic. He spoke from the heart rather than the head" (Brommel, *Eugene V. Debs*, p. 208), and "rather than rely on documents and figures, Debs based the strength of his arguments upon the experiences that he had had and the accounts others related to him" (*ibid.*, p. 203). Moreover, Debs did not appeal to philosophy or biblical scripture to support his "arguments" since they were not the source of his ideas – ideas which instead were incubated in literature and brought to life through experience. As Brommel states, "Debs's early experiences provided the material for his ideas on labor, socialism, and war . . . [as did his] avid reading of [Victor] Hugo's accounts of war, poverty, and revolution" (*ibid.*, p. 219). Debs had the gift of persuasion and "believed that anyone who upheld [the same] ideas could further labor's cause *by speaking on behalf of them*" (*ibid.*, emphasis added). Truly, he was a pragmatist after Rorty's own heart – rhetoric, not theory, was apparently the key to success, and literature, not philosophy, was the source of inspiration.

More worrying for my thesis is the Gibbardian account, as we will see, of his participation in his community's normative practices, and how this gave rise to his own normative judgments and acceptance of certain fundamental values and concepts such as "manhood." Thus Salvatore states:

> the conjunction of personal identity and public position, the definition of worth in terms of performance of duties and responsibilities in society, was the core of Terre Haute's expressed values. *Manhood was defined in public fashion, through one's actions as a citizen, a member of a specific community, and as a producer of value for one's family and the community and in one's personal relations with others.* Manhood found its clearest expression within a very small personal circle . . . The very concept of manhood hinged on the ability of any given individual to assume in his localized social group personal responsibility for his deeds (p. 19, emphasis added).

11

It seems that his values developed and were accepted by him because of the good they did for a specific community – Terre Haute in the late nineteenth century – and their ability to enhance cohesion within that community, and yet they seemingly did so without any explicit grounding in "truth," or in their ability to capture "the way things really are." In Debs's case, we seem to have a perfect example of Gibbard's theory of normative influence and the "organic" emergence of norms. At first glance, the biography of Eugene Debs seems to offer a strong case for, rather than against, neopragmatism and non-cognitivism. Yet if we take a closer look at some of the details, we will see where these models begin to fall apart. But first let me lay out the main arguments of Rorty and Gibbard.

2.2 ALLAN GIBBARD'S NORM-EXPRESSIVISM

2.2.1 *Introduction*

The first challenge to my position comes in the form of Allan Gibbard's theory of norm-expressivism which claims that to call something rational is to express one's acceptance of norms that permit it (Gibbard, *Wise Choices*, p. 7). Since moral judgments are, according to Gibbard, judgments about what moral feelings it is rational to have (*ibid.*, p. 6), his theory is not only a noncognitivist one about rationality, but about morality as well: the terms "rational" and "moral" are only expressive and not descriptive since they do not pick out any specific property. In Gibbard's theory, then, something is morally wrong if and only if it is rational for one to feel guilty for performing some action, or for another to resent one for doing it (*ibid.*, p. 42). But since calling something rational only expresses one's acceptance of certain norms, to call something morally wrong expresses one's acceptance of norms that associate guilt and resentment with certain actions. The meaning of normative terms, according to this view, is given by saying what states of mind they express. Gibbard's aim is to explain our normative judgments and practices without referring to normative facts.

The initial justification and motivation for a noncognitivist approach (ostensibly) is that it better captures what it is we do when we make normative judgments; for example, it is better able to explain the element of endorsement in normative judgments for which, says

Gibbard, descriptive analyses cannot account (*ibid.*, p. 10). Clearly, the test Gibbard appeals to in adjudicating between rival theories is which one is able to make better sense of our practices and explain our ordinary experience, which explains his concern to show, for example, that norm-expressivism does not "miss something in ordinary claims to objectivity" (p. 154), or, more broadly, in ordinary normative talk. It will be important to see whether his noncognitivist theory is in fact able to meet this challenge, or whether it leaves wholly mysterious certain aspects of our "ordinary" experience.

Gibbard presents a formidable challenge to anyone seeking to defend moral realism. The noncognitivist story he tells about our moral practices and moral judgments shifts the burden of proof not only to those who would support a cognitivist account of moral judgments and beliefs, but also to those who insist there is a distinctive class of facts to which our moral and normative judgments correspond. Beginning with the claim that the key to our moral nature is coordination (p. 27), Gibbard goes on to construct an account of our normative life, of the source and authority of normative judgments, that makes no reference to normative facts to which our normative capacities are typically thought to respond (p. 107). Echoing a line of thought from Gilbert Harman,[8] Gibbard makes the stronger claim that even if there were normative facts, they would play no explanatory role (p. 121). Clearly, these are fighting words for any moral realist. My aim, however, is not to take on the challenge directly, as others have done,[9] but instead to offer a more specific critique of his work in relation to my examination of commitment, and in so doing to try once again to shift, or at least ease, the burden of proof he places on moral realists. To this end I focus primarily on his accounts of normative objectivity and commitment, and bring into question whether noncognitivism is in fact capable of offering the best explanation of our moral practices. In the remainder of this chapter I do not offer a final refutation of Gibbard's position, since the tools I need to do this will be developed

[8] G. Harman, *The Nature of Morality* (New York: Oxford University Press, 1977).

[9] See, Nicholas Sturgeon, "Gibbard on Moral Judgment and Norms," *Ethics* 96 (1985): 22–33, as well as "Nonmoral Explanations," in James Tomberlin (ed.), *Philosophical Perspectives* vol. VI: *Ethics* (Atascadero: Ridgeview, 1992), pp. 97–117; and Peter Railton, "Nonfactualism about Normative Discourse," *Philosophy and Phenomenological Research* 52 (1992): 961–8

in the course of the discussion. Rather, I try to locate the gaps in his argument and analysis of ordinary normative practice and suggest that these gaps are best filled by a cognitivist–realist account of commitment.

2.2.2 Norm acceptance and commitment

Between Gibbard's system of normative control and what I have described as the state of being committed or having commitment, there seems to be considerable overlap in a number of areas. First, to accept a norm, says Gibbard, is "to be disposed to avow it in unconstrained normative discussion" (p. 74) and the state of accepting a norm "is identified by its place in a syndrome of tendencies toward *action and avowal*" (p. 75, emphasis added). Now a disposition to action is one of the central elements in my account of commitment – indeed, one factor that provides the basis for a later comparison of commitment with intention. Commitment as described by others also bears a striking similarity to norms. In his discussion of intention and commitment, Robert Audi states that in intending to do something one is also committed to doing it in the sense that "one is in a state of overall inclination . . . [and one is] disposed to assert that [one] will perform it."[10] Commitments and norms involve dispositions to action and avowal. Second, commitment and norms permit coordination,[11] which is, according to Gibbard, why systems of normative control were naturally selected (p. 64). And, third, commitments and norms help us to make sense of what we are doing: "We experience our lives in normative terms, in terms of things it makes sense to do, to think, and to feel" (p. 8). Similarly, says Gibbard, "[t]he important thing about norms . . . is the sense of meaning in life that comes from accepting them" (p. 216). This seems to reflect one of the central features of commitment, namely, its role in self-understanding in both the mundane sense of helping one understand *what* one is doing, and in the richer sense of infusing life with meaning, of helping one understand *why* – in a profound sense – one is doing what one is doing.

---

[10] Robert Audi, "Intention, Cognitive Commitment, and Planning," *Synthese* 86 (1991): 364.

[11] Through commitment it makes it easier to plan one's own future actions, as well as for others to make plans based on one's commitment.

2.2.3 Commitment, self-understanding, and identity

Because my criticisms of Gibbard and Rorty will rely in part on the relation of commitment to self-understanding and identity, I should at this point say more about what this relation is.

The above division of self-understanding between a mundane and profound sense reflects two views of self-understanding found in David Velleman's and Charles Taylor's works. Self-understanding and the "intellectual desire" to make sense of oneself to oneself figure prominently in Velleman's *Practical Reflection*. Velleman distinguishes between self-awareness, which involves only prima-facie descriptions of one's conduct – revealing the "what" of one's actions – and self-understanding, which he defines as an "interpretive or explanatory" description of one's conduct – revealing the "why" of one's actions (Velleman, *Practical Reflection*, pp. 15–16). Velleman develops his arguments on the thought that there is an "intimate connection between self-knowledge and the nature of agency" (*ibid.*, p. 18). Like Charles Taylor, Velleman sees the desire for self-understanding (as self-interpretation) and the quest for self-knowledge as constitutive parts of human agency (p. 207). What is important for my purposes is that the self-understanding which is operative in Velleman's account is more than a description of one's actions, but takes the form of an explanation and, as just mentioned, an *interpretation*. We thus seek to know not just what it is we are doing, but to understand our behavior in terms of the motives underlying it (pp. 25, 27).

According to Velleman, the desire for self-understanding plays an important role: when one cannot think of why one is doing what one is doing, this desire "restrains" one from doing it (p. 27). The response toward this kind of reflective puzzlement over our actions, instead of always restraining action, can also take the form of self-inquiry – one asks oneself, "What am I doing?" In either case, says Velleman, both responses manifest a desire to know what one is doing.[12] Self-understanding, says Velleman, derives from one's ability

---

[12] Velleman acknowledges that we are not ceaselessly seeking reflective insight and actively avoiding reflective puzzlement. Rather, this intellectual desire should be understood as a "guiding desire" which, although not in the foreground of our deliberations or thoughts, still has directive control, like the desire to avoid pain (p. 35). It is in this sense that we have such a desire, and it becomes more acutely manifest when we realize that we do not know the motives for the action we are currently performing.

to explain what one is doing (p. 47) and, more importantly, has motivational effects. Thus, if we take self-understanding as meaning a general awareness of one's motives, then to the extent that commitments make these manifest we can say they enhance self-understanding by bringing to our attention what these motives are. To realize or fulfill a commitment often requires one to overcome certain obstacles or to renounce various temptations and, depending on how formidable the obstacles or how inviting the temptations are, one will be led (or forced) to reflect upon, reconsider, evaluate, and perhaps more clearly articulate to oneself one's motives for forming or sustaining the commitment.

Charles Taylor, however, develops the "profound" sense of self-understanding – a form of self-understanding which enables us to develop coherent stories of our lives and provides us with an orientation according to which we can pursue goals. For Taylor, forming commitments is a necessary part of being a full human agent: it is on the basis of one's commitments that one develops the "frameworks" of meaning which are essential to human agents for making sense of their lives (*SS*, pp. 19, 27), since such frameworks allow one "to determine from case to case what is good, or valuable, or what ought to be done" (*SS*, p. 27). In other words, commitments provide certain fixed points around which a framework can be developed that allows one to rank and also evaluate one's different goals, motives and perhaps even values. In so far as this framework helps one make sense, or understand, one's actions and beliefs, and since this framework depends upon one's commitments, we can say that commitment, too, is related to self-understanding.

Thus, whether we seek self-understanding, that is, seek to "make sense" of ourselves in Velleman's mundane sense of trying to make sense of our actions and behavior, or in Taylor's profound sense of making sense of the ensemble of one's actions and behavior – of one's life – we can see how self-understanding and commitment are related.

The relation between commitment and identity should be fairly clear. As seen in the biography of Debs, and in our own experience, the way we identify ourselves to ourselves as well as to others is often through our commitments. Borrowing a distinction from Paul Ricoeur between two senses of identity – namely, *idem* identity, by which is understood sameness and permanence through time, and *ipse* identity, which refers to the maintenance of the self through, for

example, keeping one's word[13] – we can see how commitment constitutes identity in both senses. In so far as a commitment provides a fixed
project through time, e.g., a commitment to a political cause or principle, something that remains constant across the changes and vicissi-
tudes of one's situation, it can be thought of as an identifying mark or
trait, and hence as a basis for identity in the *idem* sense; and in so far as
the commitment is taken up and maintained by the person herself, it is
a source of identity in the *ipse* sense as well. Moreover, commitment
often involves, according to the literature in psychology, and as I shall
later argue, identification *with* certain norms, ideals, or values. As a
result, commitment can be thought of as that *in* which one recognizes
oneself (returning to Ricoeur's language, a form of *idem*-identity since
it represents a trait), as well as that *by* which one recognizes oneself
(and so a form of *ipse*-identity since it implies a maintenance of the
values, norms, or ideals).[14]

2.2.4 Problems of method

Returning to Gibbard and commitment, we see that we have two
competing stories – one noncognitivist and antirealist (or "non-

---

[13] Paul Ricœur, *Oneself as Another*, trans. Kathleen Blamey (Chicago: Chicago University
Press, 1992), pp. 116 ff; *Soi-même Comme un Autre* (Paris: Seuil, 1990), pp. 140 ff.
(henceforth, *OA*).

[14] *Ibid.*, p. 121. Ricoeur here speaks of character as the limit point at which *idem* and
ipse are indiscernible. It might be the case that commitment serves as a second limit
point.
  It is worth noting that psychologists have also remarked on the relation between
commitment on the one hand, and self-understanding and identity on the other. They
tell us that commitment, defined in terms of "psychological attachment," results from
"identification with the attitudes, values or goals of the model; that is, some of the
attributes, motives, or characteristics of the model are accepted by the individual and
become incorporated into the cognitive response set of the individual," and that one's
commitment "will reflect the degree to which the individual internalizes or adopts
characteristics or perspectives of the organization." The important point to draw from
these quotes is that commitment is not simply adherence to a set of norms or goals,
but involves the transition to adopting these as one's own. But it is through the
processes of internalizing and incorporating other attributes, perspectives, goals or
norms that one develops or modifies one's self-definitions and identity. One finds
similar claims in the study of management recruits. See O'Reilly III and Chatman,
"Organizational Commitment," 492–9; and Buchanan, "Building Organizational
Commitments," 535.

factualist") and the other cognitivist and realist (or "factualist")[15] – of two psychological states – norm acceptance and commitment – which seem to share, according to this cursory review, many of the same roles. The challenge Gibbard poses to my argument should be clear: here is a mental state, norm acceptance, which fulfills all the roles of commitment, but does not require any realist beliefs about value or truth in order to be effective. Two questions then are in order: first, is accepting a norm the same as being committed? And second, is a noncognitivist account of norm acceptance capable of rendering intelligible all of our moral practices? Let me focus on the second question, assuming for the time being that the states of accepting a norm and being committed are functionally similar with respect to the roles mentioned above. Given this, we can narrow the focus of the second question by asking whether Gibbard's noncognitivist theory is able to explain fully in what sense claims of objectivity are made and supported. One can think of these questions as two different ways of posing a challenge to Gibbard's account. The challenge consists in demanding a consistent and intelligible explanation of how norms can fulfill their prescribed roles *and* of how claims of objectivity are possible, *all in light of norm-expressivism*. Thus, we can ask: given that norms must play certain roles in avowal, action, and self-understanding, and given norm-expressivism, can Gibbard explain the ascription of objectivity to certain judgments and claims? Or one can shift the focus and ask; given the conditions for ascription of objectivity to certain judgments, and given norm-expressivism, can Gibbard explain how norms can still fulfill their roles? Part of my argument will be that Gibbard cannot reconcile the roles norms must play with the requirements of objectivity within a norm-expressivistic framework. Although objectivity is an issue on which Gibbard spends considerable time, I think it is a topic worth reexamining.

One obstacle to confronting Gibbard's argument, especially for someone wanting to defend moral realism, is posed by his method. He tells us on two occasions that he is not offering an analysis of what it is *to be* rational (or, for that matter objectively valid) but, rather, an analysis of what we do when we *judge, think or believe* something to be rational (or again, objectively valid) (Gibbard, *Wise Choices*, pp. 8, 46).

[15] The factualist/nonfactualist distinction is from Railton, "Nonfactualism about Normative Discourse.

18

The book offers, after all, a theory of normative judgment. But it is this approach of describing only the psychological dynamics underlying such judgment that leaves one puzzled, as it has Nicholas Sturgeon, as to whether in the final analysis the story is an antirealist one. One is tempted to settle the issue by asking not what it is we do when we say something is objectively valid, but what it is for something to be objectively valid *tout court*. But in doing so we seem to step outside the framework of Gibbard's argument. However, I think one can resist this temptation and still operate under the rules Gibbard sets out. Keeping in mind the restrictions imposed by his approach, my criticism will be that his argument relies on the unexamined assumption that we already accept certain claims as being objective (which we obviously do). Given that we accept something as objective (or given that we accept a specific norm), he can then move on to describe what it is we do when we *treat* something as objective (or when we accept a norm). But this hides, or at least ignores, the original question of how we come to attach objective status to judgments in the first place and of how we accept the norms we do,[16] and so also prevents him from answering an important question he himself poses, namely, what it is to *think* a claim objective (*ibid.*, p. 189). In short, we want to know (in more general terms) how in fact we come to accept a norm, what is involved in accepting a norm which plays the roles ascribed to it, and not only what it is we do when we have already accepted a norm.

For a noncognitivist, the restriction of the theory to the psychology of normative judgments is perfectly in order, since, by their lights, there is nothing more to tell about normative judgments other than what it is we do when we use them. Yet clearly Gibbard's argument is not

[16] Perhaps it is better to ask: In virtue of what do we say something is objectively valid? Or, why do we accept the norms we do? The answer to this second question, which is for me more interesting, seems to have as one of its criteria objectivity. For this reason, I shall focus initially on the first question. To answer the question of how we come to attach objective status to judgments might require an explanation of what it is for something to be objective. The very question Gibbard explicitly sets aside at the outset is, I think, an important one that needs to be asked if we are to understand fully our normative and moral practices. Yet, given the structure of his argument, this criticism will only be used to indicate the limits and incompleteness of his analysis. The criticism is not that he has not done what he said he would not do, but that he cannot complete his proposed analysis without a fuller story about objectivity.

premised on the "truth" of noncognitivism, since he seeks to establish an argument in its favor. As a result, he will need to offer more than just a nonfactualist account of our use of the terms "rational" and "objective'; more precisely, he will need to show how noncognitivism can explain (a) how we attach objectivity to certain judgments in a manner consistent with its own principles, and (b) how accepting a norm can fulfill its roles in the light of the explanation of (a). Call this the "self-transparency" test. If he is successful in explaining both (a) and (b) nonfactually, then he will have delivered a strong argument answering the realist's misgivings mentioned above as well as providing an even greater challenge to my own factualist account of commitment.

My argument, briefly, is this: Gibbard provides an inadequate explanation of how we attach objectivity to judgments and the basis of our claims to authority and acceptance-independent validity for certain judgments, since he relies on the unexamined brute facts of commitment and norm acceptance. Indeed, these brute facts are crucial for a norm-expressivistic account of, for example, the distinction between ideals and requirements of rationality, conversational demands, and relativism. More importantly, if we try to give a norm-expressivistic account of these facts, we see that norm-expressivism instead of describing what we are doing in our ordinary normative practices, is describing what we are doing wrong; that is, norm-expressivism, if consistent, devolves into an error theory.[17] Yet given the self-transparency requirements above, it follows that under norm-expressivism norms and commitments cannot fulfill the roles typically ascribed to them, e.g., in self-understanding. The chapter concludes by setting the stage for the introduction of a cognitivist–realist theory that can account for these brute facts that norm-expressivism can only assume rather than explain. The cognitive–realist theory of commitment enters at the point where norm-expressivism falls short of a full explanation of our normative practices.

2.2.5 Error theories and self-transparency

Before moving on to Gibbard's main arguments, let me expand on two of the above points: the self-transparency test and the problem with error theories.

---

[17] See Mackie, *Ethics*, ch. 1.

The justification for the demand that Gibbard be able to explain how norms fulfill their roles and how claims of objectivity are possible, in light of the principles of norm-expressivism, is two-fold. The first concerns two of the virtues of theory construction, namely, unity and economy. Typical of many irrealist theories of ethics, Gibbard's norm-expressivism is what Hilary Putnam might call a two-level theory in which there is a bifurcation between what it is we do and believe, on the one hand, and what theory tells us is really going on, on the other. There is a fundamental *disunity* between the different levels of explanation. I claim, however, that a realist account of our normative practices, such as commitment, has the advantages of both unifying our explanations, since our practices do not need to be shielded from our explanations, and achieving greater economy by postulating a *single, comprehensive*, and, as it were, *self-transparent* theory that explains what we believe and why, as well as how we act on those beliefs.

Now this argument from economy or simplicity is itself founded on the second justification, namely, the need to take into account the first-person perspective in the explanation of human action and practices. Why should this requirement matter? For one, Gibbard himself makes use of the first-person perspective. At the outset of *Wise Choices, Apt Feelings*, Gibbard states: "The way *we see* norms should cohere with *our* best naturalistic account of normative life" (p. 8, emphasis added). That is, the way in which we, as participants in various normative practices, attach objectivity to judgments, and how we accept norms, must be consistent and cohere with the principles of norm-expressivism. Gibbard is not doing descriptive anthropology, in which his observations as a nonparticipant of some alien culture would probably *not* cohere with the way they – the members of the other culture – saw their norms. Despite the fact that Gibbard makes self-transparency a test of adequacy for his own theory, one may still question whether such a test is valid. We can answer that in so far as Gibbard, or any philosopher for that matter, seeks to provide a sketch of the psychological dynamics of agents, of our mental life, that sketch would be woefully inadequate if it did not take into account the role of self-consciousness, i.e., first-person awareness. As William Child[18] insightfully notes, many accounts of the mental

18 W. Child, *Causality, Interpretation, and the Mind* (Oxford: Clarendon Press, 1994).

21

do ignore the distinctive role of self-consciousness: they think of beliefs and desires from a purely third-person perspective; they conceive of propositional attitudes as constructs in a theory for explaining peoples' behavior in exactly the same way as we treat centers of gravity or mass, say, as constructs in a theory for explaining the behavior of inanimate bodies (Child, *Causality*, p. 35).

Clearly, though, our goal is not to explain the behavior of inanimate bodies, but the *actions* of individuals. It is here that we touch on a much deeper problem regarding the nature of explanation in action theory. Although a full development of the problem, and its resolution, will have to wait until chapter 5, let me sketch what the problem is.

The misdirected tendency to adopt a third-person perspective is rooted in an explanatory paradigm in action theory which is exclusively causal. Yet exclusively causal explanations fail to acknowledge that what are to be explained are not simply events in the world, but human actions, and that in order to understand – to explain – these actions requires reconstituting the agent's own understanding of them. Actions have meaning, and meaning is always *for* a subject. Thus, rather than isolating the action-events and locating them in a causal succession, we need instead to provide an explanation and understanding an agent herself would reach of her own actions.[19] That is to say, we need instead a first-person rather than a third-person account of our normative practices. However, a full defense of this claim is not yet needed, since Gibbard himself seems to invoke the first-person criterion.

The problem with error theories also has two sources: one from Gibbard; and a second from economics, an increasingly favorite refer-

---

[19] In the introduction to his book, *Les Bourreaux Volontaires de Hitler* (Paris: Editions du Seuil, 1997), Daniel Goldhagen emphasizes the necessity of describing actions from the perspective of the agent, as opposed to an outside observer, in order to explain accurately and to understand fully (as fully as is possible) the events that took place. He states: "La juste description des événements que nous traitons, la reconstitution de la réalité phénoménologique des tueurs sont capitales pour l'explication. C'est pour cette raison que j'évite l'approche *clinique* [emphasis added] et tente de reproduire l'horreur, le caractère abominable des événements pour les bourreaux . . . De telles scènes, et non les descriptions aseptisées des massacres qu'on nous présente le plus souvent, étaient la réalité de bien des agents du génocide" (pp. 30–1). In historical explanation, the third-person perspective imposes severe limits on explanation and understanding.

ence for those working in action theory and ethics. Gibbard is, as we shall see shortly, reluctant to place error on the side of practice when it collides with theory. Rather than saying ordinary use or understanding is mistaken, Gibbard tries to accommodate them by reformulating his theory, as seen in his worry that norm-expressivism cannot distinguish conflicts of personal ideals and requirements of rationality (Gibbard, *Wise Choices*, p. 167 ff.). In addition to Gibbard's reluctance to adopt an error theory, there are considerations weighing against such a theory: most importantly, an error theory requires that we violate the self-transparency test and that we ignore, or forget, the principles the theory posits in order to maintain our practices successfully. This can be expressed more formally if we turn to economics.

The validity of error theories – theories according to which individuals can be systematically mistaken by the lights of a given theory, without the stability of the system being affected, despite the incoherence between the practice and the theory which it models – has received considerable attention from those working in the field of rational expectations in economics. Given the predominance of economic models or economically inspired explanations in ethics, whether in the form of game theory, decision theory, Pareto optimal equilibria, etc., it might be illuminating to see what economists have to say regarding the tenability of error theories in ethics – a model that has become orthodoxy among many noncognitivists and antirealists.

Now one of the distinguishing features of theories in the social sciences is that they are self-reflexive: they can influence the behavior of the agents they model, unlike theories in the natural sciences. Rational expectation theory, which has taken root during the past twenty years, explores in part what the consequences are of this peculiar reflexive feature of economics. According to Pierre-André Chiappori,[20] there are two senses in which we can understand the hypothesis of rational expectations: a "naive" and a "sophisticated" sense (Chiappori, "Anticipations rationelles," p. 65). What is interesting for our purposes is the latter, which imposes a methodological constraint of coherence between different logical levels of explanation. According to Chiappori:

---

[20] P.-A. Chiappori, "Antcipations Rationelles et Conventions," in André Orléan (ed.), *Analyse Economique des Conventions* (Paris: Presses Universitaires de France, 1994): pp. 61–78.

a model is compatible with the hypothesis of rational expectations if it is not self-destructive: it must keep its relevance *even if the agents are aware of the model and use it in their predictions.* In other words, what this hypothesis refuses is any representation which endows agents with beliefs that the logic of the model itself renders erroneous (*ibid.*, p. 66; original emphasis).

Clearly, error theories in ethics fail this constraint. First, they endow individuals with beliefs, for example, beliefs in the existence of moral facts, that the theories themselves declare false. Second, and this is the argument of the present book, if the agents became aware of the (non-cognitive, antirealist) model and used it in their deliberations, their behavior would radically change; such models are, I will argue, self-destructive.

The complexity of error theories and their cognitive implications are seldom appreciated, or recognized, by their proponents. Paul Dumouchel,[21] however, has drawn out some of the presuppositions and implications of such models. Drawing on F. A. Hayek's work on spontaneous orders – systems in which "the rules which govern the actions of the elements of such spontaneous orders need not be rules which are 'known' to these elements; [and for which] it is sufficient that the elements actually behave in a manner which can be described by such rules,"[22] – Dumouchel provides a useful classification of different types of such systems. In the first type, the system can only exist if the agents who constitute it have a false representation of it; that is, if they knew the rules by which they actually abide and which make the system possible, they would not agree to them. Dumouchel calls this an "Irrational System" ("Social Systems," p. 3). In a "Rational System" the agents could consent to the rules; hence, they can have a true representation of the system. Finally, Dumouchel calls a system which can exist only if the agents know and abide by the constitutive rules a "Reasonable System."[23]

---

[21] P. Dumouchel, "Social Systems and Cognition," Centre de Recherche en Epistémologie Appliquée, Ecole Polytechnique, unpublished paper.

[22] F. A. Hayek, *Law, Legislation and Liberty* (Chicago: University of Chicago Press, 1973), p. 43, quoted in Dumouchel.

[23] Part of Dumouchel's program is to draw out the political and cognitive implications of these types of systems. Moreover, he claims that such systems, in addition to being social systems, are also *cognitive* systems since representations and semantic information have a functional role in the stability and preservation of the system itself, and hence cannot be described in nonintentional terms.

Now there are two important things to notice here. First, the description of our normative practices, or our moral systems, resembles to a considerable extent the spontaneous orders described by Hayek and used by Dumouchel. The idea of an emergent system of social interactions, governed by rules of which the agents of the systems are unaware, is roughly Gibbard's account of the development of rules, or norms, governing and coordinating our interactions. Second, an error theory regarding our moral practices is essentially the description of an Irrational System. The question Dumouchel poses regarding the very possibility of Irrational Systems, and hence a question that supporters of error theories would need to answer, is the following: "[H]ow can the agents of an irrational system follow any rules, if they cannot *know* the rules which they are following?" (*ibid.*, p. 11).

One possible answer, as Dumouchel notes, is to say they are following unconscious rules. This solution, however, is fairly controversial; but for the purposes of argument, we can grant this possibility. To say the agents of the system are following unconscious rules is to attribute to them representations of the system which are different than the representations of the observer formulating the motivating rules which guide the participants-agents of the system. In other words, as Dumouchel states, "they do not share the same description of the system," which means that the observer is *outside* the system described (*ibid.*, pp. 13–14).

Now, for anthropologists or sociologists describing the habits and representations of an isolated or autonomous culture or social system, whether it be the Yanumani in South America, or a group of scientists at the Scripps Institute in La Jolla, the division between the levels of description of the system – the "point of view of an element of the system, of an agent who is inside the system, and . . . the point of view of an outside observer" (p. 14) – seems admissible. But what are we to say of the case in which the "observer" inhabits the social system herself, as is the case of philosophers describing *our*, in the inclusive sense, normative practices, of which morality and rationality are a part? The answer is, I suggest, that she cannot be describing an Irrational System, a system in which the motivating and prescriptive rules differ: a system in which the representations the agents in the system have, herself included, of the system itself are false. For if such were the case, she either could no longer be part of the system, or else the system itself would be destabilized, since the agents could not then accept the false representations. Error theories are, we see once again, self-destructive.

If what I argue in the following chapters is correct regarding the conditions of commitment, then norm-expressivism must be an error theory, which in turn means that it leads to a bifurcation between theory and practice – to two-level thinking. To the extent that a cognitivist–realist account avoids this, not only does it have the advantage of being self-transparent, but also of being much simpler.

2.2.6 Normative objectivity

With the criteria for an adequate explanation now defined, we can return to Gibbard's arguments. Gibbard begins his discussion of objectivity by looking more closely at what is involved in saying something is a requirement of rationality. He isolates three features: first, to say a norm is a requirement of rationality is to take the norm as applying independently of one's acceptance of it; second, as a requirement of rationality, it must be more than an "idiosyncratic existential commitment"; and third, as such a requirement, it purports to be an interpersonally valid claim and not simply an opinion – the claim of rationality carries with it an element of authority (Gibbard, *Wise Choices*, p. 155). Gibbard's goal is to explain within a norm-expressivistic framework the objective pretensions in our normative talk. In this explanation, as we shall see, commitment plays an important role. The path to this goal follows two stages: the first stage examines normative authority from the point of view of the audience; the second addresses the same issue but from the perspective of the speaker. I shall focus mainly on the latter.

Gibbard's examination of objectivity begins with the apparent acceptance-independent validity of certain normative judgments, and he presents us with the example of an ideally coherent anorexic to help highlight how claims to objectivity work. Our norms tell us that starving oneself to death is irrational whether or not one accepts those norms, while the anorexic's norms clearly do not. Even though she does not accept our norms and is guilty of no incoherence in the manner in which she abides by hers, we still think she acts irrationally: we think our norms are valid independently of our acceptance or her rejection of them. The problem is to explain her "irrationality" when she does not accept our norms: to explain the acceptance-independence of norms – norms which are only expressions of states of mind, recall – thereby showing how norm-expressivism can capture normative authority.

One possible solution is to say that the disagreement is just a conflict of personal ideals rather than a problem of rationality. This solution, however, reveals a deeper problem: on a norm-expressivistic account "all personal ideals are matters of rationality" (*ibid.*, p. 167) since to uphold an ideal is to express one's acceptance of certain norms, which is, by Gibbard's definition, to make a claim to rationality. The problem is that norm-expressivism seems unable to distinguish between thinking something a requirement of rationality and being committed to it as an ideal, despite the fact that in ordinary language we often do make such a distinction: one can be committed to certain ideals without seeing it as a requirement of rationality that others be so committed as well.[24] To help distinguish between ideals and requirements of rationality, Gibbard posits what he calls an "existential commitment": "a choice of what kind of person to be, in a fundamental way, come what might, which the chooser does not take to be dictated by considerations of rationality" (p. 168).

Existential commitments, or ideals, might come into play, suggests Gibbard, when we accept higher-order norms (those that govern the acceptance of other norms) that permit the acceptance of lower-order, mutually incompatible norms; that is, the higher-order norms do not dictate the acceptance of a unique set of lower-order norms. Thus, in choosing the lower-order norm, we do so not as a requirement of rationality – since there is no higher-order norm requiring its acceptance – but as an instance of existential commitment. Depending on which lower order norms one accepts, one can be in disagreement with another person without it being the case that either person is irrational. With existential commitments at hand, Gibbard can now distinguish between ideals – norms whose acceptance is not required by higher-order norms – and requirements of rationality – norms whose acceptance is so required. This apparently solves the initial threat to a norm-expressivistic account.

---

[24] Here one sees Gibbard's reluctance to adopt an error theory. For another solution would be to say that our ordinary understanding is just wrong, and that in fact there is no distinction between personal ideals and requirements of rationality.

This now brings us to a second problem, namely, how to explain standpoint-independent validity. As Gibbard notes, in judging the (ideally coherent) anorexic to be irrational, one is doing more than expressing one's acceptance of certain higher-order norms prohibiting self-starvation: one is also claiming authority for the norms one accepts by asserting that they apply validly to her (p. 171). This claim to authority involves, says Gibbard, placing a demand that she (or one's audience, generally) accepts what one is saying, as well as an implicit claim that one has a basis for such a demand (pp. 172, 173). Gibbard's analysis now turns away from the above example and toward these demands for acceptance – what he calls "conversational demands." Although his examination of conversational demands starts from the point of view of the audience, the more interesting questions arise from the first-person, speaker perspective.

A speaker thinks his claim objective, according to Gibbard, if he can "sincerely" demand of others that they accept it, i.e., "if he can make the demand openly and without browbeating" (p. 191). This amounts to being open to revealing the grounds of one's demand as well as being capable of supporting it with a "coherent epistemic story" (p. 194). Gibbard summarizes his argument as follows:

> If a person is fully coherent, then he accepts something as an objective matter of rationality only if the higher order norms he accepts ascribe it a standpoint-independent validity. The line of reasoning was roughly this: a speaker treats what he is saying as an objective matter of rationality if he can demand its acceptance by everybody. More precisely, the test is this: could he coherently make his demands, revealing their grounds, and still not browbeat his audience? (p. 193)

But is this what it is for a speaker to think a claim objective? For Gibbard this is the important question for norm-expressivism to answer (p. 189). Although one might offer an accurate description of what it is for *someone else* to treat a claim as objective, this "says nothing about what objectivity means" (p. 189). To answer that requires, in part, that we find out what it is to think a normative claim objective. Yet the passage just quoted regarding objectivity and the demand for acceptance seems rather to describe criteria by which *we can judge whether someone else is treating his claim as objective*, but it does not describe, *from the first-person perspective of a speaker, what it is to think a claim objective*. It is not by making sincere demands of others that one recognizes that one thinks one's own demands are objective matters of rationality, although when one sees *others* making such demands one can conclude, by Gibbard's criteria, that they must think their claims are objective since they are treating them as such. Indeed, once we consider a certain judgment to be objective in Gibbard's sense, we then go on to treat it in the way he describes. But this leaves unresolved the initial problem of what it is to think something an objective matter of rationality in the first place. This is particularly problematic for Gibbard since the expressivistic strategy made the question of what it is to think a claim objective one of the important questions to answer (p. 189). It would seem that Gibbard does not move beyond a third-person account of what it is to treat a claim as objective.

Consider the statement: "he accepts something as an objective matter of rationality only if the higher order norms he accepts *ascribe it a standpoint-independent rationality.*" Now this ascription was to be explained by the capacity of the agent to make sincere demands. The question, why, or in virtue of what is standpoint-independent validity ascribed to a norm? – a question whose answer would tell us what it is for an agent to think something objective – is answered instead by drawing our attention to the fact that the speaker makes sincere demands. Again, though, this only tells us, as *observers*, how to recognize when a speaker ascribes such validity to his judgments. The question now becomes; why, or in virtue of what, does one feel entitled to make such demands? The key question is whether Gibbard can answer this without referring to facts, or truth, and still explain how norms are connected to dispositions to action, avowal, and to self-understanding. Gibbard, I argue, instead simply assumes as a given fact that we do make these demands, and that we do ascribe standpoint-independent validity to certain claims. And it is only on the basis of these assumptions that he is able to explain (norm-expressivistically) certain behavior related to treating norms as objective. This fact of ascription is, however, left unanalyzed and is a potential fault in his argument. In short, we see another brute fact that plays a crucial role in Gibbard's norm-expressivism. To the extent that the problem of how we come to accept a norm as an objective requirement of rationality, one which will guide action and provide self-understanding, has been left unanswered, Gibbard's argument, I suggest, does not succeed in establishing a case against moral realism. It is possible that these brute facts – of commitment and objective ascription – can only be explained within a realist framework about values.

A similar appeal to the brute fact of commitment also underlies Gibbard's discussion of relativism, as I will show in the next section. In all of these cases there is an *ad hoc* flavor to the account: at the crucial points where an explanation is needed, Gibbard simply invokes the "fact of commitment" or the "fact of acceptance," and never addresses how or why it is that we accept certain commitments or norms, or in virtue of what we ascribe objectivity to certain judgments – we just do. The key question is whether he can make this move and still explain how norms function in our lives and fulfill the roles they play in avowal, action, and self-understanding. By way of answering this question, let me develop further how these brute facts figure in Gibbard's theory, and why they open the way for an alternative, cognitivist–realist account.

Let us return to the case of making a conversational demand, but from the perspective of the person making it. We may ask what the agent understands herself to be doing in making such a demand. Gibbard says, rightly, that this involves a claim to authority and objectivity, but he then goes on to analyze criteria by which we recognize the agent's objective attitude, so to speak, and leaves unexamined the source of objectivity and authority.[25] Assuming the noncognitivist framework, what can be said about how the agent understands *her own* conversational demand on others?

In getting others to accede to her demand, she needs to provide some basis for it in the form of an "epistemic story." Now we could leave aside all questions of truth and matters of fact, if her only goal in making the demand was to get others to share her state of mind. Truth might emerge as part of the epistemic story, but only as a way

---

[25] I am not pressing Gibbard for a descriptive account of objectivity, of what it is to be objectively rational, but I am instead asking how it is one comes to ascribe this status to certain judgments. As a result, I am still operating within the confines of his argument and am not begging the question against him. Simply to object that he fails to describe what objectivity is would be illegitimate since he says at the outset that this is not his goal. One can ask, however, whether such a description is necessary in order for us to understand fully our moral practices and how norms fulfill their roles. For the time being, though, I restrict my analysis to the framework originally described by Gibbard. I thank Bryan Van Norden for bringing this potential objection to my attention.

of convincing others to accept the demand; that is, although some stories might have a realist flair, with references to truth and facts, they are at bottom pragmatic. But convincing others is not all that is involved in making a conversational demand, as Gibbard recognizes. He places an important restriction on such demands by saying that the speaker herself must sincerely accept the demand (and its basis). The story she tells others, then, must be the same story she tells herself, i.e., the justification for believing the claim she makes. It is at this point that we run into trouble. Assuming noncognitivism, her story cannot include any reference to truth or a domain of facts in virtue of which her demand or claim is valid. Without these, however, it is unclear how we are to understand her ascription of standpoint-independent validity and objectivity to her demand, let alone why she should then think others should accept it, since it is often in terms of what is independent of our beliefs, desires, and attitudes that notions such as "truth" and "facts" are defined. Does she then make her demands only to encourage consensus and, if so, why is it important to consider certain particular demands and not others? Now if believing is part of accepting, and if she accepts the basis of her demands, then to suggest that she is only interested in encouraging consensus or getting others to share her state of mind neglects a crucial feature of what it is to be a "believer," namely, to have an interest in acquiring true beliefs, and not just the most popular beliefs, or even beliefs that others would easily or readily accept (though these may be considerations as well). Without the vocabulary of "truth" and "facts," how does an agent explain and justify to herself the beliefs she has, and their objective status? And how does she understand the process by which she came to hold them and why she is now disposed to act on them and persuade others to accept them?

Following a norm-expressivist account of the source of normative authority, one encounters a failure of self-understanding, in Velleman's sense described above, on the part of the agent in so far as she is incapable of answering the above questions. She understands neither how she acquired these norms, nor why she is now disposed to avow them, other than through a story which recounts her exposure to "normative influence": but the story of normative influence treats the emergence and acceptance of norms like an organic, unreflective process – as if normative influence were something some people exude and others catch, like a cold, through exposure.[26] It seems that an agent could only be mute on these points. In so far as she has no story to tell herself, then she has no basis for the demands she places on others, and so cannot make sincere demands. It is precisely at this point that Gibbard invokes the fact of acceptance. But, on closer examination, it is by no means clear how this fact is to be explained. Noncognitivism leaves it wholly mysterious as to why we accept the demands we do, and how we ascribe objectivity to them.

In short, it seems that under a noncognitivist theory, norms cannot play at least one of the roles assigned to them, namely, that of self-understanding. In my discussion of commitment, I will argue at length that self-understanding, as described above, involves realist beliefs. Understanding what it makes sense to do, I claim, involves beliefs about what in fact is the case and what is true. But I leave the argument for these assertions for later chapters. Suffice to say at this point that our ordinary understanding of what it is to accept a demand, or a norm, and what it is to make a sincere demand on others, involves claims of truth regarding the belief that the norm or demand is "getting it right."

Consider once again the coherent anorexic. How can one explain the authority of one's own judgment that what she is doing and the norms she accepts are "crazy," to use Gibbard's word. In claiming this kind of fundamental authority, says Gibbard, one is at the same time claiming "to be 'seeing' something that she doesn't: that the fundamental norms she accepts just don't make sense" (p. 175). Here, I think, Gibbard misdescribes, or misleadingly describes, the situation. What we claim to be seeing is not that her norms do not make sense –

---

[26] Speaking on normative influence, Gibbard says, "We may have little choice in the matter; we simply *are* influenced in a fundamental way by what those around us think. Mutual influence . . . is part of what accounts for the very existence of normative discussion" (p. 177). Although he does say that we try to decide whether it makes sense to be influenced in this way, I would suggest that what are involved in "making sense" are questions about which norms are "getting it right." One can elicit a realist strain in Gibbard's thought. Gibbard might say that one would understand one's acquisition of, and adherence to, certain norms in terms of a process of normative discussion and inquiry. But this normative discussion will involve distinctions, Gibbard admits, between which judgments are warranted and which judgments are correct (p. 215). But this distinction is central to all realist accounts, particularly those opposing a pragmatic reduction of truth. In short, the story of normative influence still seems to involve some reference to truth.

they do since we have no trouble understanding them – but rather that her norms are *mistaken*. What does not make sense to us is how a person who is as coherent as she can be so fundamentally *wrong*. One's claim to authority in these cases is premised, I suggest, on thoughts like "getting it right," "being wrong," or "having a clear grasp of the facts." If these are the kinds of things we are "seeing" in our claims to authority, then norm-expressivism will be hardpressed to explain it.

As "there is no class of facts which make normative judgments normative" (p. 113) according to norm-expressivism, there is no sense in which one "sees," for example, that something is wrong, except, of course, a mistaken sense. But then our ordinary claims to authority which involve this kind of "seeing" must be, according to Gibbard's theory, fundamentally mistaken. If our ordinary claims to authority are "realistic," for lack of a better word, and if norm-expressivism tells us that in fact they are baseless, *and we know this*, how then do we make sincere demands? Once again, in virtue of what do we demand acceptance of our judgments by others? To the extent that norm-expressivism, as a noncognitivist theory, precludes us from explaining why we accept the moral claims we do by saying, for example, that they reflect the way things really are, it fails to describe accurately many of our ordinary normative and moral practices such as forming commitments, accepting norms, asserting authority, and demanding acceptance, all of which seem to involve such notions as "getting it right," "being wrong," etc. The result is that noncognitivism must cast itself as an error theory. Gibbard, then, cannot be describing what it is we are doing, but rather must be describing what it is we are doing wrong. If the cognitivist (and moral realist) have ordinary practice on their side, then the burden of proof shifts to their opponents.

I should stress that the argument so far is not a refutation of Gibbard's position nor of noncognitivism generally, but more an indication of the inadequacy or incompleteness of his explanation of our normative practices – one which is engendered by his method. In discussing conversational demands and claims to authority, Gibbard focuses attention on (1) "how conversational demands can work in normative life," and (2) "what role they play in normative discussion" (p. 173). What I have suggested is that for a fuller, more explanatorily powerful account of our normative practices we need also to examine what the basis of these demands is and how we come to make them. By focusing exclusively on the dynamic *process* of making demands without considering their source, Gibbard leaves open, as we shall see, the possibility of a cognitivist–realist story that need not invoke the fact of acceptance (or the fact of commitment), but rather will be able to explain it.

The point to bear in mind so far is that his reliance on the "fact of acceptance" (and as we shall see, the "fact of commitment") renders his argument for a noncognitivist theory problematic. Indeed, the opacity of this fact obscures his later discussion of parochialism and relativism.

2.2.7 Parochialism

Continuing his discussion of normative objectivity, Gibbard examines another, fairly broad, dimension of our normative practice in which we restrict the extension of normative judgments and the scope of conversational demands for acceptance between groups who may have different standards of normative judgment. In these cases one can treat a judgment in one of two ways: either as parochial, in which one excludes certain groups from being potentially competent normative judges; or as relative, in which case one sees that one's own way of life might not be right for others (and vice versa) without it being the case that you are wrong or the other is wrong. Parochialism and relativism serve as two general categories of our normative practice. It is the task of norm-expressivism to explain how we make certain judgments in the context of these two frameworks. I argue that parochialism fails and that relativism ultimately relies on the crucial, but unexplained, fact of commitment.

If we consider two different groups (Greeks and Scythians, using Gibbard's example), each of which, as a group, is coherent in the judgments it makes based on the higher-order norms it accepts, then "[a] Greek treats a judgment as parochial, *vis-à-vis* Scythians, if he confines his demands on its behalf to a group that excludes them" (p. 205). Greeks think that an ideally competent normative judge is one "who knows enough that no further true beliefs would lead him to change his mind on normative matters, and who has engaged in dialectic to the point where no further dialectic will show him incoherent or make him give up normative judgments he now holds (p. 205)" (Gibbard calls this state "dialectical equilibrium"). Call this the first definition (D1) of a competent normative judge. Gibbard later introduces a second definition (D2) in his discussion of parochialism: "A potentially competent judge is someone whose judgment would carry weight if he had all the properties a competent normative judge must have. *These properties must be generic, not matters of being a particular person or in a particular group*, or of bearing a special relation to the speaker" (p. 208, emphasis added). Now a Greek's judgment is parochial *vis-à-vis* the Scythians "if he thinks that a Scythian, even if he met all generic qualifications for ideal normative judgment, would still be a poor judge." When we consider D1 and D2 together, we must ask how any parochial judgments are possible.

Gibbard notes that the Greek must himself consider it "illegitimate" to demand of the Scythians that they share his judgments, but he allows that a Greek can apply his norms to the lives of the Scythians in discussions with fellow Greeks (p. 208). However, I think that this restriction of normative discussion is still too wide, given the definitions a Greek accepts regarding competent judges. In discussing with other Greeks the lives of the Scythians and making normative judgments about them, the Greek is claiming that such judgments would be made by an ideally competent normative judge. By D2 above, such a judge is defined in terms of purely generic features, which means that the standards of competence cannot be Greek-specific, and the Greeks realize this according to D2. Yet, they exclude Scythians from influencing their normative discussion for no other reason than that they are Scythians. In other words, the Greek, by Gibbard's story, employs normative judgments in discussion which he knows could not be made by an ideally competent normative judge. Even in restricting his judgments regarding Scythians to a Greek audience, his judgments still fail to carry any normative weight since they would not be judgments made in dialectical equilibrium – they are subject to revision by the influence of further true beliefs, namely, that Scythians are potentially competent judges. Without an epistemic story as to why Scythians cannot be competent judges – one that does not simply repeat the fact that they are Scythians – Greeks cannot consistently make normative judgments regarding Scythians to themselves or others. Parochialism, as defined by Gibbard, is untenable. Gibbard recognizes as much when he states that "[i]t might seem that parochialism collapses into relativism" since in excluding a group from influencing normative discussion we must give evidence of a generic property they lack; but in doing so "we are claiming normative expertise, [and] not treating our judgments as parochial" (p. 213). When it comes to normative judgments, relativism seems to be the only mode of discourse.

2.2.8 Relativism and the "fact of commitment"

The above examination of parochialism does more than bring out a problem in Gibbard's analysis which he himself acknowledges in passing. Gibbard gives us the option between parochialism and relativism as two broad conceptual frameworks to help us understand some of our normative practices. Parochialism fails – if we accept Gibbard's account, then we cannot make the judgments we do. That leaves relativism. But I want to argue that this, too, fails as an interpretive model since it rests on a fact Gibbard assumes, but leaves largely unexplained: the fact of commitment.

Relativism is defined by Gibbard as roughly the view that one's own way of life might not be suitable for others, and vice versa, though we are both probably right in choosing the way of life that we do (p. 205). One way of explaining this, says Gibbard, is through "communitarian commitment" (p. 208): "[t]hrough communitarian commitment, whatever norms emerge by consensus within the community come validly to apply within that community" so that in being committed to a certain community, or in upholding certain commitments, some norms will apply validly for me that might not apply for others. For Gibbard, the commitment seems to consist in the acceptance of "higher order norms that say to abide by one's communitarian commitments" (p. 209). The norms that now emerge through consensus within the community acquire a new status in that they are now held for a reason: namely, that these norms are part of an "ethos" to which they are committed.

This account of communitarian commitments should strike one as incomplete: there is a missing link between the lower-order norms that emerge through consensus within my community and my acceptance of higher-order norms directing me to abide by these lower-order norms. Gibbard tries to fill in this gap with the opaque concept of commitment. Once he posits the fact of our commitment to a community – one that consists in our acceptance of higher-order norms – he is then able to explain how judgments can be relativized to groups: once I am committed to my community, it makes sense for me to abide by certain norms even though it would not make sense for others to do so, since these norms are not part of their "ethos." But what justifies

invoking this fact of commitment? If we are to reach a better understanding of how this kind of relativism is possible, rather than a general
description of how it works, we need to know how such commitments
come about. Once again we should be suspicious of the noncognitivist
sleight of hand: by drawing our attention to the superficial dynamic
between higher-order norms, commitment, and lower-order norms,
we are distracted from examining what is going on below. We need to
ask, once again, what these communitarian commitments involve.

Communitarian commitments, Gibbard tells us, like existential
commitments, are possible only for a person who accepts higher-
order, "voluntaristic" norms: norms that "direct one to be governed
by whatever norms one designates to oneself by thinking or feeling in
certain ways about them" (p. 209). I belong to a certain community,
and within that community certain norms emerge through normative
discussion – for example, norms calling on us to be kind to strangers,
or to look twice before crossing the savanna. Now if I am committed
to this community, I then accept higher-order norms directing me to
abide by these norms of kindness and prudence. What is it about this
commitment and its grounds that then leads me to accept such norms?

Gibbard seems to be aware of a potential problem in his formulation of commitment when he poses just this question regarding the
ground of the communitarian commitment itself (p. 210). He
answers by saying that the relativism he sketches must be partial: "The
highest order norms of a relativist must have some non-relative
status" (p. 210). This is surely a curious statement, since it seems to be
a concession to some form of realism in that it allows that the validity
of certain norms is not indexed according to persons or groups but,
rather, holds for a wider community. But if this is so, it leaves us some
room to claim that, with respect to these norms, there is a fact of the
matter regarding the validity of their acceptance. And this in turn
permits us to say that, with respect to action falling within the scope
of these norms, some of them are right and some of them are wrong,
and this too is a matter of fact that expresses more than my acceptance
of certain norms. For whether or not I accept the norms that permit
(or forbid) those actions, they are still the right (or wrong) actions to
perform. And this last claim is certainly beyond the bounds of noncognitivism. Gibbard's argument, far from excluding moral realism,
rather points in its direction, or at least provides fertile ground for its
development.

If we look more closely at these commitments and their associated higher-order norms, we find further room for a realist story. Our higher-order norms, says Gibbard, will be backed by a "deep rationale" for the acceptance of the everyday norms by which they tell us to abide (p. 214). Relativism concerns this rationale which provides an epistemic story supporting the lower-order norms and why it makes sense for "us" to abide by them and not others. As this rationale addresses the higher-order norms, and the higher-order norms are formed or accepted only after we have formed the communitarian commitments, it seems likely that the reasons for which we form or justify the commitments might be the same reasons given in the deep rationale for the higher-order norms. Commitment is an essential step in Gibbard's account of relativism, one of the central domains of normative practice for which his noncognitivist norm-expressivism was to offer a complete account. Therefore, if it is possible to give some sort of realist–cognitivist story regarding commitment, one will overcome Gibbard's challenge by showing that norm-expressivism is unable to accommodate our ordinary normative practices since it cannot explain the key step of commitment. As it is the task of the book to offer this realist story, let me only indicate at this point the ample opportunity Gibbard leaves for its development.

In order for the Greeks to become relativists, says Gibbard, they would need "a story of how the norms that apply to a person depend on features of his community" (p. 208). "One such story," he adds, "would give a leading role to commitment" (p. 208). In light of its "leading role," we would expect from Gibbard an examination of commitments, how we come to have them, and what they involve. Gibbard instead moves right past these issues and simply assumes the fact of our having such commitments. Instead of an argument or analysis, we are asked only to "[s]uppose the Greeks think communitarian commitments valid" (p. 208). Without any story as to why the Greeks should think this or what thinking this involves, we are free to offer our own. By appealing to this fact of commitment without offering an account of what it is, Gibbard opens the way for an alternative, cognitivist–realist account.

2.2.9 Conclusion

Recall that there were three main axes which, taken together, were meant to support Gibbard's overall argument. These were his accounts of (1) norm-expressivism (noncognitivism generally), (2) the role norms play in self-understanding (as well as in action and avowal), and (3) normative objectivity. The test of his argument was whether, given norm-expressivism, (2) and (3) could be held simultaneously.

Now in order for these three axes to bear the weight of Gibbard's argument successfully, he must assume the fact of commitment and norm acceptance. Without this fact, Gibbard must either abandon (2), or say that our ordinary understanding of (3) is mistaken, or admit that norm-expressivism is the wrong account. But since his method is to draw on evidence from common-sense beliefs, vocabulary, and observation (p. 56), he would be unwilling to say that our ordinary understanding of (3) is mistaken. And since he clearly wants to retain norm-expressivism, the only option is to say that norms cannot play a role in self-understanding, and as a result to concede that norms and commitments are not functionally similar. But this leaves open the possibility of a realist account of commitment and so defuses what I took to be Gibbard's challenge to my argument regarding commitment and its requisite realist belief structure. This is, of course, not the only option. One could say that the ordinary understanding of objectivity as I present it is mistaken, and thus try to reconcile once again the three axes mentioned above, but in a way that departs from Gibbard's work. In some ways, this is in fact what Richard Rorty tries to do in his discussion of the liberal ironist in *CIS*; that is, to show that one can accept norms, be committed, make sincere demands, and be wholly indifferent to questions of truth and facts of the matter (or, as he would say, problems of accurate representation).

2.3 RICHARD RORTY: CONTINGENCY, IRONY, AND SOLIDARITY?

2.3.1 Introduction

In *Contingency, Irony, and Solidarity*, Richard Rorty paints a picture of a liberal utopia whose cultural hero is the strong poet – one who creates herself through her own descriptions yet finds solidarity with others on the basis of a shared vulnerability to pain and humiliation. The new society of ironists, built on the ruins of foundationalism and constructed outside the borders of essentialism, is still capable of supporting community through a shared abhorrence of cruelty. As attractive and appealing as Rorty's new society is, emphasizing as it does novelty in self-creation and allowing the individual to define her role without ever being defined by it – a society in which, as Marx might say, "it [is] possible for me to do one thing today and another tomorrow, to hunt in the morning, fish in the afternoon, rear cattle in the evening, criticize after dinner, just as I have a mind, without ever becoming hunter, fisherman, shepherd or critic"[27] – we should perhaps be a little suspicious of the happy coincidence that the destruction wrought by neopragmatism of the old society's epistemological and metaphysical superstructure has yet left its most beautiful monuments intact: Freedom, Creativity, and the classic Pain and Suffering Vanquished. Yet, it seems very possible that it is only on the basis of realist assumptions on Rorty's part – that in fact not everything is language and some things withstand redescription – that these monuments can serve as landmarks to his utopia. Although the tension in Rorty's work between his antiessentialist pretensions and "realist-sounding" assertions is worth careful examination, the question I want to draw attention to at this point, by way of highlighting where the main arguments regarding commitment will lead, is whether his portrait of the liberal ironist is recognizably human, or if the combination of radical doubt with solidarity can only be realized through a kind of schizophrenia. Rorty, it seems, would have us say with him, "There is no God, and Mary is His mother."[28]

2.3.2 Rorty's antirealism

The quest for objectivity, according to Rorty, is yet one more remnant of the realist/foundationalist enterprise: an attempt to ground our beliefs in transcultural, transhistorical, and transcendental foundations. Rorty urges us to drop the metaphysician's talk of representation, reference, and correspondence[29] and instead adopt a vocabulary in which truth is not located in some nonlinguistic realm, but is

---

[27] Karl Marx, *The German Ideology*, Part I.

[28] I take this quote from W. W. Bartley, *The Retreat to Commitment* (LaSalle: Open Court, 1984), in his description of George Santayana, p. 6.

[29] R. Rorty, *Objectivity, Relativism, and Truth* (Cambridge: Cambridge University Press, 1991), p. 5 (henceforth, *ORT*).

identified simply by "what is good for us to believe" (*ORT*, p. 22). Having a true belief, says Rorty, is having a successful rule for action (*ORT*, p. 66). Like Wittgenstein, he seeks to cure us of our urge to search for unifying theories, whether they be of truth, meaning, or knowledge. As a result, he rejects the demand to provide his own substantive theory, complete with necessary and sufficient conditions determining criteria for knowledge and truth. To do so would be to use the tools of the tradition he wants to overcome. Instead, his method will be one of redescription, of casting old vocabularies in a bad light until they fall into disfavor and new vocabularies are adopted. When Rorty says we should no longer talk of truth as awaiting discovery he insists he is not putting forth the positive thesis that truth is not out there (*CIS*, p. 8), but, rather, that it would simply *better serve our purposes* to talk in a new idiom.[30]

One of Rorty's main targets is the philosophical model which takes language to be a medium between the self and reality (*CIS*, p. 11). For Rorty, there is no privileged standpoint outside of language that will provide us with a clear and unobstructed view of reality. Given that the history of language is just the history of metaphor – the contingent, arbitrary emergence and disappearance of idioms and descriptions – a history unguided by any fixed points of human nature or things in themselves, we come to see why forms of expression and changes in vocabulary are all that matter. Without these fixed points there is no sense either in looking for something "beyond the reach of time and chance" (*CIS*, p. xv) that will ground our beliefs, or in asking for criteria that determine which are the right language games to play. All we can do, says Rorty, is face the contingency of even our most

---

[30] Here we have the first sign of a mistake running through *CIS*: conflating the efficacy of a method with the dispensability of a theory. This mistake is pivotal since it allows Rorty to concentrate on the persuasive force of a certain discourse and leave behind substantive questions of theory. Although parody and *ad hominem* are effective means of persuasion, they are not typically taken as marks of truth, pragmatic or otherwise. Though we may grant that truth is what is good for us to believe, it does not follow that all that matters for a theory is how effectively it persuades us. His view that avoiding cruelty is the most important thing, combined with the not surprising fact that probably more people have been moved by reading Orwell's *1984* than the *Journal of Philosophy*, leads him to conclude that metaphysics and epistemology have no role and should simply be set aside. This is, however, a *non sequitur*. His appropriation of philosophy's artifacts betrays, I think, a reliance on the metaphysics he shuns as well as a significant element of realism underlying his argument.

central beliefs and so become ironists ourselves. Although Rorty's arguments against realism are, I think, suspect and open to criticism,[31] I want to turn to a different problem, namely, the possibility of explaining and retaining certain "moral" practices within his neo-pragmatist "theory" of truth. The question I want to address is what it means to embrace irony.

2.3.3 Irony or solidarity

One of the most serious challenges Rorty faces is, as mentioned above, to combine the two central themes of his book – irony and solidarity – and to show how ironic solidarity is not only a human possibility, but an enviable one.[32] Against the backdrop of his antirealist, or anti-essentialist, program, Rorty defines the liberal ironist as one who: (1) has "*radical* and continuing doubts about the final vocabulary she currently uses";[33] (2) realizes that "argument phrased in her present vocabulary can neither underwrite nor dissolve these doubts"; and (3) thinks that "her vocabulary is [not] closer to reality than others" (*CIS*, p. 73, emphasis added). Yet, despite these radical, indissoluble doubts the ironist is still able to combine commitment with her sense of contingency (*CIS*, p. 60). But this must give us pause: what does it mean

[31] There is, for example, an uncharacteristic seriousness in this business of irony which fits ill with the "spirit of playfulness" that would most naturally accompany the ironist's "power of redescribing" (*CIS* p. 39): a seriousness of purpose in avoiding cruelty as the worst thing one can do and advocating freedom and autonomy as the most prized (and essential?) tools of the trade. This seriousness in irony betrays, I think, a realist spirit in Rorty. See also, Alessandro Ferrara, "The Unbearable Seriousness of Irony," *Philosophy and Social Criticism* 16 (1990): 81–107.

[32] Although the problem here is expressed in terms of the combination between irony and *solidarity*, rather than commitment, the problem extends to the latter as well, for two reasons: first, solidarity can be thought of as a particular kind or form of commitment, so that the possibility of ironic solidarity touches on the possibility of ironic commitment; and, second, although Rorty does not explicitly address commitment itself, he does speak of the possibility of being a liberal ironist and still maintaining one's convictions and dedication to certain principles or groups, which are, as I discussed in the introduction, different forms of commitment as well. Within this context, "solidarity" and "commitment" are interchangeable.

[33] Rorty defines "final vocabulary" as the words in which we express praise and contempt, and "formulate . . . our long-term projects, our deepest self-doubts and our highest hopes." The words of one's final vocabulary are "as far as [one] can go with language; beyond them there is only helpless passivity or a resort to force" (*CIS* p.73).

to have *radical* doubts about one's most central beliefs[34] and yet be able to remain committed to them or be willing to endorse any actions that might be called for on their basis?

To help motivate this sort of misgiving, consider again the case of Eugene Debs. He was committed to political and social causes that were highly unpopular among the general public, including his neighbors and former friends. As part of his commitment he undertook a number of actions that put him at great personal risk. Suppose he came to have radical doubts about his commitment: not simple misgivings about the efficacy of his actions, about whether he was really making a difference, or whether anyone really cared, but *radical, indissoluble* doubts about the commitment itself and the central beliefs which supported it – he came to doubt the very principles on which the commitment was premised. And now suppose he remained "committed" to the cause, despite his doubts and knowledge of its attendant risks. How shall we understand such commitment?

Let us try this thought experiment. Keeping everything Debs did in his life exactly the same, suppose now that he is in fact a liberal ironist called Twin Debs. Now Twin Debs does not believe his commitments rest on any "facts" about the world or human nature, they do not purport to be true in any interesting (nonpragmatic) sense, but, rather, he recognizes their radical contingency, lack of grounding, and failure to represent anything "real." That said, he does everything the original Debs did. He suffers sunstroke after speaking for two hours to workers in the stifling heat in Montana (Brommel, *Eugene V. Debs*, p. 50). He pushes himself to the point of physical and emotional exhaustion, and suffers frequent bouts of sickness (Salvatore, *Eugene V. Debs*, p. 276), in order to defend and promote principles which lack any grounding. At the age of sixty-three, "fully expecting arrest" (*ibid.*, p. 291), Twin Debs speaks out against American war activities. And when later sentenced to ten years in prison, despite the deep personal toll prison life takes on him, "he [forbids] any special pleading for himself at the expense of other political prisoners . . . [and] reject[s] any suggestion that he accept a release conditioned on the promise to cease future political activity" (*ibid.*, p. 327). But why?

---

[34] This is not, importantly, equivalent to having fallible beliefs, or beliefs we think are mostly true – ones which we would be unwilling to deny, yet whose truth we cannot guarantee.

When he can simply adopt a new final vocabulary, and when the cost of not doing so is so high, how do we explain his continued commitment to his beliefs and principles? Equally important, how does Twin Debs understand himself? What does a sixty-three-year-old man say to himself in prison, isolated from the friends and family he loves, with freedom so easily within his reach, in order to explain why he sticks by groundless principles? Why is he so serious when instead he could be so playful? It is not ego. Who would blame a man after a lifetime of sacrifice for not wanting to spend his final years in prison? He is not a martyr: he never had much tolerance for religious fervor and was by no means a religious zealot.

Again, how shall we understand the commitment of a liberal ironist? Should we perhaps say the commitment only manifests an unwillingness to come to terms with the doubts or a deliberate refusal to acknowledge them; or that it is a form of self-deception or wishful thinking – that by pursuing the "commitment" the doubts will disappear and he will recapture the assurance he once had? Or that the "commitment" is rather the continuation of a familiar pattern, the submission to an inertia built up over years that one cannot now resist? Or should we say that the doubts were not as radical as originally thought, that they were overstated and exaggerated doubts which resulted more from frustration than a questioning of one's principles, and if exposed to a little more thought and reflection would have disappeared? This inclination to reinterpret either the "commitment" or the "doubt" stems from our inability to reconcile the continued, genuine commitment with the presence of such doubts. At this point we need to examine Rorty's understanding of commitment and solidarity. Unfortunately, he has little to say.

The closest Rorty comes to explicating what he means by either of these notions is in the following sentence: "if the demands of a morality are the demands of a language, and if languages are historical contingencies rather than attempts to capture the true shape of the world or the self, then to 'stand unflinchingly for one's moral convictions' is a matter of identifying oneself with such a contingency" (*CIS*, p. 60). There are two things to notice here.[35] First, one should notice that

---

[35] There are actually three things to notice, the third being Rorty's identification of commitment with "unflinching support." For ease of exposition I shall adopt Rorty's assimilation of the terms, though it should become clear in the discussion that they differ.

Rorty simply redefines what commitment will be once we accept that contingency runs all the way down. He avoids asserting that commitment will remain as we have typically experienced it or play the same role in our lives as it once did, whatever that experience or role may have been. Although I will return to what I take to be the importance of commitment and some of the assumptions which accompany it, suffice it to say at this point that all Rorty has said is that in the ironist utopia there is still commitment, but it refers to something else, namely, identifying with contingency.[36] Clearly, though, the concern is not whether the word "commitment" survives, but whether the possibility of forming deep, long-lasting attachments – to principles or persons – remains. Second, one should be aware that at this point in *CIS* Rorty has not yet defined the ironist in terms of radical doubts. Consequently, the question he addresses here is only whether commitment is possible in the face of *contingency*. We can, without too much difficulty, answer with him in the affirmative. Consider a marriage. Unless one holds strongly to the idea of soulmates, of being destined to meet the one you love, a marriage would seem to be a perfect example of a contingent, yet deeply committed, relationship. But the real problem is whether we can "unflinchingly support" convictions of which we have radical doubts – whether we can commit ourselves ironically without winking.

Rorty is sensitive to what I take to be the central question of the book – whether it is psychologically possible to be a liberal ironist (*CIS*, p. 85). Yet in the remainder of the work we never receive a satisfactory answer. At best we are simply invited to trust Rorty that it is possible since "as far as [he] can see" there is no problem (*CIS*, p. 87). There is, however, reason to think that ironism as Rorty defines it leads to stasis, and that for solidarity and commitment to emerge there would have to develop a radical split or detachment of the ironist from her actions; that is to say, Rorty is guilty of a kind of "theoretical akrasia," or "intellectual schizophrenia."

Rorty tells us that the ironist not only sees her most central beliefs as contingent, but has radical, indissoluble doubts about them, and that although she worries that her own self-descriptions may be wrong, she can offer no criteria for determining how or in what way (*CIS*, p. 75). One thing to notice here is that the very notion of doubt, and the

---

[36] That is, identifying with whatever contingent practice, system, etc., happens to have emerged, without thinking that it captures anything about "the way the world is."

worry that one's self-descriptions may be wrong, are both premised on the idea that there is "something to get right." It is only in the context of this (modest) realism, which holds out the possibility of there being right answers, that radical doubt makes sense. As for the compatibility of commitment with irony, recall that commitments were characterized by their stability and critical revisability as well as their figuration in self-understanding, identity, and governance of action. If we try to explain these roles of commitment within a theory of irony, we immediately encounter a series of problems.

One problem is to understand what reason one would have to sustain a commitment based on a central belief that was very possibly false and unsupported by one's other central beliefs since, *by one's own acknowledgment*, they have no greater share in truth. One would be unable to defend a belief for which one could offer no criteria for what it would mean for the belief to be wrong or right. In what way, then, could it withstand exposure to criticism? Perhaps Rorty would remind us that questions of truth would no longer be the exigent questions for liberal ironists. But then, given her indifference to truth, it would seem that her commitments and the central beliefs upon which they are based are simply chosen; that is, she decides to believe, for example, that inflicting cruelty is the worst thing one can do. But, if this is so, we must be given a more complete story of the terms in which the liberal ironist understands her commitments. For when we acquire beliefs, we typically aim to acquire beliefs that are true: being a believer means, as Peter Railton and others suggest, having an interest in truth. As a result, we cannot simply decide to believe something at will without regard to its truth, since doing so would involve having a belief one *knows* does not represent or reflect the truth, which is not possible for "believers" whose interest is truth.[37]

Rorty clearly denies this picture. Ironists, he says, "do not take the point of discursive thought to be *knowing*, in any sense that can be explicated by notions like 'reality,' 'real essence,' 'objective point of view,' and 'the correspondence of language of [*sic*] reality'" (*CIS*, p. 75). The question thus remains: in terms of what does the liberal ironist understand her commitments to such things as avoiding cruelty? It is on this point that the playful spirit of irony and the

---

[37] See Bernard Williams, "Deciding to Believe," in *Problems of the Self* (Cambridge: Cambridge University Press, 1973).

ironist's power of redescription exhaust themselves and must fall back on the facts which language cannot describe away but, rather, must try to represent. Rorty says as much in an earlier passage in *CIS*: "Faced with the nonhuman, the nonlinguistic, we no longer have an ability to overcome contingency and pain by appropriation and transformation, but only the ability to *recognize* contingency and pain" (*CIS*, p. 40; original emphasis). This is a curious choice of words for one for whom everything is language and who chides the "metaphysicians" who "do not believe that anything can be made to look good or bad by being redescribed" (*CIS*, p. 75); it suggests that even for the liberal ironist, in order to explain certain commitments – such as the commitment to the liberal ideal of avoiding cruelty – some appeal must be made to things which withstand and limit redescription, and which we must instead try to *recognize*. When it comes to pain, cruelty, and humiliation, the ironist's rhetoric regarding values and truth changes from creation to discovery. Contrary to what Rorty says later, the point of some discursive thought for ironists is still to know.

Another problem for Rorty is to explain not only our understanding of our commitments in the context of irony, but also our understanding of our own commitment-based actions; that is, he must give a more complete story of how a belief which is held so untenably, of whose truth we are so unsure and whose conditions of truth we are unable to formulate, could play a role in helping us understand the reasons and motives for certain actions, i.e., how it could play a role in self-understanding. Without anticipating too much of the work to be done in later chapters, let me briefly sketch what the problem is. Borrowing from David Velleman the definition of self-understanding as involving, at least in part, an understanding of the motives and reasons for one's action and an ability to explain and make one's actions intelligible to oneself, and assuming, as Velleman does, that when we fail to reach this understanding of our actions we stop doing whatever it is we are doing, since we like doing things we understand, we can ask whether Rorty's ironists ever reach this sort of self-understanding given their radical doubt, or if they are in a state of "perpetual puzzlement."[38]

Return to the above example of Twin Debs who has radical doubts about his commitments. Once again, these doubts go to the very

---

[38] Velleman, *Practical Reflection*, p. 27.

heart of his central beliefs: he worries that he may be radically wrong about the principles he holds and comes to think they no longer represent the truth since he cannot offer any test by which he could know, or have reason to believe, that they are right. The doubts refer, not to the success of his actions, but to the value of his commitment (or what he is committed to) and the truth of the beliefs associated with it. But Twin Debs is a liberal ironist and retains his commitment: he continues to take risks, make sacrifices, and expend time and energy for the cause. A natural question to ask is why. If his central beliefs are very possibly false – if the principles he supports are just wrong – would he not be at the very least more hesitant or, what is more likely, unwilling, to undertake an action required by the commitment and its supporting belief? In these kinds of cases it is a commonplace to offer as a motive or reason for action that "It was the right thing to do," by which one often means "I believe X is right (or good or true), and doing Y is a way of realizing X." This is probably the most natural way for any agent to explain her actions. But once doubt infects her central beliefs and she can no longer offer these reasons, how does she understand why she is doing what she is doing? Perhaps she just likes doing these things, but in light of their highly counter-prudential outcomes, her desire hardly rationalizes the action. In the absence of an explanation of her actions, there is a breakdown in self-understanding which, in turn, according to Velleman, puts a stop to action. The consequence of embracing irony is, I suggest and will later more carefully argue, reflective puzzlement about one's own actions.

The best argument for these claims comes once again from examples. Debs's final vocabulary (to use Rorty's phrase) consisted of such concepts as "manhood," "the dignity of the individual," "justice," and "the evil of suffering." Although these concepts were, admittedly, formed through experience and the influence of literature rather than philosophy and robust moral theories, we can still trace a realist foundation to these concepts, the absence of which impedes our understanding of the "story" of Debs's life.

Debs's involvement in labor struggles, his opposition to war, and his advocacy of women's and minority rights were premised on his respect for *individual dignity* and the abhorrence of suffering. Speaking against American involvement in the war, Debs stated that "the profits of the munitions industries never justified the *human suffering* caused by war" (Brommel, *Eugene V. Debs*, p. 147, emphasis added). In his speeches, Debs commonly made appeals to "fair play, happiness, security, honesty, freedom, pride, honor, loyalty, and other *basic human needs*" (*ibid.*, p. 205, emphasis added). We see time and again statements to the effect that while strikes were ostensibly organized for political and economic goals, they were in fact based "primarily in defense of [the laborers'] *rights as individuals*" as well as their "individual dignity" (*ibid.*, pp. 61–2, emphasis added).[39] These kinds of arguments are made by the workers themselves. As Salvatore states, "the increasingly harsh treatment meted out by foremen and managers undermined [the workers'] *basic self-dignity* . . . The wage cuts, although cruel, might have been bearable, one woman argued, but for 'the tyrannical and abusive treatment we received from our forewoman'" (p. 127, emphasis added). The point here is that the actions that political and social activists like Debs and others took on behalf of their principles were informed by certain *objective* beliefs. It was not that they denounced their treatment simply on the basis of their American citizenship, for example, but rather on the basis of their status as one human being, as one person, among others. Indeed, they were equally concerned for the plight of Russian workers at that time (Salvatore, *Eugene V. Debs*, p. 212). Debs saw the real harm done to real people. Granted, his commitments were not molded in the context of an overarching moral theory; but he did see them, we can surmise, as responding to things "in the world" – namely, human beings, certain social conditions, and the measurable effects these conditions had on them. Looking more closely at his actions and speeches we can go so far as to say that Debs did not view his commitments as the arbitrary product of his culture or community – as an organic extension of the normative practices inculcated in him in his youth – but as based on reflectively endorsed principles that withstood criticism and were believed to be "true" in the sense I have been using.

His commitments responded to the demand for objectivity – a demand which only makes sense in the context of realism. Debs felt the pull of consistency, publicity, and universality on the principles he held. We have already seen part of this in his extension of the notions of dignity and respect to women, blacks, and immigrants, and not just

---

[39] Cf. Salvatore, *Eugene V. Debs*, p. 293: "Ultimately the central issue, as always for Debs, revolved around the *individual*" (emphasis added).

white American males. The demand for objectivity forced him to reconsider his ideas and explore the implications of some of his commitments. For example, although he "found it difficult to break during these years with the dominant racial attitudes of the culture that had formed him . . . Debs nonetheless came to oppose immigrant restrictions, in part because of his *deep belief in free speech*" (*ibid.*, p. 105, emphasis added).

This example highlights our inclination to explain our commitments, and to reach an understanding of them, in terms of beliefs which we take to be true, or to approximate closely to the truth. This is not to say that these beliefs are basic beliefs, incorrigible and indefeasible, but beliefs whose truth does not depend on consensus or on the prevailing attitudes of one's time or culture: beliefs whose truth is indicated by their ability to withstand exposure to critical, rational evaluation; by their coherence with other beliefs we have regarding, for example, the conditions of human well-being; and by our consistent endorsement of them in our actions. In short, there is reason to think, *contra* Rorty, that commitment and action based on that commitment are predicated on the thought that we are, in some sense, "getting it right" – a thought which liberal ironism rules out. If, however, radical doubts infect all of our most central beliefs, we are left without grounds for pursuing any course of action except through a Herculean act of will of which not even the strong poet might be capable. The radical doubt that defines the ironist is in fact paralyzing.

2.3.4 Conclusion

What emerges from this discussion is that one of the central points of contention in the debate over moral realism is what beliefs are required for commitment and what their content might be. Rorty's emphasis on the possibility of radical *doubt* and the contingency of our *beliefs*, together with his attempt to reconcile these with solidarity, underscore the centrality of the question of what roles, if any, beliefs play in commitment and what those beliefs might be. Indeed, it is only in the light of this last question that the problem of the psychological possibility of liberal irony arises. Rorty wants to retain commitment and solidarity while rejecting moral realism. He constructs a picture of a new kind of agent, the liberal ironist, who does not simply suspend belief, but entertains radical doubts. Yet she is still able to find solidarity and even fight for principles unto death.[40] It is unclear though how (and Rorty offers no insights) one is to reconcile the subject who acknowledges that her beliefs are very possibly wrong and is unable to articulate how they might be true, with the subject who acts in accordance with those beliefs.[41] The conclusion that will emerge in the subsequent chapters is that one cannot reconcile these two subjects; that is, ironism is impossible on the assumption of a unitary subject and so crucially depends on what has been called "intellectual schizophrenia." "Theoretical" and "practical" beliefs cannot be held simultaneously within the same subject if solidarity and commitment are to be possible under ironism. The only way to be both an ironist and participate in commitment would be through a radical split between the agent and her actions. In short, the rejection of moral realism constitutes a real threat to commitment. To the extent one wants to retain it as an important element of our lives and something that needs to be accommodated by any broad metaethical theory, one has to concede the conditions which make it possible, and

---

[40] See *CIS*, p. 189.

[41] It is interesting to compare Rorty's neopragmatism with Sextus Empiricus' Pyrrhonian skepticism. In *Outlines of Pyrrhonism*, (trans. B. Mates [New York: Oxford University Press, 1996], HP 1.10), Sextus tells us that the skeptic's goal is *ataraxia*, "an untroubled and tranquil condition of the soul." The way the skeptic attains this state is through the suspension of all beliefs regarding the nature of things. The skeptic acts only on the impression made upon him by the appearances. However, as Myles Burnyeat and J. Annas point out, we see a radical division taking place within the skeptic: on the one hand there is the subject who acknowledges the impressions affecting him but withholds belief about their truth; and on the other hand is the subject who acts in accordance with the appearances. We find the skeptic saying to himself, "It is thought within me that p, but I do not believe that p" (M. Burnyeat, "Can the Sceptic Live His Scepticism?" in M. Schofield *et al.* (eds.), *Doubts and Dogmatism* [Oxford: Clarendon Press, 1980], p. 53). The skeptic stands outside himself only as an observer of his actions and does not inhabit them as a deliberator or judge. "He becomes," says Annas, "the uncommitted spectator of his own actions and impulses" (J. Annas "Doing Without Objective Values: Ancient and Modern Strategies," in M. Schofield and G. Striker (eds.), *The Norms of Nature* [Cambridge: Cambridge University Press, 1986], p. 22). A similar radical division between the acting and the observing (or theorizing) subject also takes place, I think, in the ironist. Note also that both Rorty and Sextus see their "philosophies" as a kind of therapy: to cure us of foundationalist longings, on the one hand, or to lead us to *ataraxia* on the other. And both claim to be antiphilosophical in that they do not put forward a positive theory, yet attempt to remain detached from all theory (*CIS*, p. 8; Empiricus, HP 1.16; Annas, "Doing Without Objective Values, " p. 20).

these include, so I will argue, realist beliefs which are explicitly rejected by Rorty's neopragmatism.

Before concluding this chapter, I want to return to the example of Eugene Debs and introduce a new one – M. Meursault from Camus' *The Stranger*. These two "case studies" will help us assess the arguments presented so far, and provide a more perspicuous context for the development of the argument that centrally locates realist evaluative beliefs within substantive commitments.

2.4 IRREALISM IN CONTEXT

2.4.1 *Debs's final vocabulary: a realist account*

Recall that Debs felt the pull of consistency, publicity, and even universality on the principles he held. I have shown how the demand for objectivity forced him on many occasions to reconsider his ideas and explore the implications of some of his commitments. A realist account of Debs's final vocabulary is further evidenced in the story we are told of how Debs tried to step outside his community's limited perspectives on many issues, e.g., race, the status of women, and immigration, and take a more objective standpoint. Indeed, Debs's life is testimony to the difficulty and struggle involved in such a task, and how it remains incomplete in many ways. Yet despite being "rooted" (Salvatore, *Eugene V. Debs*, p. 106) in important ways in his culture, he still attacked its prejudices and tried to "transcend the ethnic and geographical difference that separated working people" (*ibid.*, p. 232). Although he initially accepted his community's norms and values, he was able to take a critical stance toward them, discern their inconsistencies, and draw out their logical implications.

The story of Debs's life speaks against not only Rorty's ironist stance, but also against the kind of parochialism and relativism Gibbard describes. Gibbard's theory of the "organic" emergence and acceptance of norms fails to explain the development and evolution of Debs's thought and commitments – a process that fits better with an objectivist–realist story and the attempt to reach a more objective point of view. Debs certainly was not simply making "sincere conversational demands" on his audience. His claims to objectivity, if we can call them that, were not just based on a "good epistemic story," but were supported instead by the thought that his commitments, and the beliefs supporting them, were "getting it right"in a way that other stories – those of the industrial capitalists, nativists, and pro-war activists – were not. They were "getting it right" because they *recognized* or took into account certain facts – most notably, the heavy physical toll and insult to individual dignity of current working conditions – that other stories ignored. It was in virtue of such facts that he ultimately accepted the norms he did, and made demands on others to do so as well. He did not mysteriously come to have these norms because of the normative influence his community exerted on him, but because they captured certain facts about human needs, and because of his critical awareness that they did so.

The structuring role Debs's final vocabulary played in his life, projects, identity, and self-understanding, in no way conforms to the liberal ironist's "spirit of playfulness" and capacity to adopt new vocabularies, nor does it sit well with Gibbard's "givenness" of commitment. Debs was involved in a lifelong project of gaining a better understanding of both himself and the meaning of what he took to be his fundamental values, such as manhood, justice, and dignity. Nowhere can we discern an ironic stance toward them. Instead of adopting new vocabularies, Debs came to a deeper understanding of the values he held,[42] critically reflecting on them, trying to reach consistency between them, and bringing them closer to the standards of objectivity. These values had a fixity they would otherwise lack if in fact they were the products of contingency, whim, or mere desire. It was through such values and the commitments based on them that Debs understood who he was (Salvatore, *Eugene V. Debs*, p. 23), and defined his identity. Despite the fact that he was born into a certain community, and was raised on their values and norms, he was at the same time able to step back from them, to avoid the parochialism – the givenness of his initial commitments – and assess them from a more objective standpoint.

2.4.2 Commitment without objective value: the case of Meursault

Suppose we take the antirealist position seriously. What would a life look like in such circumstances? There are two ways we can approach

---

[42] Cf. Mark Platts's notion of "semantic depth" in *Ways of Meaning* (London: Routledge and Kegan Paul, 1979), ch. 10.

this: first, we can consider someone like Eugene Debs and try to make sense of his commitments in the absence of any realist beliefs about value; and, second, we can consider someone without such beliefs and ask what kind of commitments they would have, that is, ask whether commitments could form in the liberal ironist or noncognitivist. The first approach I have undertaken in the discussion of Rorty. I now follow the second approach, but in order to do so I shall have to turn (tellingly) to fiction.

Consider a character who in fact values nothing, who has no substantive beliefs about values, in part because nothing matters in any deep sense: everything is contingent, absurd, the product of historical circumstance and chance. What does his life look like and what kind of commitments does he have? The richest description we can find of such a character comes from Camus' novel *The Stranger*.

The picture of the world we get through Meursault's eyes is flat, and lifeless. His detachment, passivity, and near alienation from the events and people around him come through in the short, simple phrases used to describe the world around and within him. His evaluations, if we can call them that, are simple to the point of being banal: "I don't like Sundays . . . I don't like [being asked questions] . . . I didn't feel like going downstairs" (Camus, *The Stranger*, p. 21). His strongest "indictments" are tied to his physical reactions: what he finds "repulsive" is not his neighbor Raymond's brutal beating of his girlfriend, but the effect that the sight of Raymond's pale, hirsute forearms has on him. Just as striking as his detachment from the world is his lack of any deep reflection. The strongest emotions he experiences are "embarrassment," "discomfort," "irritation." In situations that others find "pitiful," like old man Salamono's repeated beating of his hairless, scabrous dog, he can only yawn. Not once do we hear Meursault express or use any evaluatively rich concepts.

Yet is not this the kind of detached, uninvolved life we would expect from the strong poet, the liberal ironist? In Rorty's picture one vocabulary has as much claim to truth as another, which is to say none. The ironist creates her life, and can do one thing today and another tomorrow, but without any criteria by which to choose her roles, since those too she creates. But this is exactly how Meursault sees his life. When asked if he had wished for another life, he responds by saying, "of course I had, but it didn't mean any more than wishing to be rich, to be able to swim faster, or to have a more nicely shaped mouth. It was all the same" (*ibid.*, p. 119). Echoing Rorty's theme of freedom, Meursault states, "I had lived my life one way and I could just as well have lived it another. I had done this and I hadn't done that. I hadn't done this thing, but I had done another. And so? Nothing, nothing mattered, and I knew why" (p. 121). This is the kind of flattening one would expect when we are denied the evaluative vocabulary we typically use to describe our projects, our principles, and the things that matter to us. When we excise the possibility of objectivity, as do neopragmatism and noncognitivism, what we are left with are characters like Meursault rather than Debs.

Consider Meursault's relation to his girlfriend Marie: "she asked me if I loved her. I told her it didn't mean anything but that I didn't think so. She looked sad" (p. 35). When the topic of marriage comes up, he has this to say:

> Marie came by to see me and asked me if I wanted to marry her. I said it didn't make any difference to me and that we could if she wanted to. Then she wanted to know if I loved her. I answered the same way I had the last time, that it didn't mean anything but that I probably didn't love her. "So why marry me, then?" she said. I explained to her that it didn't really matter and that if she wanted to, we could get married (p. 41).

One has the sense that he is watching himself live his life, that he is merely going through the motions with nothing of himself vested in them – that he is a detached observer of himself. Indeed, Meursault nearly says as much through his reaction to a young reporter during his trial for killing an Arab. He notes the reporter's "two very bright eyes, which were examining me closely without betraying any definable emotion. *I had the odd impression of being watched by myself*" (p. 85; emphasis added).

The point of this discussion is to draw a portrait of a character for whom there are no fixed points, no substantive values through which one constructs a life, makes sense of one's actions, or reaches some sort of self-understanding. When we take seriously what neopragmatism and antirealist theories of value have to tell us, when we look closely at a life lived by those principles and move beyond the glib reassurances about the possibility of ironic solidarity, or the brute fact of commitment without reflection, the portrait we eventually sketch resembles M. Meursault, not Eugene Debs.

The examples of Debs and Meursault are not meant as a final proof against Rorty and Gibbard, but as a means of orienting the reader's intuition toward the realist theory of commitment I develop in subsequent chapters. In the more philosophical arguments that follow, it will be useful to think back to these two cases in order to gauge the plausibility of the theories discussed.

2.5 RORTY AND GIBBARD: CONCLUSION

Upon closer examination of their noncognitivist and neopragmatist positions, the compatibility of commitment with their background assumptions regarding, for example, the purely expressive role of normative judgments, or the strictly pragmatic nature of "truth," is brought into question. Most importantly, the discussion has revealed the need for a more careful analysis of commitment in a number of areas, including: (i) the role beliefs play in commitments; (ii) the connection between these beliefs and the other roles and functions of commitment in, e.g., self-understanding and stability; and (iii) what the content of these beliefs might be.

The two guiding questions with which we started – whether Rorty offers a psychologically plausible story (given the dynamic of certain mental states such as commitment), and whether Gibbard misses something in ordinary normative talk and practice – can now be answered. To the first question, the answer is "no": given what we take to be the roles of commitment, and our (provisionally) naive understanding of how commitment fulfills these roles, the plausibility of the liberal ironist depends on a radical split in the subject – a separation of the agent from her actions. The answer to the second question is "yes": Gibbard does not explain, and in fact leaves it wholly mysterious, how we ascribe objectivity to certain judgments, and in virtue of what we make sincere demands. If we accept his theory of norm-expressivism, a large category of our ordinary normative practice becomes unintelligible. Now since these two questions were in fact proposed by Rorty and Gibbard themselves as tests of their respective theories, if the answers I have given are correct, there is considerable room left for a defense of moral realism – a defense which I offer by way of an examination of commitment.

3

Commitment and intention

3.1 INTRODUCTION

The previous chapter opened up the debate over commitment and its relation to moral realism, and helped bring into focus some of the main points of contention, most notably the role of beliefs in commitment and the restrictions on their content. By way of addressing these issues and isolating the central points for analysis, I want to draw out and extend as much as possible a comparison between commitment and intention, since precisely the same problems have been raised with respect to intention as will be addressed concerning commitment. As we shall see, there are a considerable number of overlaps between the two.[1]

---

[1] The action-theoretic approach to commitment might be contested by those who would prefer a phenomenological analysis as found among so-called "continental" philosophers. Yet, as hermeneutic criticisms have shown us, phenomenological analyses face the general problem that in identifying a certain experience and in bracketing its particular instances in favor of its common features, it makes use of considerable knowledge of the defining structure of the experience which is only supposed to be reached at the *end* of the phenomenological process of description, reduction, and variation. Thus, rather than a means of attaining *original* knowledge, phenomenology instead seems to be a method of elucidating *implicit conceptions* of what it sets out to describe. As Bernet *et al.* state, a "phenomenological description of the continuous experience of a thing is . . . guided by a preconception of the very object which is yet to be constituted." Clearly, this undermines phenomenology's attempts at deriving *a priori* necessary truths on the basis of the pure descriptions of the essences of given objects or structures of experience, since it eliminates as fiction the ideal of pure description. In the case of commitment, then, to the extent that one wants to remain "phenomenological" in one's orientation, perhaps it is better to set aside a rigorous phenomenology, in the manner of Peter Kemp's work, in favor of what P. M. Cryle describes as a "pseudo-phenomenological" approach in which "to talk of the essence of commitment is not to appeal to an *eidos* that can be reliably seen and verified as an invariant through all the variations of commitment that are effected: it is rather an

As I have noted, the term "commitment" is used in a variety of contexts with a variety of meanings. Among moral and political philosophers one finds references to the importance commitment plays in structuring our lives and reinforcing the basic good of self-esteem. For virtue ethicists commitment serves as a crucial basis for integrity. Sociologists have taken an interest in commitment as a way of examining consistent patterns of behavior in individuals. Organizational psychologists use it as an indicator of productivity and pro-social behavior. And action theorists have seized on the term to explain a complex sort of intention. Thus a first task of this present chapter will be to defend the position that these different commitments, from which the general description of commitment was derived, have more in common than their nominal similarities in order to ward off objections that the analysis of commitment I offer has been caught in a pun on its various uses.

A second task that needs to be undertaken before moving on to the discussion of beliefs is to show that commitment is a distinct category requiring its own proper analysis; more specifically, to show how and in what ways commitments differ from policies, plans, and intentions. This is not a purely taxonomic exercise; rather, by locating the differences between commitment and policies, or commitment and intention, one will at the same time locate the operative elements of commitment, which in turn will help elucidate its structure as well as direct the developing examination of commitment itself. One of the main questions I address here is whether in fact commitment can be distinguished from intention, or if commitment is simply a "resolute" intention. If it were found that commitment is completely reducible to intention, or is a subset of intention, then one would have immediate answers to a host of questions. For example, there is the question I address in chapter 4 of whether belief constraints apply to commitment. Given the assumption that commitment is a subset of intention, one would only need to see whether constraints apply to intention to find the answer (although this is a highly controversial

appeal to that which we, as writer and reader, can perceive as typical." See Rudolf Bernet, Iso Kern, and Eduard Marbach, *An Introduction to Husserlian Phenomenology* (Evanston: Northwestern University Press, 1993), p. 123; and P. M. Cryle, *The Thematics of Commitment* (Princeton: Princeton University Press, 1985), pp. ix–x.

issue in itself). Or, in asking whether all these various "commitments" have anything in common, one would only need to be able to characterize them all as intentions in order to reach an affirmative answer. Whatever questions arose with respect to commitment could be answered simply by looking at what the case for intention was. But the assumption that commitment is a subset of intention is not without problems. For example, if it were true that every commitment is also an intention, then in being committed to a political cause, say stopping the war or abolishing apartheid, one would then also have to *intend* to stop the war or *intend* to abolish apartheid; but it is not clear that these are the sorts of things one can (rationally) intend to do. Thus, clarifying the relationship between intention and commitment is methodologically useful as part of the "bottom-up" approach – in which the examination of commitment, its structure and conditions, proceeds with the least normatively weighted concept of commitment, as found in the philosophy of action, and works toward the substantive commitments of moral philosophy – and is also necessary for determining the general plausibility of the claim that the different kinds of commitment share a common structure and that the analysis I offer is not the result of an unfortunate ambiguity of language. I argue that although intention can serve as a useful model for studying commitment, a general theory of intention, even one that incorporates policies, is unable to provide an adequate explanation of it.

This chapter seeks to elucidate the structure and role of commitment understood in its least normative sense, that is, simply as a state of "being settled upon" some course of action. Chapter 4 further develops this structure in considering "substantive" commitments – commitment to principles, political causes, and interpersonal commitments – and their associated belief constraints. I argue that all these commitments share a basic structure, but as one moves from the limited conception of commitment in the philosophy of action to the fuller conception of commitment concerning moral philosophers, an important component of commitment is added, namely, its constitutive role in self-understanding and identity. By juxtaposing and comparing commitment and intention, I hope to enrich our understanding of commitment and its associated belief structure.

3.2 COMMITMENT AS A KIND OF INTENTION

The similarity between intention and commitment as described earlier[2] becomes immediately apparent when we look at Michael Bratman's definition of intention. The three central features of intention are, according to Bratman: (i) a conduct-controlling pro-attitude; (ii) a disposition for its retention without reconsideration; and (iii) its role as an input to reasoning in the formation of further intentions.[3] Bratman states explicitly that commitment is crucially involved in future-directed intentions. Commitment (in the narrow sense) has a volitional and reason-centered dimension. The former provides the conduct-controlling pro-attitude whereas the latter provides both the stability (or inertia) of intention and the requisite means–end reasoning (*IPP*, pp. 16–17). For Bratman, "an intention to act is a complex form of commitment to action" (*ibid.*, p. 110). It might be thought that while intention is "open-ended," commitment is more settled and thus a kind of "locked-in" intention.

Robert Audi also remarks on the close relation between intention and commitment.[4] In intending to do something, says Audi, one is at the same time committed to doing it: "One is motivationally committed in that one is in a state of overall inclination . . . And I am cognitively committed in the sense that . . . I am disposed to assert that I will perform it, to take my performing it as a premise in reasoning, and to deny claims that I will fail" (Audi, "Intention, Cognitive Commitment, and Planning," p. 364). Although Bratman and Audi differ with respect to what an intention involves, they agree that it is closely associated with commitment. The question then is how to distinguish commitment from intention.

One way of comparing intention and commitment is by examining some of the roles they play, and then moving on to any constraints that might apply to having an intention or a commitment. I shall begin with the former.

---

[2] Recall that commitment was characterized by three main features: its stability over time while remaining potentially revisable (under critical, rational scrutiny); its action-guiding force; and lastly, its role in self-understanding and identity.

[3] Michael Bratman, *Intention, Plans and Practical Reason* (Cambridge, MA: Harvard University Press, 1987), p. 20 (henceforth, *IPP*).

[4] Audi, "Intention, Cognitive Commitment, and Planning."

From Bratman we have that intentions are conduct-controlling, resistant to reconsideration, and serve as elements in practical reasoning. Alfred Mele also notes that intentions are important in coordinative plans, that they initiate and sustain action and that they prompt and end practical reasoning.[5] This last point is also made by Stuart Hampshire and H. L. A. Hart who state that forming an intention typically terminates inquiry.[6] This list is extended by Bratman once again. He remarks that in addition to their characteristic stability and the fact that they are often parts of larger coordinating plans, intentions also extend the influence of rational reflection over time, thus promoting coordination; they support associated beliefs in their successful execution and so allow others to plan on us and allow us to plan on ourselves; they pose problems for further planning in terms of means–ends reasoning; and, lastly, they act as filters on further intentions by screening inconsistent options in the light of our prior intentions.[7] Combining and summarizing the above points, we have a modified version of Bratman's list:

1. Intentions are stable though revisable.
2. Intentions are conduct-controlling: they both initiate and sustain action.
3. Intentions can prompt and terminate practical reasoning.
4. Intentions impose consistency and coherence constraints: they serve as filters on admissible options, and require means–ends reasoning.
5. Intentions play an important role in both inter- and intra-personal coordination. They serve as elements in an agent's own larger coordinating plans, and also make it possible for others to plan on the agent.

We now have to see how commitment compares with intention on these five points.

Consider, first, some simple forms of commitment: for example,

---

[5] A.Mele, *Springs of Action* (Oxford: Oxford University Press, 1992), ch. 8. Hugh McCann makes the same point in "Settled, Objective and Rational Constraints," *American Philosophical Quarterly* 28 (1991): 26.

[6] S. Hampshire, "Decision, Intention, and Certainty," *Mind* 67 (1958): 1–12.

[7] M. Bratman, "Intention and Personal Policies," in James Tomberlin (ed.), *Philosophical Perspective*, vol. III *Philosophy of Mind and Action Theory* (Atascadero: Ridgeview, 1989), p. 451.

being committed to solving a difficult puzzle, or to seeing one's plan through. Clearly, (1) above is satisfied since it is the very stability that allows us to recognize it as commitment. Someone who gives up on a puzzle as soon as it becomes challenging, or abandons a plan as soon as it encounters obstacles, is not a person we would describe as being committed. Yet, we do recognize the possibility of revising commitments. For example, a student's commitment to becoming a lawyer will probably influence her to follow one curriculum over another, to join the debate team rather than the chorus, etc., and this influence will extend over a period of months and probably years. Yet she may come to realize that law school is not right for her, or that she is not the kind of person who makes a good lawyer. And so she revises, perhaps with considerable difficulty, her commitment. Although there is much to be said on the differences in revision for commitment and intention, especially in the case of substantive commitment, suffice it to say at this point that we typically acknowledge the possibility of revising stable commitments. With respect to (1), commitment and intention are alike.

Regarding (2), the conduct-controlling aspect of intention, it almost follows analytically from what is ordinarily understood by 'commitment' that it, too, can initiate and sustain action. Indeed, Benn and Gaus define an "action commitment" as a course of action appropriate to a belief.[8] For example, a detective may be committed to solving a case and so, determined to leave no stone unturned and believing Mr. Green to be a suspect, will initiate the appropriate course of action. This seems fairly uncontroversial. Moreover, commitments typically sustain an action in so far as the commitment remains: the detective will continue to investigate provided, other things being equal, he remains committed to solving the case. Commitments also satisfy (3). The commitment to finishing a paper by tomorrow will terminate reasoning about whether I should start it now. And in connection with (4) it should also be clear that commitments will prompt practical reasoning. Drawing on the detective once again, his commitment to solving the case will prompt him to think about how to go about gathering evidence (a form of means–end reasoning). Commitments will also act as a screen filtering out inadmissible options. One's commitment to solving a difficult puzzle might

---

[8] Benn and Gaus, "Practical Rationality and Commitment."

preclude one from forming other commitments, for example, finishing that paper.[9]

We can also grant quite easily that commitments figure in plans. And like the intentions described in (5) above, commitments certainly permit inter- and intra-personal coordination and perhaps even fulfill this role more effectively than intentions since they are typically more secure: knowing you are committed to finishing that paper tonight, I can plan appropriately. Similarly, given one's own commitment to finishing the paper, one will know how to plan for the rest of the day. These cases of commitment seem amenable to being components of plans. Yet if we consider substantive commitments, like stopping the war or promoting racial harmony, it is not clear how these would figure into our standard plans, apart from saying they are part of our rational life plans; but this surely overextends the notion of planning used in action theory.[10] Despite this one difference, there seem to be strong similarities between commitment and intention with respect to the above roles – in the language of action theory, commitment and intention look to be functionally similar.

I want to turn now to the question of how, if at all, commitment and intention differ and whether commitment can be reduced to intention.

3.2.1 Commitment and intention: differences

One way of trying to pull commitment apart from intention is to consider instances where an agent is committed to (doing) *A* and to ask

[9] As a historical aside, it is interesting to note that this comparison between intention and commitment is further supported by a description of commitment Gabriel Marcel offers in *Du Refus à l'Invocation*. With uncanny prescience, Marcel describes some of the main features of commitment that action theorists were later to describe, though under the rubric of "intention." According to Marcel, commitment, like intention, figures in planning by (i) requiring that one adapt future behavior to the commitment; (ii) filtering out from possible consideration certain courses of action, and (iii) offering stability through an active will toward nonreconsideration. Once again we see that commitment mirrors the roles attributed to intention. See Marcel, *Du Refus à l'Invocation*, p. 211. It is also worth comparing what Marcel says about deciding not to put a commitment in question with Bratman's discussion of reflective versus nonreflective (non)reconsideration of prior intentions (Bratman, *IPP*, pp. 64 ff.).

[10] I shall return to the problem of the relation of substantive commitments to plans in the comparison of commitments and personal policies.

whether we can also say that she intends to *A*. Consider the following cases of commitment.

1. A student is committed to finishing a paper.
2. A detective is committed to solving a case.
3. A person is committed to solving a puzzle.
4. A student is committed to becoming a doctor.
5. A protester is committed to stopping the war.
6. A person is committed to a friendship.

For each of these we can ask whether one can also intend the object of the commitment. In case (1), saying the student is committed to finishing seems to allow us to say that she also intends to finish. It certainly would be odd for her to say, "I'm committed to finishing this paper, though I don't intend to." However, the oddity of being committed to something without intending that "something" loses its force as we move down the list. Does the detective intend to solve the case? Perhaps, if he is very confident in his elementary skills of deduction. But consider (5): can one say that the protester *intends* to stop the war? No. The verb "intends" applies to events or outcomes which we can directly influence or control.

One might object that this denial assumes that all intentions are intentions to act, a view which has been challenged by Bruce Vermazen.[11] He argues that there are such things as "nonact intentions" whose object is "someone else's action or a mere state of affairs" (Vermazen, "Objects of Intention," 252) and which are not simply elliptical expressions of intending to bring about the state of affairs (*ibid.*, p. 253–4). On Vermazen's view, for example, the conditional, "If anyone reads my epitaph, I intend him or her to reflect on the fragility of life," is a legitimate intention even though the prospective action is not the intender's action. According to Vermazen, then, being committed to stopping the war or, better, being committed to world peace, could be read as an intention that a state of affairs obtains, despite my objection that one cannot *rationally* intend such things. But Vermazen adds a caveat which blocks an immediate translation of such commitments into intentions.

"[A] necessary condition," says Vermazen, "for having a . . . non-act

---

[11] B. Vermazon, "Objects of Intention," *Philosophical Studies* 71 (1993): 223–65. I thank Michael Bratman for drawing my attention to this issue.

intention appears to be that the agent believe the state of affairs that the intended proposition is about to be potentially controllable by her" (255, also 261). This is not to say that intending that p "require[s] *intending* that one control the circumstances that make p true . . . but [it] does require that one think it possible that one control those circumstances" (256). Using Vermazen's example, one can intend to host a pleasant picnic (a necessary condition being fair weather), provided one believes that one can control the weather. Returning to the above commitment, then, one can be committed to world peace and also intend that there be world peace, provided one believes that world peace is a state of affairs one can control. Yet the question is then whether this is a belief a *rational* agent would possess. I suggest it is not, and as a result one cannot translate the commitment into an intention. Even if there are non-act intentions, the limits on what an agent can rationally believe set limits on what an agent can rationally intend. And since the objects of certain commitments are states of affairs typically beyond an agent's control, such commitments cannot be immediately read as intentions, non-act or otherwise. That is, my claim does not crucially depend on the assumption that all intentions are intentions to act. [12]

Returning to (6) above, the commitment to a friendship, in this case it is not at all clear what, if anything, is intended in being so committed. As we move toward the more substantive cases of commitment, commitment no longer seems to track intention since the content of what is intended cannot be read off directly from the commitment.

The problem may simply be one of generality; that is, while what one intends applies to a specific action, the object of commitment can be very general. A possible solution to the problem might be to say that the more general commitments have intentions embedded within them: while being committed to stopping the war does not entail intending to stop the war, it does entail certain actions (not necessarily known in advance), and whatever those actions are one intends to perform them. In other words, one might say that commit-

---

[12] For a related discussion, see Wayne Davis, "A Causal Theory of Intending," *American Philosophical Quarterly* 21 (1988): 50. Note also that intending to A typically involves having a plan to A. But it is unlikely that the protester can be said to have a "plan" to stop the war. Protesting is a way of registering her opposition, and not necessarily a step in her plan to end the war; cf. Gilbert Harman, *Change in View* (Cambridge, MA: MIT Press, 1986), p. 84.

ments of this type are simply general intentions whose content needs to be further refined in order to elicit the embedded intentions and, once that is done, one will have once again a nice parallel (if not reduction) of commitment with intention. Bratman performs a similar "reduction" of personal policies by showing that they can be thought of as "intentions that are general in an appropriate way" (Bratman, "Intention and Personal Policies," p. 466). It is worth examining whether commitment might be reformulated as a kind of policy and hence as a general intention.

3.2.2 Commitment and personal policies: the reduction

Bratman notes that although personal policies, such as always buckling one's seatbelt or always studying a foreign language over the summer, are not normally elements of partial plans (since "plans typically concern particular, more or less specifically characterized occasions," while policies are "general with respect to their occasions of execution" (*ibid.*, p. 444), policies still fulfill the main roles of intention: they promote coordination, they are stable, they pose problems for practical reasoning, and act as filters on the admissibility of options. Moreover, says Bratman, we form policies for roughly the same reasons we form intentions: to extend the influence of rational reflection over time and to facilitate coordination (*ibid.*,p. 452). As a result, a personal policy can be thought of as a kind of intention.

Bratman offers a useful distinction between kinds of policies which will help in the comparison with commitment. He distinguishes "situation-specific" policies, or "ss-policies," from "situation-indefinite" policies, or "si-policies." The former are policies of "acting in a certain way whenever one is in a certain type of situation. An ss-policy is a general intention to A whenever C" (p. 458). Si-policies, however, "do not specify a recurrent kind of situation in which one is to act, but rather are policies to act in certain regular ways over an extended period of time" (*ibid.*). Si-policies seem to capture many of the more substantive commitments. Recall that the problem of translating the commitment to stopping the war, or the commitment to a friendship, in terms of intention was that such commitments did not specify either any specific action or any specific occasion for action. (Am I committed to stopping the war *only* while I am protesting or *only* if I protest? Is one committed to a friendship *only* while acting as an exemplary friend?) The idea of regular action over time is a useful way of characterizing such commitments without specifying a unique action or occasion for action which constitutes the commitment.

David Velleman in *Practical Reflection* also gives strong reasons for thinking that commitment, as I have described it, could be thought of as a kind of policy. What he says about policies – which he defines, like Bratman, as "plans to the effect that we shall act in a particular way on every occasion of a particular kind" (Velleman, *Practical Reflection*, p. 307) – reflects to a considerable extent what I have said about commitment, particularly with respect to some of its initial differences from intention. Commitments, I have noted, were more general than intentions and often directed toward principles whose attendant actions were not clearly specified. Just as one can have a commitment to stopping the war without knowing fully in advance what specific actions one might have to take, so also, says Velleman, one can have:

> a policy of standing up for truthfulness, say, or never tolerating lies. Of course, such a policy would be rather vague, given its reliance on phrases like "standing up" and "not tolerating." But most long-range plans are vague, in that they commit the agent to a course of action whose precise specification will require subsidiary decisionmaking, and a policy of never tolerating lies would be vague in precisely this way. The agent who adopted such a policy would be leaving open precisely how not to tolerate particular lies on particular occasions. Such openness about the details of execution would not rob the policy of its informativeness or practical force (*ibid.*, p. 308).

However, there is more to suggest a comparison between commitment and policies in Velleman's discussion than their shared "vagueness" with respect to future action. Velleman goes on to claim that policies are the kinds of plans "worth including in our self-conception" (p. 307) since the adoption of such policies "promotes the agent's self-understanding" (pp. 308–9) by enabling her to better comprehend her behavior. The one feature which I said was definitive of commitment, namely, its role in self-understanding, turns out, in Velleman's view, to belong to policies as well. This becomes particularly problematic given Velleman's instrumentalist, antirealist theory about values. Although I will return to Velleman's conception of self-understanding and his instrumentalism about values in chapter 5, let me say *briefly* why his theory poses a problem. He agrees that one's self-conception is comprised of certain fundamental values – from which one can infer that such values bear some relation to policies – yet he also claims that these values are only settled, stable desires and in no way reflect "the way the world is."[13] The problem, therefore, is that if (a) commitment can be cast as a kind of policy, and if (b) the role of values in policies and their connection to self-understanding can be explained in instrumentalist and antirealist terms, then (c) an argument for moral realism based on the conditions of commitment will be effectively blocked. Clearly, it is too early to tackle (b) since I have not yet discussed the connection between self-understanding and commitment, let alone the role of values in commitment. Instead, I want to turn to (a). The distinction between commitments and policies is an important one.

Taking stock of the discussion so far, it looks as though a general theory of intention, one which incorporates si-policies, might be capable of offering an account of commitment in all its forms: from the intention-like commitments such as finishing a paper, to more substantive commitments. Given Velleman's extension of the roles of commitment in self-understanding to policies, together with Bratman's reduction of policies to intention, it appears that commitment can be assimilated to a theory of intention. We need to look carefully at whether the identification of commitment with si-policies (or with policies in general) is valid.

3.3 COMMITMENT VERSUS POLICIES

One way we might try to distinguish between commitments and policies is by comparing them on certain shared features such as defeasibility, flexibility, and revision. While commitments need to be revisable and open to reconsideration in order that a steadfast determination to a course of action or principle does not become a blind obsession, what is involved in revising commitment is, I will argue, considerably different from revising policies. Before discussing the problem of revision and reconsideration, I shall start with the

---

[13] Velleman, *Practical Reflection*, pp. 282–3; 292; 294.

comparison of the defeasibility and flexibility of policies and commitments.[14]

3.3.1 Defeasibility

Policies are defeasible, according to Bratman, in the sense that circumstances will arise "in which one will appropriately block the application of the policy to the particular case" without abandoning the policy (Bratman, "Intention and Personal Policies," p. 456) – one can block the policy without having to reconsider it.

Here, policies closely model commitments. One's commitment to solving a case or winning a conviction can be blocked or overridden due to the circumstances in which one finds oneself without involving an abandonment or reconsideration of the commitment itself. One blocks one's commitment-based actions due, not to any changes in one's values or beliefs about the original circumstances of the commitment, or reasons for forming the commitment but, rather, to circumstances one faces in one's current situation. One does not reconsider the commitment, but only refrains from acting upon it. This matches the conditions for revision and reconsideration we normally think apply to commitments (to be discussed in section 3.3.4); namely, unexpected changes in circumstances *do not* typically warrant reconsideration of the commitment. Consequently, the commitment can remain stable though it is not acted upon. In other words, there will be occasions on which one does not act in accordance with the commitment without reconsidering it – without reconsidering its supporting beliefs, reflecting on one's values, and in general reexamining the reasons behind the commitment.

One might object that there is an important difference between the defeasibility conditions that apply to policies and those that apply to commitments, particularly the more substantive ones. Policies, the objection goes, are defeasible just in urgent situations, or those in which it is physically dangerous to carry out the policy, while commitments may require performance on the agent's part even

---

[14] The term "defeasible commitment" has already been used in discussions bearing on the relation between commitment and integrity. See for example John Keke, "Constancy and Purity," *Mind* 92 (1983): 499–518; Lynne McFall, "Integrity," *Ethics* 98 (1987): 5–20; Cheshire Calhoun, "Standing for Something," *The Journal of Philosophy* 92 (1995): 235–60.

when they pose a nontrivial risk. After all, did I not say that commitments often require counter- (not-on-balance) preferential and counter-prudential actions? Such an objection, however, does not do justice to the versatility of the policy theory itself. If one has a policy of helping friends in need, what one counts as an exception will depend on a number of factors: what kind of help she needs; whether it is a pressing need; what other obligations one has at that time; how important those obligations are; whether the friendship will be jeopardized by not helping, etc. But similar questions would be raised concerning a commitment to the friendship.

For both policies and commitments, then, one weighs the relative imports on the demands for action. But it is important to keep in mind that, in making a decision against acting in accordance with the policy or commitment, one is not necessarily making a decision against the policy or commitment itself. For example, if a friend needs help in getting to the airport, but I have an important meeting at the time, I could go to the meeting instead of driving her to the airport without either having to abandon my general policy of helping friends in need or bringing into question my commitment to the friendship. The stability of commitments and policies does not mean one either has to act upon them consistently without fail or give them up. Neither policies nor commitments are to be enforced "no matter what," and what counts as an exception to their application will vary depending on what is at stake.

3.3.2 Flexibility

Recall that si-policies "do not specify a recurrent kind of situation in which one is to act" (*ibid.*, p. 458). Such policies, says Bratman, exhibit "general occasion flexibility": the policy of exercising regularly leaves open the question of whether to exercise on any given opportunity – it does not require that one exercise whenever presented with the opportunity to do so (pp. 459–60). As a result, refraining from exercising on one particular occasion does not mean one has come to question or reconsider the policy, but only that one has exercised the flexibility of the policy itself. "An si-policy," notes Bratman, "need not be all-consuming" (p. 459). Although commitments also need not be all-consuming, one needs to examine whether they exhibit the same kind of flexibility.

For some commitments, e.g., being committed to finishing a paper sometime this summer, there will be the same kind of flexibility: not finishing the paper on June 15 does not mean I have either abandoned the commitment or that I am seriously questioning it – I am just not going to finish it that day. But as one moves down the list on page 64 from the intention-like commitments of finishing a paper to the more substantive commitments of stopping the war or being committed to a friendship, one notices more acutely the divergence between commitment and its proposed reduction basis of intentions and policies. Although substantive commitments need not be "all-consuming" – one need not always be protesting the war, or always be acting like an exemplary friend or spouse – it does not seem to be the case that one can, on "*any particular opportunity*," invoke the flexibility characteristic of policies in order not to act on such commitments. In other words, it looks as though there are constraints on when one can flexibly refrain from acting on one's commitments; unlike policies, commitments seem to be more rigid – there seem to be more occasions when exercising the flexibility does in fact constitute reconsideration or revision. There are test cases of commitment in which a failure to act is not simply an instance of flexible nonenforcement – when not helping a friend just means questioning the friendship. This might be a result of the more limited range of conditions under which commitments can be revised which in turn narrows the standard for what counts as a stable commitment (see section 3.3.4 below).

But in making this distinction, one has to be careful to match the right kinds of policies with the right kinds of commitments before comparing constraints on flexibility: just as there are a range of commitments, from the intention-like to the substantive, so, too, is there a range of policies. One's commitment to finishing a paper might be like one's policy of exercising once a week, while one's commitment to a political cause might be like one's policy of never negotiating with terrorists.[15]

There are, certainly, minimal constraints on policies that derive analytically, as it were, from the concepts of "flexibility" and "stability" themselves: one must act on a policy at least once – unrestrained flexibility is not compatible with stability (one might call this an "end-

---

[15] Rachel Cohon's example.

point" constraint). In the case of at least the more substantive commitments, this constraint is too weak. But is this the only constraint on policies, or are there instances when, as with substantive commitments, flexibility entails revision or reconsideration?

The above negotiating policy provides just such an example. Never negotiating with terrorists (though more like an ss- than an si-policy) is just as, if not more, rigid and just as intolerant of exceptions as many substantive commitments. To capitulate to terrorist demands is to abandon the policy. One cannot on any particular opportunity – arbitrarily, as it were – refrain from acting and still retain the policy. When one compares the appropriate policies with the appropriate commitments one sees that in both cases there is a range of flexibility. Just as there are test cases for commitment in which flexibility entails revision, so too are there test cases for policies.

3.3.3 A closer look

In light of the above discussion, it looks as though policies might in fact adequately account for the kinds of commitments I have described. The attempt to distinguish policies from commitments turns out to be somewhat more difficult and to require more attention than originally thought, especially in light of David Velleman's assertion that policies figure in our self-conception and aid self-understanding. Faced with this problem, there are two approaches one could take. As the distinction between "policy" and "commitment" becomes less clear, we are at first tempted to see this simply as a question of semantics, and to return instead to the functionalist approach outlined earlier. *The first approach thus tells us to focus on the psychological state* defined by a certain constellation of roles – stability, self-understanding, etc. – and to analyze the conditions that make successful execution of these roles possible: whether we call this state "commitment" or "policy-holding" is not immediately to the point. Yet such a move at this stage of the argument is, I think, premature and, perhaps worse, deflationary. In bypassing the preliminary distinctions between intentions, policies, and plans on the one hand, and commitments on the other, in order to get to the central arguments regarding the conditions of the psychological state defined by this cluster of roles, one loses the point of the argument as a whole: namely, to examine this concept of commitment which occupies a central place among, and is given equal importance by, a wide range of moral and political philosophers, with the hope of constructing an argument for moral realism. Although a large part of this argument will rely on a functional analysis, if we immediately jump to this analysis and simply investigate "the state" which plays the roles in self-understanding, stability, etc., without first connecting it to commitment, we deflate the argument for moral realism: "How quaint," an opponent to moral realism might think, "that there should be such a state requiring realist beliefs about value. But why is this important?"

One needs to keep in mind that the goal is not simply to identify first certain psychological states and then attach labels to them, but also to start with the concepts we do have and use – such as intention, policy, commitment – and to try to discover and understand, when appropriate, their associated psychological states. We have to work in two directions at once: from the concepts to the mental states and back again. Although the functionalist approach occupies a central place in this work and is indispensable as a method of analysis in this context, it should not be invoked too quickly as a response to the challenge posed by the combination of Bratman's and Velleman's theories of intention, since it forces us to feign disinterest in the distinctions between intentions, policies, and commitment that we should first try to understand. As concepts which figure prominently in the literature of the philosophy of action, it is important to demarcate the scope of their application.

The second approach is the one I have been pursuing and want to develop a little further since it will help locate more precisely those roles on which commitment and policies differ. It seeks a stronger clarification of policies by way of reaching a more accurate comparison with commitment. To this end it looks more closely at the ways in which the term "policy" is used and in what contexts, it examines why we form policies, and finally returns to the question of what is involved in breaking them. By doing this first one will be in a better position to assess the question of whether commitment is a kind of policy and hence a generalized intention. This is not, once again, a purely semantic point. The goal is not to stipulate a definition of "policy" or "commitment," but to try to complete our understanding of these concepts.

Although there are certain surface similarities between policies and commitments with respect to their flexibility and defeasibility, we need to examine whether they share deeper affinities in terms of how they are formed and revised.

Recalling Bratman's distinction between ss-policies, which require a specific action in a specific situation, and si-policies, which specify only the action and not the situation, one can generalize and define a policy *simpliciter* as having two parameters: an "action" parameter and a "situation" parameter. Each parameter can be defined either "ambiguously" or "unambiguously." There are then, in principle anyway, four kinds of policies.

    1. Ss- policies are one type.

As "a general intention to A whenever C," they are unambiguous in both parameters. When Velleman defines a policy as "a plan that we shall act in a particular way on every occasion of a particular kind" (Velleman, *Practical Reflection*, p. 307) – call this his v1–policy – he too places policies in this first category.

    2. Si-policies are a second type.

They are ambiguous, by definition, with respect to the situation in which they are to be carried out.

    3. Policies like never tolerating lies are a third type.

These policies (call them v2–policies, after Velleman's example) are ambiguous in terms of the action parameter but not the situation parameter. A policy of never tolerating lies is "vague" in that it commits the agent "to a course of action whose precise specification will require subsidiary decisionmaking" (*ibid.*, p. 308). The situations in which it must be enforced are unambiguous, namely, in any instance of lying, though what one is supposed to do in these cases is not antecedently apparent.[16] Thus, we have examples of three of the four in-principle types of policies. But what of policies that are ambiguous in both parameters?

I said earlier that si-policies might serve as proxies for substantive commitments since such commitments were often vague in terms of the situation or situations in which they need to be acted upon. But

---

[16] Si-policies and v2–policies are inversely related: the first is ambiguous with respect to its situation but not its action, while the second suffers ambiguity of action but not situation.

such commitments are not always only vague or ambiguous with regard to their situations, but potentially also with regard to their actions, especially in the case of commitments to ideals or moral principles. These commitments might in no way specify either how or when one should act. Suppose I am committed to a political cause, say saving the rain forests or improving human rights. What does it entail that I do and in what circumstances? Are there only certain types of actions to be performed in specific kinds of situations that will count as fulfilling or meeting my commitment? If I am reluctant to risk physical injury by chaining myself to a tree or lying down in front of bulldozers, but choose instead to disseminate information and raise public awareness about the problem, am I really not committed to its resolution? Perhaps a better example is a friendship: what actions on my part and in what situations are required or entailed by this kind of commitment? As noted in the above discussion on flexibility, there is a wide space for individual decisions with respect to the what, when and where of commitment-based actions.

4. Commitments *might* thus be thought to be an example of the fourth type of policy which is ambiguous in both parameters.

We are most familiar with policies at the institutional level: businesses, universities, and governments have policies. All of the reasons for which institutions have and form policies seem also to apply to individuals. Having a policy, whether for an institution or an individual, promotes efficiency and coordination. (This fact was already remarked upon by Bratman and Velleman.) It saves members of the organization from repeatedly making individual decisions and from potentially arriving at different conclusions. So too with individuals. By imposing uniform and regular standards of decision and action, policies coordinate and so also enhance planning.[17] In imposing such standards, policies also guarantee fairness and impartiality since the same decisions will be made under all similar circumstances.

---

[17] It was in this sense that Velleman said that policies promote self-understanding. By having a policy I will always have a reason for a future action bearing on the policy. Moreover, policies induce a regularity in my action and a stability in my behavior so that I can expect not to be surprised by something I am doing; that is, I can expect not suddenly to be doing something which appears unmotivated or without reasons and which would therefore interfere with self-understanding in Velleman's sense.

Individuals might also adopt policies for the same reasons. For example, by having a policy of never lending money to friends or doing business with family, one can (at least try to) take the sting out of rejecting a friend's financial need or a relative's business proposition by invoking one's policy: one's refusal has nothing to do with them personally, it is just the way one does things.

Here one gets a clearer indication of a possible distinction between policies and commitments, which is brought out by the fact that the vocabulary of "policies" is most naturally spoken by institutions and organizations than by persons.[18] There is a certain *impersonal* nature to policies which commitments generally do not share. To say one has a policy of never tolerating lies, as opposed to being committed to honesty, implies a certain distance from what is espoused – as though one has less of a personal stake in it. Imagine explaining to a friend why you performed a certain favor for them in terms of your *policy* to do such things. The "distancing" inherent to policies is a vestige of its institutional heritage.[19] When this term is extended to individuals it undergoes some distortion: a distortion which may account for the confusion between, and attempted assimilation of, commitments and policies.

Keeping with the institutional model, we can compare what happens when policies are changed or abandoned. Organizations, like individuals, have a range of policies that could be plotted on a scale of significance: from policies prohibiting smoking or requiring certain dress codes, to policies regarding equal opportunity in employment and affirmative action. When an institution changes its policies located on the low end of the significance scale, we think nothing of it. To the extent that institutions may be said to have a "character" (we do at times speak of the character of a business, or the character of a university), such revisions occasion no reassessment or reevaluation of

---

[18] In origin policies refer to a state or government and connote something which is advantageous and expedient. See the *Oxford English Dictionary*.

[19] I imagine that the moral life of liberal ironists or Pyrrhonian skeptics follows quite closely the institutional model. They do not have moral beliefs so much as moral policies: general rules for action to be executed under the appropriate circumstances. The notion of "distancing" is an apt description since they have, I argue, no personal stake in the policies or beliefs as a result of the larger skeptical or neopragmatic framework in which these "beliefs" are formed.

the institution's character. But now suppose a business or university abandons its policy of affirmative action in hiring, for example, or admissions. Such a change, of course, brings about considerably more reassessment than a change in the more mundane policy of dress codes. One does speak of a change in character in this case by saying such things as "The university has taken a hostile attitude toward minorities," or, "The company has become insensitive to the problems of discrimination." Although I do not intend to draw any conclusions on an anthropomorphized view of institutions, we can still ask why changes in different policies bring about different responses.

The reason I focus on institutions is to try to drive a wedge between policies, on the one hand, and self-conception and self-understanding, on the other, and to show that the reason why policies seem to mimic commitments, especially in certain cases of policy revision, is that policies are often manifestations of underlying commitments. So when we say the character of the university or business has changed, what do we mean? Certainly not that there has been a change in its self-understanding or self-conception – such a statement overextends the analogy of institution-as-individual. A more likely story is this: what causes the radical reassessment of the "character" of the institution when it abandons these more significant policies is that we see such policies as being *grounded* in a way in which other policies are not. While most policies can be explained in terms of expediency, efficiency, and prudence, these policies cannot (an affirmative action policy would probably fail most of these tests). Rather, they seem grounded in certain principles and beliefs, and what alarms us about the abandonment of the policy is that it brings into question the company's or university's *commitment* to the underlying principles and their assessment of them as valuable principles worth defending and promoting. The way we describe a change of policy and what is involved in doing so mirrors that of commitment precisely because these policies are mediated by commitments.

When we extend policies from institutions to persons we elide the space occupied by underlying principles: we too easily and readily connect policies directly to self-understanding and self-conception and ignore their (possible) mediation by commitment. What I suggest is that we form certain policies against the background of certain commitments. Besides the institutional reasons for forming policies –

efficiency, coordination, impartiality – we have other reasons based on substantive beliefs or principles. My policies of never tolerating lies or of standing up for truthfulness might grow out of a commitment to fairness, justice, or the importance of honesty. My policy, then, provides a specific basis for acting on the commitment; that is, it disambiguates one of the parameters by specifying either a particular action or a particular situation.

Although the defeasibility and flexibility of policies generally match those of commitment, we need to take a closer look at the revision and reconsideration of policies *vis-à-vis* commitment, since it is here that the real difference between them is to be found. The motivating idea is that commitments reflect a greater personal stake of the agent in what she is committed to than do policies. Though policies might gain stability because of their relation to one's self-conception, this relation is tenuous at best, and the effects on one's self-conception in the face of policy revision is innocuous at worst.

3.3.4 Commitment revision

It is argued that in the case of intention, revision or reconsideration is justified if either (1) one has mistaken beliefs about the original circumstances in which the intention was made; (2) the circumstances in which one finds oneself are not what one expected; (3) one's desire-belief reasons for acting change; or (4) one's values change (Bratman, *IPP*, p. 67). Now if, in keeping with the general reductive approach above of casting commitment as a kind of policy and hence as a form of intention, we wish to extend this account to commitment, some modifications will have to be made. First, let us see if in fact all the above conditions of revision apply to commitment. Condition (2) seems idle since commitments, like si-policies, are vague with regard to the occasions on which they require action, so that to speak in terms of unmet expectations is inappropriate. Moreover, as a steadfast determination to a course of action, commitments are meant to be carried through regardless (to a considerable extent sometimes) of changes in circumstances. In fact, they may be formed with an expectation that circumstances will change in unexpected ways. Condition (3), also, seems not to apply. Often, commitments require us to make choices or perform actions which are counter-preferential[20] and even counter-prudential. Take the student who is committed to finishing her paper. It is 8:00 p.m., she has not yet finished the paper, and a friend calls offering a free ticket to the last performance of a sold-out concert she wanted to see. Despite a change in her immediate desire-belief reasons for staying and writing a paper versus spending an enjoyable evening at the concert, reconsideration of her commitment is not warranted since forming such a commitment is done precisely in order to override unexpected changes of one's desire-belief reasons for acting. Or consider the person committed to a political cause. The fact that her commitment requires counter-prudential actions, perhaps risking arrest or professional censure, does not by itself provide grounds for revision of her commitment; indeed, it is the counter-prudential nature of her actions that allows us, in part, to recognize this as a case of commitment. This leaves conditions (1) and (4).

Condition (4) is, I think, the most salient condition for revision and reconsideration of commitment. Although I will argue for this point at length when discussing belief constraints on commitments, it seems plausible to say that commitment involves some kind of valorization of an object or end. If this changes, i.e., if what we value changes, then it follows that our original commitment should (or will) change as well.[21] Finally, (1) most clearly applies: if the student mistakes the due date of the paper; if the detective mistakes the nature of the crime; or if a spouse mistakes the feelings of his or her mate, then reconsideration is called for. To the extent that conditions (1) and (4) provide grounds for reconsideration and revision, they also provide a rough

[20] Counter-preferential in the weak sense: as opposing one's immediate desires and inclinations and not as opposing one's on-balance, or all-things-considered, preference.

[21] There might be the problem that the criterion of value change will permit too much in the way of revision. The student who abandons her commitment to finishing her paper and opts for going to the concert may rationally have done so if she no longer "values" finishing the paper, but instead "values" going to the concert. That is, one can avoid the counter-preferential costs of commitment by making one's values track desires and therefore be able to revise one's commitments at will. I will argue, however, that the value attached to commitment does not derive exclusively from the fact that the agent happens to desire the object of commitment; that is, the first-person, subjective desires are not the basis of the evaluative element of commitment. This will be discussed in chapter 4.

definition of the stability of commitment: barring changes in what one values, and provided that one's beliefs about the background circumstances of the commitment itself are either true or not known to be false, the commitment will be stable.[22]

It might be objected that condition (2) still plays an important role; for example, one might commit oneself to a strenuous exercise regimen only to develop an illness later which prevents one from exercising.[23] This problem, however, falls under condition (1): one had a mistaken belief that one's health in the original circumstances of the commitment would not deteriorate. When we form commitments (as we do intentions) we expect certain "enabling conditions"[24] to hold (or at least do not believe they will fail to hold), e.g., that one will be in good enough health to exercise.

Conditions (1) and (4) then provide a rough sketch of two criteria for (a) what constitutes rational reconsideration of a commitment, and (b) what justifies revision of commitment. In the case of intention, it is argued that we have habits or dispositions of (non)reconsideration, since as resource-limited agents the cost of deliberation in terms of lost time can be high: such agents cannot afford always to deliberate over whether to fulfill their intentions whenever there is a "prima-facie" trigger of reconsideration due to some change in beliefs. To say, however, that the mechanism of (non)reconsideration of commitments, particularly substantive ones, rests on underlying *habits* is misleading. In the first place, the constraint on time is not as pronounced with such commitments – it is the fact of having ample time to deliberate about whether to perform

---

[22] This suggests that, like intentions, commitments are retained due to habits or dispositions of nonreconsideration – that being committed is somehow a passive, inertia-driven state. Such a picture of commitment is mistaken. The "state" of commitment is more active and commitments are retained and sustained, not out of a habit or disposition, but as a result of reflective endorsement on the agent's part toward the objects of commitment. Although Benn and Gaus deny this, I think they were correct in originally suggesting that for the "vast range of our action commitments – political, religious, selfish, altruistic – some kind of personal affirmation or active commitment to an end may still be called for," in "Practical Rationality and Commitment," 258.   [23] Rachel Cohon's example.

[24] "a condition whose presence I believe to be required for my being able to *A*": Michael Bratman, "Davidson's Theory of Intention," in Bruce Vermazen and Merril B. Hintikka (eds.), *Essays on Davidson: Actions and Events* (Oxford: Clarendon Press, 1985), p. 20.

actions based on the commitments that poses problems for the agent (consider Hamlet). Second, the costs involved in reconsideration and revision are not exclusively costs in expected utility. Rather, when one revises a commitment, one reassesses one's values which constitute, in part, one's self-conception. The things we value and how we rank them say something about who we are. Quoting Rawls on Josiah Royce: "an individual says who he is by describing his purposes and causes, what he intends to do in his life."[25] There would seem to be much more reflection and deliberation built into the revision process since so much more is at stake, namely, the kind of person one takes oneself to be.[26] Even in the case of revision of more mundane commitments one's self-conception is involved: am I the kind of person who finishes their projects or studies law? Is this the kind of action or vocation someone like me would perform or choose? Reconsideration is called for if there is a change in beliefs supporting the original commitment, or a change in beliefs regarding the value of the object of commitment (or the commitment itself). Revision is justified if the evaluative beliefs directly oppose the commitment, or if one's self-conception changes.[27]

Now the conditions for revision and reconsideration of policies are broader: in addition to (1) and (4) above, one also has (2) one finds oneself in unexpected circumstances; and (3) one's desire-belief reasons for acting change. I want to argue that what supports the inflexibility or rigidity of substantive commitments is their relation to the agent's self-understanding and self-conception, while the inflexibility of policies is not necessarily, or very seldom, so related, despite Velleman's assertion to the contrary.

---

[25] John Rawls, *A Theory of Justice* (Cambridge, MA: Harvard University Press, 1971), p. 408.

[26] This is, admittedly, a rather vague phrase which I have translated elsewhere as "self-understanding." Through "self-understanding" a person is able to trace a continuity through her life, to build narratives around things she has done, to understand herself as the kind of person who does or would do certain sorts of things, and to draw on it as a source of identifying who she is to others and to herself. In simpler cases, self-understanding can also mean, as Velleman states, simply knowing the "why" of one's actions.

[27] Consider a student committed to becoming a lawyer. She may revise this commitment if she thinks either that law is not a worthwhile profession, or that she is not the kind of person who becomes a lawyer, whether or not the legal profession is worthwhile.

To try to align the reader's intuitions with this general claim, consider how one typically talks about policy formation, justification, and revision. One can come to have a policy by simply *adopting* it – what was not one's policy before, now is. One adopts the policy of never negotiating with terrorists, of never talking with strangers, of learning a new language every summer. But policy adoption does not require the same self-assessment or reflection on the part of the agent as is involved in forming a commitment. In fact, a policy can be adopted which conflicts with one's self-conception and does not reflect one's most stable desires – what Velleman calls values. One can revise or abandon a policy simply on the basis of pragmatic or prudential reasons without it affecting one's self-conception. The agent's view of herself as a certain kind of person, as a person with a certain set of values, is separable from the policies she adopts to a degree that is not the case for commitments: policies can be formed, revised, abandoned in light of what is personally, politically, economically exigent (see conditions (1)–(4) above).

Consider the kindly, sentimental, old professor who desires nothing more than being on the friendliest terms with his students and likes nothing more than seeing them happy. He knows that this makes him highly vulnerable to being manipulated and, what is worse, his students know this too. Rarely a class goes by when a student does not deftly shift the lecture to fond reflections on better days spent in the company of famous scholars. When it comes to grading, the professor knows after years of experience that his first assessment of a term paper, though tough, is always correct. But when confronted with the weepy, pouting bloom of youth, he can rarely resist such pleas. Maybe he did not take into account their sincere effort, their stellar character, and the fact that they have so much enjoyed his class. He does not like giving bad grades, he does not like seeing his students unhappy, and nothing feels more natural, he would like nothing more, than doing what will please everyone. Instead he adopts a policy of never discussing grades, for he knows that otherwise he will never stick to his original decisions. Now, clearly, such a policy does not reflect his self-conception. He does not like the policy; he sees himself, as his students do, as a kind-hearted old man. And if he were to drop this policy, there would be no reassessment of his self-conception or self-understanding. On the contrary, the abandonment of the policy would be in keeping with his self-conception. This example shows the detachment that exists between policies and the person. Where policies are more closely coordinated with a person's self-assessment and self-conception it is usually because of underlying principles to which he or she is committed. In these instances, policies are a manifestation of some sort of commitment. If, for example, the kindly old professor was committed to treating his students fairly, or providing them with the best education which included giving them an honest evaluation of their work, we could understand how his policy would be more closely coordinated with his self-conception. But in the absence of any mediation by commitments, there is a gap between policies and one's self-conception or self-understanding because of the generally impersonal nature of policies discussed earlier.

Yet this gap does not exist for commitments. One typically does not talk of "adopting" a commitment precisely because it is much more integrally related to the agent herself. Revising or abandoning a substantive commitment necessarily involves, based on the conditions listed above and as we shall see in subsequent chapters, a deeper reassessment of one's self-conception and deeper reflection on the value, and not just the exigency, of the commitment itself. Counsels of prudence alone never justify reconsidering a substantive commitment, while they may be sufficient grounds for revising policies. Policies and commitments might be thought of, respectively, as the accidental and essential features of the subject. While policies are to some extent descriptive of the agent, commitments are definitive.

The difference between commitments and policies might best be described with a spatial metaphor: substantive commitments lie nearer the center of who the agent is, while policies are found at the periphery. Although there will be occasions in which one must act on the basis of the commitment or policy, or be forced to reconsider them, the failure to act on the commitment occasions a further reconsideration of one's self-conception or a reassessment of one's values, both of which further destabilize the commitment, while reconsideration of the policy ends with the policy itself – the reconsideration does not reverberate to the center. Granted there are instances when flexibility entails instability for both substantive commitments and policies, but what underwrites the stability of commitment is the stability or continuity of one's self-conception.

One comment and one objection are in order.

Bratman notes a disanalogy between policies and intentions in that the latter, while not the former, typically figure as elements of plans. Now commitments seem to be caught on both sides of the fence: intention-like commitments, like finishing a paper, can be elements of plans while substantive commitment will not be. Yet substantive commitments also differ from policies in that they form a framework or background against which plans are made, and in this respect once again resemble intentions. While policies may be said to serve as landmarks among the possible courses of action one might follow, substantive commitments, to extend the metaphor, shape the topography of the terrain itself and in this way might be said to be part of one's rational life plan as mentioned in section 3.2. One does not run up against a (substantive) commitment in pursuing some course of action but, rather, one's course of action is informed, or guided, by the commitment itself, just as one's intended path is guided by the lie of the land. Substantive commitments help shape and define one's self-conception, how one identifies oneself to oneself and to others, in a way that policies do not. It is in this sense that such commitments are interwoven with, and have an orienting role in, our lives.

One might object that the divergence between commitment, on the one hand, and intentions and policies, on the other, is due not to any limitations in the reduction basis, but to the fact that an artificial structure has been imposed on these different cases of commitment in an attempt to construct a unified theory of commitment. Yet, the objection would go, "being committed" to finishing a paper and "being committed" to a friendship are simply puns on the words "being committed." The reason the intention model fails to accommodate all types of commitment is that commitments are not all of the same type – there is no common structure which any model can capture.

The motivating assumption to the objection is that commitment, like policies, can be "reduced" to, or at least explained by, a theory of intention. But this oversimplifies the nature of the relation between commitment and intention. As I remarked earlier, some commitments can be characterized as a kind of intention, especially in those cases in which the content of what one intends can be read off directly from the commitment itself (again, consider finishing the paper). But in being committed to solving a puzzle or stopping the war, what one intends is not clear; yet this is not to say that these are different kinds of commitments altogether, since some state of intention is still involved. Such commitments will entail specific actions under appropriate circumstances and the agent will intend those actions. Although these actions cannot be fully specified in advance, whatever actions they are, the agent will intend those. In other words, intention is always embedded within the commitment. What does one intend in being committed to stopping the war? Certainly, one does not intend to stop the war. However, the commitment may call on one to participate in a protest, distribute literature, send a letter to one's representative, etc., all of which are intentional actions. So whether the intention lies at the surface (as in intention-like commitments) or lies deeper within (as in substantive commitments), there is an intention to be found. But the fact that intentions are embedded in commitments does not mean that commitments are composite intentions, or that intentions are more basic than commitments. What should emerge from the discussion so far is that intention and commitment are related in a number of ways, but that relation is complex and not easily characterized as one of subset to superset, or species to genus.

The reason commitment diverges from policies and intention as one moves down the list offered on p. 64, is due, not to the lack of a common structure of commitment, but to the increased presence of the fourth component of commitment, namely, self-understanding. The comparison of intention with commitment is useful up to a point; specifically, the point at which the constitutive role of commitment in self-understanding and identity becomes more important.

3.4 CONCLUSION

Intention and commitment, as we have seen, share many similarities with regard to their roles and functions: they are stable; they control conduct; they play a role in practical reasoning; and they can facilitate coordination. However, important differences emerge as soon as we press a reduction of commitment to intention. Commitments are typically more general than intentions, and their criteria for revision and reconsideration are more constrained. Although there are important overlaps between commitment and intention, there are also important differences; while they meet on certain points, they diverge on others. And the point at which they diverge is on the role of self-understanding and identity: the structuring and orienting role commitments have in our lives.

One might still ask whether commitments are simply principled policies which are doubly ambiguous in terms of action and situation, or whether policies are unprincipled commitments with only one free parameter. At a certain point, the argument will turn on semantics, and if pushed far enough it will be forced to stipulate a definition of each one – to make a *de facto* ruling on what we shall call policies and on what we shall call commitments. What I have tried to do, however, is develop the analysis as much as possible before it devolved into a question of definitions. This conceptual analysis has given us some important insights into their underlying differences and pointed the way to other areas of investigation – notably, the revision process of commitments and policies, the connection between commitment, on the one hand, and value and self-conception, on the other – and it has also provided a launching point for the functional analysis to follow in the next chapter. Once again, we see that beliefs and their relation to commitment will be an important topic, as well as the different conceptions of self-understanding and its connection to commitment. Perhaps it is best to conclude with some definitions to help us keep our terms straight. What I will call simple policies proper (ss-, si-, and v2–policies) do not play a role in the kind of self-understanding at issue in the present discussion and of interest to most moral philosophers, and so cannot fulfill the roles of commitment. As a result, the complex policies Velleman gestures toward would be better understood as a kind of commitment or as resting in some way on unexpressed commitments of the agent.

If we come across something which is stable over time, guides action, and plays a role in a person's self-understanding and identity, we shall call that commitment. If its revision and reconsideration either occasion or in some way depend upon a reassessment on the person's part of "who she is," then it is better described as a commitment than a policy. If the person has a personal stake in its fulfillment, realization, or maintenance, that too will be called a commitment rather than a policy or general intention. The point to argue will be that in order for commitment to play these roles there must be present realist beliefs about value. This is the subject of chapters 4 and 5. Thus, when Velleman says there is something called a "policy," which is like an intention, and figures in an agent's self-conception and self-understanding, we can either split hairs about labels or just agree, for convenience, to call this "commitment." Yet when he adds that a "policy" plays these roles *and* is able to do this in the absence of realist beliefs about value, and instead needs only stable desires, then we enter a real point of contention. For it is my argument that what we typically call a commitment – the state that has the above functions and roles – functionally requires such beliefs.

The examination of the differences between policies and commitments has helped to focus and bring to light some of the central elements of commitment to be discussed in the following chapters. We have seen that values seem to play an important role in commitments, in part because of the personal stake we have in them and also because of the personal reassessment their reconsideration and revision occasion. We need to take a closer look at what place values occupy in commitments and what we mean by value. Are they simply expressions of what a person thinks is important for herself, or are they more "objective"? We have also seen that the important link to be articulated is the one between commitments and self-understanding and self-conception. These are the central topics of chapters 4 and 5.

4

Commitment and belief

4.1 BELIEF CONSTRAINTS

4.1.1 *Introduction*

The aim of the present chapter is to bring the structure of commitment into finer focus by examining what belief constraints apply to commitment and what the content of these beliefs might be. In chapter 2 we saw that this was one of the main steps toward an argument for moral realism. The question of what agents can believe while still remaining committed was a central point of contention in the discussion on Rorty and Gibbard. Recall that I claimed that their neopragmatist and antirealist metaethics were incompatible with the requirements for the possibility of commitment itself. The goal now is to show that (1) beliefs do in fact figure in at least the substantive commitment, and that (2) these are (what I called) realist beliefs. Naturally, I shall begin with (1). Chapter 5 will address (2).

4.1.2 *The cognitive component of commitment*

Before moving directly to the examination of beliefs and commitment, there is the preliminary question of why we should even think that there is a cognitive component to commitment at all: that is, why should we think of commitment as anything more than a strong desire or a form of self-expression?

One immediate difference between commitments and desires is that the former, while not the latter, are sensitive to the demands of consistency and coherence. I might have a desire to lose weight and eat chocolate, to finish a paper and go see a movie. Similarly, I can have a desire to smoke and know it is unhealthy. Our desires, unfortunately, are usually insensitive or unresponsive to the demands of consistency and coherence. One's commitments, however, typically aim at coherence with the other commitments and beliefs one has. A commitment to promoting civil rights, for example, is consistent and coheres with a system of beliefs regarding the natural equality of all human beings, the need to respect the dignity of all persons, etc., while a commitment to national socialism is not. A committed Nazi would probably reject one or both of these beliefs. Although commitments might come in conflict with one another because they require divergent actions within a certain situation,[1] they still aim at general consistency with one another. One's commitment to principles of nonviolence would preclude one from developing commitments to violent political causes, for example. Consistency and coherence are two reasons for thinking commitments are more than desires.[2]

Moreover, when it comes to commitments we often find ourselves giving reasons for and against them. We deliberate about our commitments in a way we would not if they were purely affective states. When we are challenged or questioned about our commitments, we try to offer justifications for them. That is, we respond to the challenge in a way which indicates there is something more to it than just a peculiar feeling we have: we reason about, assess, reflect upon, and justify our commitments in a way that is similar to our response to challenges to our beliefs.[3] Robert Adams, in his article "Moral

---

[1] This should not be thought of as a conflict of "oughts," a topic which has been widely discussed. Rather, I want to consider cases in which the actions deriving from the commitments are incompatible, though the commitments themselves are not. The point is that the principles supporting the commitments must be consistent even though they may lead to conflicting actions. For example, a commitment to pacifism and a commitment to helping those in need, though not inconsistent principles, might lead to a conflict in which one has to resort to violence in order to protect an innocent person from harm.

[2] Gilbert Harman makes a similar point in distinguishing intention from desire in *Change in View*, (Cambridge, MA: MIT Press, 1986), p. 83.

[3] One might object that we partake in the same activities with respect to "feelings" of anxiety, panic, or depression. If we reflect, assess, and reason about these feelings or emotions, why could we not do it with commitment and call that another kind of feeling or emotion? The problem with this objection is its failure to recognize the deep cognitive component to anxiety, panic, and depression which forms the basis for treatments such as cognitive psychotherapy that aims at changing one's beliefs and thought patterns. In his article "Depressive, Anxious and Intrusive Thoughts in Psychiatric Inpatients and Outpatients," *Behavioral Research and Therapy* 30 (1992): 93–102, D. A. Clark remarks that it was:

> Aaron T. Beck's research on cognitive factors in anxiety and depression
> [that] first noted that clinically depressed patients engage in a repetitive

Faith,"[4] raises similar points in his discussion of the cognitive aspect of moral faith. Perhaps the most important distinction he draws between moral faith and feeling, and which I think also applies to the distinction between commitment and feeling, is that there is "an intention central to moral faith, an intention of respecting something more commanding, and at least in some cases more external to the self, than mere personal preference and feeling" (Adams, "Moral Faith," 84). He goes on to say that:

> [t]his is the most important reason for speaking of moral faith as a sort of "belief," and it is connected with *the possibility of error*. It is characteristic of the sort of faith I am discussing to acknowledge a sort of possibility that one could be mistaken in it – typically, a possibility that one could be mistaken and never know it . . . I must recognize that I could be tragically mistaken, mistaken in a way characteristic of false *beliefs* . . . Faith confronts a temptation to doubt precisely because such possibilities of error must be recognized, and in a way respected" (*ibid.*, 84, emphasis added).[5]

> > pattern of self-denigration he labeled negative automatic thinking. In depression, this automatic thinking consists of repetitive, persistent and uncontrollable thoughts or images involving loss or failure within the personal domain. To the depressed individual these thoughts are highly plausible, absolute and pervasive in nature (93).

According to Alan Stoudemire, cognitive psychotherapy views "the patient's conscious thoughts as central to producing and perpetuating symptoms such as depression, anxiety, phobias, and somatization," and the way it treats depression is by teaching the patient "to become more aware of their negatively biased automatic thoughts and to recognize . . . that negative affects are generally *preceded* by such thoughts" (p. 437, emphasis added). In the next phase of therapy, says Stoudemire, "the emphasis shifts to a detailed exploration of the patient's *cognitions and their role in perpetuating depressive feelings* . . . Psychotherapy then focuses on the attitudes and assumptions that underlie the patient's negatively biased thinking" (p. 439, emphasis added). See Alan Stoudemire, *Clinical Psychiatry for Medical Students* (Philadelphia: J. B. Lippincott, 1990).

[4] *The Journal of Philosophy* 92 (1995): 75–95.

[5] Although there are some interesting parallels that might be drawn and distinctions that could be made between faith and commitment, particularly as it is formulated by Adams, I shall need to leave them aside for now. My argument for moral realism by way of commitment would work well in the analysis Adams offers of moral faith, and accords well with his own suggestion that some sort of realist picture about ethics is needed to account for moral faith. (It might be interesting to compare this to Kant's postulate of practical reason in *Religion within the Limits of Reason Alone* [New York: Harper and Row, 1960] and *Critique of Practical Reason* [Chicago: University of Chicago Press, 1976].) Adams says:

The "intention of respecting something more commanding" in the case of commitment is revealed by our participation in such activities as justifying our commitments, of giving reasons for them, etc. What underlies such activities is, as in the case of moral faith, the possibility of being wrong about, or of making an error in, one's commitments. The whole process of inquiry into, and adjudication between, the various justifications and reasons we give is premised on the thought that one might be wrong. If we accept this, then there is reason to think that there is a cognitive element to commitment since it is the cognitive component which is responsive to reason-giving, justification, and inquiry. What the exact import of the possibility of error is will be developed. It is certainly too early to say that such a possibility in turn rests on certain realist beliefs (though I think it does). The only conclusion I want to draw at this point is that to the extent commitment involves justification and reason giving, which in turn imply the possibility of error which is a feature of beliefs, we have reason to think that commitment is more than mere desire or expression of personal preferences.[6]

> the possibility of an objectively appropriate or inappropriate relation to reality is precisely the aspect of moral belief most subject to metaethical doubts, and also the aspect that seems to me most important to the nonegocentric character of moral faith. *So long as we must acknowledge this possibility in our faith, it is hard for me to see what would be gained by eliminating belief from our conception of faith* (Adams, "Moral Faith," 85, emphasis added).

This last phrase is, in a nutshell, the argument I want to develop.

[6] One of the earliest and most extended descriptions of commitment, or *engagement*, is provided by the French religious existentialist, Gabriel Marcel, principally in the texts *Etre et Avoir (EA)*, *Du Refus à l'Invocation (RI)*, *Homo Viator (HV)*, and *Présence et Immortalité (PI)*. Marcel asks how one can commit one's future and highlights the fact that in making commitments one tends to abstract from the potentially variable elements of one's current situation, e.g., one's feelings, desires, and dispositions. He thus brings out a tension between the supposition that commitment is based on a feeling or desire and the fact that commitment is partially unconditional, that it will be met regardless of one's future inclinations. In order to explain the possibility of commitment *in light of the assumption that it is based on a current disposition*, we would have to accept, according to Marcel, one of two alternatives: either "one poses arbitrarily an invariability of one's feelings which is not really in one's power to establish"; or, "one accepts in advance having to accomplish at a given moment an act which does not reflect at all one's interior dispositions at the time when one will have to act" *(EA, 70)*. The implausibility of either alternative is meant to establish the untenability of the hypothesis that commitments are formed solely on the basis of an affective disposition. The argument is a *reductio* of the position that commitment rests

4.1.3 Beliefs: The functionalist approach

Trying to locate the beliefs that figure in our commitments is a formidable task. By way of a first step I want to return to the theory of intention since considerable work has been done in this area in trying to determine the relation of belief to intention. While some have argued that intention is a special kind of belief (J. David Velleman), others claim that intending to perform a certain action only entails the belief that one will so act (Stuart Hampshire, H. P. Grice, Robert Audi), and still others think intending is independent of such beliefs altogether (Donald Davidson, Alfred Mele). In short, there is an important debate in action theory over the demands of belief on intention, and it is from this debate that I want to draw some insights into the role beliefs play in commitment. One caveat, though, is in order: although I will use some of the arguments regarding the relation of intention to belief in order to set the stage for my argument regarding belief constraints on commitment, what I say is neutral with respect to the existence or nonexistence of demands on belief for intention. If it were established that in fact belief constraints do not apply to intention, yet do apply to commitment, this would only help the arguments in chapter 3 regarding the difference between commitment and intention. If, on the other hand, constraints applied to both intention and commitment, though this would support the reductionist view that commitment is a special kind of intention, it would

on a disposition and is, for Marcel, an important step in establishing the transcendent basis of commitment in universal values. See especially the examples in *EA*, pp. 56–7, 66–7. It is interesting to compare these examples with Gregory Kavka's Toxin Puzzle in which one must form an intention to do something which one knows in advance one will have no reason to do when the time of action arrives. See Gregory Kavka, "The Toxin Puzzle," *Analysis* 43 (1983): 33–6. Finally, I should note that Paul Ricoeur locates Marcel's discussion of commitment and the dilemma of sincerity vs. fidelity in the context of Marcel's broader theory of availability, and does not connect it to universal values. Ricoeur understands Marcel's discussion as a means of underscoring the essentially intersubjective nature of commitment and as further evidence for his own (Ricoeur's) argument regarding the role of the other in the identity of the self. While I readily agree with Ricoeur that commitment for Marcel is related to identity, this role cannot be explained exclusively in terms of "availability." Since Marcel connects identity to authentic commitments, and explains these in terms of supreme values, one must seek to explain what, if any, relation exists between the latter. See Paul Ricoeur, *Oneself as Another*, p. 267.

by no means prove it given the differences discussed in the preceding chapter. Although the question of whether beliefs figure in intention is important, it is not necessary for my discussion of commitment at this time. In what way, then, can the debate in the theory of intention be useful to the analysis of commitment?

4.1.4 The intention model

The debate over belief constraints on intention turns on the question of whether in intending to *A* one must also believe one will *A*. Assuming some similarities between intention and commitment, this belief naturally suggests itself as a constraint on commitment. But recall that the cases with which we are principally concerned are instances of commitment to a political cause, commitment to a moral principle, and commitment in a friendship. Although it is true that when we take ourselves to be committed in such cases we typically understand that we are committed not just in word, but also in deed, the connection between the commitment and the action is not as direct as it is in intention. One intends to carry out some specific action, e.g., going to the concert. But a commitment is to something more abstract – a principle or ideal rather than specific actions on our part – and only calls for action under certain circumstances, e.g., when the principle is violated. One might be committed to the principles of justice and equal rights, and yet be lucky enough to live in a world where these are never violated so that direct action on the basis of one's commitment is never required. More importantly, it is not always obvious what one must do in order to satisfy the commitment. Unlike intention, it is unclear what one must believe one will do in having the commitment. Perhaps we can reformulate commitment in order to benefit from the intention model.

Recall that in chapter 3 a similar problem arose with respect to the generality of commitments when we tried to formulate commitment as a kind of intention. In order to overcome this problem and extend once again the intention model to commitment, we tried to elicit the embedded intentions and recast commitment as a general intention. We might try something similar here. To say one is committed to a principle or cause – the wrongness of lying or the importance of equal rights – is to say one is committed to *telling* the truth and *keeping* one's promises, or committed to *treating* people as equals and *fighting* discrimination. In other words, one can translate commitment to principles and causes into commitment toward *categories* of action without significant loss of meaning. Although the action of commitment lacks the specificity of the action of intention, we can now, according to this suggestion, compare the belief constraints of the two using the following general formula: one intends/is committed to *A* only if one believes one will *A*.

But this will not work. Although one now has an action as the object of commitment, one need not believe one will fulfill the action in order to have the commitment. Take the commitments of stopping the war or finishing the paper. Does one need to believe one will stop the war or finish the paper to be committed? Not necessarily. Using this model, the most one could say is that one believes one will *attempt* the proposed action (if one needs to), but not that one believes one will *succeed*. Yet this is a very weak constraint to impose on the beliefs associated with commitment. Little of interest follows from this since it makes almost no discrimination between what would and would not count as a commitment. Provided one always believed one would attempt the proposed action, one could have a commitment to virtually anything. But what counts as an attempt? The belief constraint that intending to *A* entails believing one will *A* is not usefully extended to commitment in its current form, but must instead be modified. The question is, in what way.

To answer this, I turn to Alfred Mele's discussion of belief constraints on intention since he offers the most useful model for the analysis I propose.[7] Following Michael Bratman, Mele outlines two general approaches to the analysis of intention. The first "begin[s] with intentional behavior and ask[s] what intention must be if it is to figure in the production or explanation of such behavior" (Mele, *Springs of Action*, p. 127). The second approach starts "by inquiring about the state of mind itself, independently of the behavior that it generates or explains" (*ibid.*). Mele's own method, he says, is a combination of the two. With respect to the question of belief, then, Mele considers in turn each of the functions attributed to intention in the literature and asks whether belief is necessary for the production of intentional behavior. Thus he considers whether the intention to *A* can initiate and sustain activity, guide and monitor behavior, coordi-

[7] Mele, *Springs of Action*, especially chs. 8 and 11.

nate activity, and prompt and terminate practical reasoning, without the aid of the belief that, in this case, one will *A*. In what follows I propose to do something similar to Mele's general approach, though with some changes.

First, although commitment and intention share many of the same roles – coordinating activity, prompting practical reasoning, etc. – the roles and features I want to examine in relation to beliefs are distinctive of commitment itself, in particular of substantive commitments. I will therefore focus principally on the stability and revisability of commitment, as well as its role in self-understanding. Second, as already noted, the beliefs themselves will be different. While I keep to Mele's general model, a good part of the details of that model will have to be changed. Third, Mele focuses on the *causal* relation between beliefs and intentional action. His test for belief constraints on intention is whether they are *causally* necessary for the *production* of intentional action. My arguments, however, will not be that one could not act on one's commitment without certain kinds of beliefs; that is, I do not argue that realist beliefs are a necessary link in the *causal* chain connecting commitment to action. A different kind of test for belief will need to be developed. Finally, in a related point, what is to be explained in the behavior, and perhaps even the notion of explanation, is somewhat different. While Mele looks at the action and asks whether it was intentional, I do not only consider the action of the agent and ask whether that was an instance of commitment. Rather, I seek also to explain that action in the context of the other roles of commitment, in part by asking how the *agent herself* understands the action. The explanation I seek is not only one of observer to subject, but the explanation and understanding an agent herself would reach of her own actions. That is, while Mele is concerned with causal explanations, I will aim instead for rational explanations as they have come to be called in the literature: an "explanation that makes sense of the thing explained . . . renders it intelligible (as opposed to merely predictable) [and] which we seek as a part of self-understanding."[8] These differences will be further explored in the

---

[8] Susan Hurley, *Natural Reasons* (Oxford: Oxford University Press, 1989), p. 285. See also p. 100. Gabriele Taylor uses a similar form of explanation in *Pride, Shame, and Guilt* (Oxford: Clarendon Press, 1985), p. 5. A full criticism of strictly causal accounts of action is given in chapter 5.

next chapter where I will show that interpretation plays a large part in these explanations, yet we can note at this point that this approach is in keeping with the constraint of the first-person perspective discussed earlier.

4.1.5 Alfred Mele on intention and belief

Mele formulates a number of possible belief constraints for intention on the basis of our common-sense understanding and ordinary use of the term. Because in intending to *A* one is generally confident one will *A*, Mele acknowledges that there is reason to think that intending to *A* entails believing one will *A*. He formulates this as

1. *S* intends to *A* only if *S* believes that he (probably) will *A* (Mele, *Springs of Action*, p. 129).

A second constraint Mele considers is a weaker version of (1). It states

1*. *S* intends to *A* only if *S* does not believe that he (probably) will not *A* (*ibid.*).

Thus (1*), like (1), is supported by a general "confidence condition" we typically associate with intention (*ibid.*, p. 148). Mele's claim is that the ability of intention to fulfill its roles in coordination, practical reasoning, etc., does not depend on the truth of either (1) or (1*) (pp. 130, 146). The way he sets out to prove this is by considering each of the roles of intention and examining whether or not they rely on such constraints. I propose to try something similar.

4.1.6 Commitment and confidence conditions

As noted above, the kinds of beliefs associated with commitment and intention are different. In being committed to saving the rain forests, or stopping the war, one need not believe that one will actually succeed in doing these things in order for commitment to fulfill its roles. Nor is it true that one must not believe that one will not save the rain forests or stop the war. One can be committed to projects that might not be realized in one's lifetime. Clearly, we need to formulate a different set of constraints. To do this, I want to use Mele's notion of confidence conditions.

Consider this example. Take a person who is committed to a political cause, say stopping the war. Her confidence is not that her commitment will result in successful fulfillment of the implied action (demonstrating, boycotting, fasting, etc. – which may be thought of as the embedded intentions mentioned earlier), nor is the confidence related to the realization of the political cause itself.[9] Indeed, she may have serious doubts about whether *her own* commitment-based action will result in an end to the war. One can imagine, without too much difficulty, asking the person whether she really thinks her actions will stop the war. If one were persistent enough (and maybe callous enough) in pressing the question, I think one could expect an answer of the form, "No, I do not really think my actions will change anything, but it is certainly worth trying." This is a familiar response, so familiar that variants of the expression are almost clichés, for example: "Sometimes you just have to stand and be counted," or, "it is the principle that matters," or again, "it is just the right thing to do." These different statements all express a confidence in the *worthwhileness* of the commitment itself or a confidence in the *value* of its object; that is, a confidence in the value of abolishing apartheid, of disarming nuclear weapons, or drawing attention to the plight of the downtrodden, whatever the political cause may be. One can have confidence in the value of these projects without being confident in one's own success in bringing them about.[10]

The above examples are, admittedly, on the morally dramatic end of the spectrum of commitments. Although these are the kinds of commitments with which I shall be most concerned, it is important to look at less morally substantive cases in order to see that the structure of commitment remains more or less the same throughout (not exactly the same since, as we move to the more mundane instances of commitment, its constitutive role in identity and self-understanding will diminish). Consider the case of being committed to completing some sort of project, for example, learning a new language. This can,

---

[9] One might say that the commitment (stopping the war) together with the embedded intention (to demonstrate) entail a belief that one will perform the implied action (i.e., demonstrating). However, I am interested in the beliefs that attach to the object of commitment or the commitment itself – the beliefs the agent has about stopping the war or about having such a commitment.

[10] An interesting question that comes up, but one I will not discuss here, is whether one can be committed to a *hopeless* cause. I think one can be. Depending on our point of view, we might call such people either stubborn idealists or fanatics. It is, I think, unlikely that an agent can be committed to something judged *worthless* by the agent herself.

at times, be a frustrating and time-consuming endeavor. The commitment carries with it a certain investment of energy and time on the agent's part with often little noticeable improvement. We can still speak of a confidence condition in this case, though what one values may not be the outcome of the commitment itself, in this example the language learned. In studying German, say, one need not think that the language itself is of value, but what explains the commitment is instead a confidence in the project or process. That is, we think the learning of a language is worthwhile because of the skills we develop and acquire. It is implausible to describe all of our commitments to various projects in terms of our valorization of the object of the commitment. In being committed to learning a language, or finishing a paper, we do not necessarily value the paper or the language, but instead probably place value on either or both of two things: (a) the skills we acquire or qualities we develop in having and fulfilling the commitment, e.g., greater self-discipline and sharper mental acuity, the ability to read a foreign language, improved facility in writing, etc.; (b) certain ideals associated with the commitment, e.g., the importance of finishing one's projects or being multilingual, which in turn might rest on an ideal of being well educated or cultured.

In short, we can still characterize commitments in terms of a confidence in either the value of the *object* of the commitment (stopping the war, saving the rain forests) or in the value of the commitment itself (the learning of a language, the finishing of a paper). In the latter case I shall say that one has confidence in the *worthwhileness* of the commitment (since one does not necessarily value the language learned or the finished paper in themselves), while in the former case I shall say that one has confidence in the *value* of the commitment. I should note that seeing a commitment as being worthwhile can, and often will, include a conception of it as promoting one's long-term self-interest.

One might raise an initial objection that an agent can fulfill a commitment simply by virtue of being committed and without any confidence in the value of the commitment or its object: one is committed to going to a meeting despite one's strong disinclination to do so, despite evidence from past meetings that little is ever achieved, and despite the thought that one's time could be better spent doing other things. No confidence of value or worthwhileness seems to attach to the commitment of, or to being settled upon, going to the meeting. In formulating this objection, however, one must be careful to distinguish commitment-as-intention from commitment-as-obligation. The first, which is the focus of this chapter, is often expressed in the passive voice: one is committed to (doing) *A*, or one describes oneself as being committed to (doing) *A*. The second sense is most aptly expressed in terms of having committed oneself to (doing) *A*, or having a commitment to *A*. Commitment, in the obligatory sense, can create its own reason for action simply in virtue of having the commitment itself and independently of what we value. Reluctantly kept promises are a familiar phenomenon. We can grant, however, that these kinds of commitments are of a completely different order from the intention-like ones. While the former express an obligation that one has made and so might be best classified as a speech-act, the latter are indicative of a certain kind of attitude and hence can be seen as a cognitive or mental state.

Now the separation of the obligation, or promissory, commitments from the intention-like commitments might be questioned by those who argue that the normative concept of commitment as a kind of obligation is in fact "embedded in the very possibility of intending."[11] For Michael Robins, the obligation commitment is primitive in the sense that "it is a relation that binds together the very concept of intention with that of volition" (Robins, *Promising, Intending and Moral Autonomy*, pp. 12, 14, 19). In fact, commitment is so basic for Robins that he seeks to elucidate intention in terms of commitment (*ibid*., pp. 42, 84), rather than commitment in terms of intention (p. 19). His approach, then, is diametrically opposed to mine which uses intention as the basic unit of comparison.

According to Robins, a commitment relates a volition with an earlier intending and so is best thought of as a "three-place operator" ranging over an intending, a volition, and an agent: from the intention to *A* one forms a commitment to an act of volition which in turn causally produces the action, *A* (p. 20). His starting point is the idea that to intend to do *A* is to commit oneself to do *A*. Under this normative theory of intention, "the intention 'binds' the agent to act at a later time or it binds the agent to later exercise his volition, to 'try' or

[11] Michael Robins, *Promising, Intending, and Moral Autonomy* (Cambridge: Cambridge University Press, 1984), p. 2.

to 'will' the appropriate bodily movements" (p. 30). According to Robins, the advantage of this theory is that it alone is able to explain how there can be a mistake in performance with regard to intentions rather than only mistakes in intentions.

Now because commitment-as-obligation is built into the intention, as it were, the conditions for revision of intention are greatly narrowed. He notes an asymmetry between the forming of intentions and the changing of them: while one can form them arbitrarily, one cannot change them at will (p. 35). Because of the binding nature of the commitment that occasions an intention, one can change an intention only if it is *mistaken*; that is, only if there is an "oversight of fact or logic which occurred at the time of the original intending" (p. 36). Otherwise, one is acting akratically, i.e., intentionally acting against one's intentions for reasons that "do not aim at correcting a mistake in intention" (p. 35). Consequently, the only permissible changes in intention are attempts at correcting what look like mistakes in the original intention (p. 85).

As a first response to Robins, one must note that this condition of revision is too narrow. Common experience tells us that circumstances often change in unanticipated ways, in which case it seems perfectly admissible to change one's intention. But if this is to count as one of Robins' "permissible changes," then it must be that the change aims to correct a mistake in the original intending. Yet in order to elicit a mistake in the original intention, some conditions specifying future circumstances must be part of the intention since it is only in contrast to these that the correction is made. However, this in turn implies that in the original intending one specified the expected future conditions for successful intentional action. That is, Robins is forced into holding the position that "intending to *A*" is always a variant of "intending to *A* if one can." Yet it is certainly unclear whether intending is like this. Similarly, it seems to leave little room for permissible changes on the basis of changes in desire-belief reasons for action. Keeping in mind that non-akratic changes in intention are based on *corrections* of the original intention, it looks as though if one's desires change, then the change of intention is permissible only if one can characterize the original intention as faulty for not having foreseen the future change of desire: one intends to *A* provided one still feels like *A*-ing. Thus Robins, in order to allow for what we ordinarily take as permissible changes in intention, must require all intentions to be long conditional intentions: I intend to *A* *if* circumstances are such that . . . and *if* I still desire that . . .[12]

In short, by making commitment a primitive, normative concept, one that is embedded in the very concept of intending, Robins is forced to burden intention with unnecessary conditionals. Moreover, given the importance of the normative concept of commitment for intention, he must place a wide range of common changes in intention in the category of akratic action, contrary to the ordinary use of intention and ordinary understanding of legitimate cases of changing one's mind. Although I think he is correct in saying there is an important obligation aspect of commitment, I do not think it is exhaustive of all the kinds of commitment there are. Ultimately, his attempt to explain intention in terms of this type of commitment leads him to mischaracterize intention. The obligation commitments are thus justifiably set aside in the current analysis.

Returning to the confidence conditions for commitment and their formulation in terms of an "attitude" regarding its value or worthwhileness, I shall now address the problem of formulating and arguing for belief constraints on commitment.

4.1.7 *Confidence conditions and belief constraints*

Recall that the conditions of confidence for intention relate to our ability to, or the likelihood that we will, carry out the specified action. As Mele suggests, this confidence can be characterized by the absence

---

[12] Robins does note the possible objection that the akrasia problem can be overcome by saying that the agent is not able to anticipate fully how he will feel when the time for action arrives. The agent's original intention was mistaken since it did not fully anticipate future circumstances; consequently, acting against the intention is not akratic since one's aim is in fact to correct a mistake in intention – a mistake that arose over the inability to fully anticipate. While he recognizes a "grain of truth" in this objection, he takes its main point to be that since the agent cannot *exactly* represent how he will feel, that representation is somewhat defective or incomplete (p. 37). And since it is *incomplete*, so goes the objection according to Robins, the agent does not act akratically. Robins's response is that the requirement of full anticipation undermines the very possibility of akrasia (p. 37). True. But the real problem is not whether agents fully or inexactly anticipate the future. Rather, it is that Robins requires too much of the original intention in the first place. Consider another way of avoiding the problem of akrasia: never think about the future. Then every intention is potentially mistaken since there will always be oversight of some fact – a natural consequence of not thinking.

of the belief that we cannot or will not do what is called for. The confidence that attaches to commitment, however, is confidence in the value of the commitment itself or its object, not simply confidence in the successful execution of any specific action.[13] If we then want to translate "confidence" in terms of "belief," it would seem that the confidence of commitment is (following Mele's model) the absence of the belief that the commitment (or its object) is not worthwhile (or valuable). The important question to answer is whether mere confidence is enough for commitment, or whether the "committed" agent must possess explicit evaluative beliefs. In other words, are any beliefs functionally required for commitment?

Mele argues against belief constraints on intention by considering whether each of the four roles of intention can be met when the belief constraint is removed. He concludes that since intention can initiate and sustain action, coordinate plans, monitor and guide action, as well as prompt and terminate practical reasoning, without any constraints on beliefs, imposing such constraints is idle. I propose to use the same method for commitment, but in order to reach a different conclusion.

The confidence conditions on commitment were expressed in terms of value. Following Mele's lead, the belief constraints can be formulated as:

> (2) *S* is committed to *A* only if *S* believes *A* is valuable or doing *A* is worthwhile,

or, the weaker constraint,

> (3) *S* is committed to *A* only if *S* does not believe *A* is not valuable or that doing *A* is not worthwhile.[14]

Let me first consider the simpler cases of the intention-like commitments in which there is confidence in the worthwhileness of the commitment. Typically in these cases value does not attach to the object of the commitment but rather to the process or state of

---

[13] I should add that in so far as a commitment requires us to act in a specific way toward its realization, it thereby involves a confidence that we will so act when the time comes. Thus "confidence of intention" is an element of "confidence of commitment" – though not the operative one – and not the other way around.

[14] Similar constraints apply when value attaches to the commitment itself, rather than the object of commitment.

commitment itself.[15] I start with cases of the intention-like commitments since they are the easiest to handle. Suppose a person is committed to learning a new language. What we must show is that either (2) or (3) above must be true in order for commitment to fulfill its roles, that is, that such beliefs are functionally required at least for these types of commitments. Rather than going through both cases, I will focus on what happens when the stronger condition (2) is false. The idea is simple: to prove that (2) is true and that evaluative beliefs are required for commitment, let us assume the contrary. Working out the details, however, is more difficult.

The first question to pose is what does it mean for one not to believe the commitment is worthwhile or to believe it is not worthwhile. Given the formulation in section 4.1.4 that what we value in these kinds of commitments is either (a) the skills we acquire or qualities we develop in having and fulfilling the commitment, or (b) certain ideals associated with the commitment, we can say that to believe that the commitment is no longer worthwhile involves one or both of the following: (i) the belief that the commitment does not in fact lead to one of the skills in (a) or instantiate an ideal in (b); or (ii) the belief that the skills or ideals described in (a) and (b) are not valuable. Take a person who is studying a new language, has been doing so for several months, goes to classes during her free Saturday afternoons and in general does all those sorts of things according to which we would describe her as committed to this project. Suppose that we convince her or somehow induce her to believe that her commitment is no longer worthwhile. Will the "commitment" still be stable and action-guiding?

If by "no longer worthwhile" we mean (i) above the answer clearly is "no." In this case the commitment to learning a new language is means-ends incoherent since it either does not develop certain skills she thought it would develop, or it does not fit her ideal, using the earlier example, of what well-educated people do. Given these facts, it is unlikely that the "commitment" would lead her to study on Saturday afternoons, let alone that she would ever retain it, since for

---

[15] In being committed to finishing a paper or learning a new language, one probably does not value the completed paper *per se*, or the language in itself, but rather the importance of finishing the paper, or the importance of being well educated of which learning a different language is a part. In this sense one thinks the commitments are worthwhile.

her to do so would appear to us as either irrational or purely inertia-driven. If it is not worthwhile in sense (i), the commitment will either be abandoned or inert. For these kinds of intention-like commitments it seems uncontroversial that a belief in its worthwhileness is required. Is it possible, though, that she might simply find it fun to study a new language and continue to do so? Of course, but if this is the only reason, we would not call it a commitment since once it stopped being fun she could simply quit. Yet commitments as we typically understand them are formed in part as an assurance that we will continue a certain general course of action even in those times when it is no longer "fun" to do so.

If the agent thinks instead that the commitment is not worthwhile in sense (ii), i.e., she does not value its associated skills or ideals, what can we say about the ability of commitment to fulfill its roles? Here we must depart somewhat from Mele's model. Recall that Mele's concern is whether beliefs are *causally* necessary for the production of intentional action. He thus considers examples of agents who act in the absence of the relevant beliefs and then asks whether their action could still be described as intentional; that is, given that they perform the action in the absence of the belief that they would, he asks whether we would still consider it an instance of intentional action. Using examples of a foul-shooter who sinks the ball in the basket while thinking she would not, or of answering a knock at the door without previously believing one would, Mele concludes that beliefs are not *causally* required: one can intentionally *A* without the belief one will *A*. However, the question of whether one can "committedly" *A* without the belief that *A* is valuable or worthwhile, is not the immediately relevant question. In order to determine whether the general action, disposition, or state still counts as a commitment in the absence of the belief that the commitment is worthwhile or valuable, I need first to examine whether this psychological state fulfills the same roles of commitment. The motivating question then is not simply whether this action would still count as an instance of her commitment given that the agent acts in the absence of the relevant beliefs; this question needs to be unpacked and elaborated. In order to do this we must look at the other features and functions of commitment – its stability and its roles in self-understanding and identity. We will need to ask what motives we could attribute to an agent who acts in the absence of the relevant beliefs, how she might understand her actions in light of such motives, whether given this understanding she would continue to act, and whether her continued action is compatible with her self-conception and serves to maintain or enhance her own self-understanding. In short, we cannot focus exclusively on the causal dimension – on whether action would follow in the absence of the beliefs – but must also examine the other dimensions of commitment. The kind of explanation I want to offer is broader in scope than the causal one Mele provides. What I aim at is a more general notion of explanation as "making sense," and the best way of making sense of something is not always expressed in causal terms.

This type of explanation is similar to the rational explanations defined on p. 95 which are used, as Susan Hurley states, by "persons . . . interested in making sense of themselves and one another, in trying to find one another intelligible" (Hurley, *Natural Reasons*, p. 100). This explanation is more apt for the kind of dialogue taking place in this book between action theory and metaethics. My claim so far is that a strictly causal account cannot adequately address the categories of analysis at issue, especially given the fact that we aim not so much at predictability as at intelligibility. In chapter 5 we will see more clearly what the limits of purely causal explanations of action are – limits defined by a science of action itself – and how these limits define in turn the role of interpretation in action explanation. At this point, however, suffice it to say that in so far as the current analysis does not seek to fill out the causal links between commitment and action, strict adherence to a purely causal model is unproductive.

Returning now to the belief constraints, I said that the agent does not believe her commitment is worthwhile in the sense that she does not value the skills and qualities it develops, or the ideals it promotes. Commitments, like intentions, guide actions, help agents plan what they will do in the future, and act as filters on possible options. If condition (2) above is false, how can commitment fulfill these roles?

Filtering Take first its role in filtering options, which is related to its stability. Returning to the example of the commitment to learning a new language, suppose this involved dedicating all of one's Saturday afternoons to sitting in a classroom. Clearly, there are any number of possible options for spending one's free Saturdays, but the commitment filters or blocks them. In the absence of any evaluative beliefs about the commitment, the only way to explain the continued filtering of options would be in terms of a strong desire to go to class on Saturdays.[16] But such an account, I suggest, either fails as an explanation of the commitment or leads back to some set of "values" that our hypothesis excluded. Very often our commitments do not track our desires and, despite changes in our immediate desires, we often retain our commitments. Moreover, we seem to be able to exercise a certain control over our commitments which we are unable to do over our desires. As noted in section 4.1.2 we can reconsider, revise, and abandon our commitments, but our desires are seldom so responsive. To the extent the commitment is beyond the person's control and influence since its continued presence depends entirely on the immediate desire of going to class which screens other options, we might say that the commitment is not hers: whether or not she likes going to class is something that happens to her, of which she is the passive spectator. Her commitments are decided for her according to her desires. This is not, however, how we view commitments: they are able to filter options even at those times when our immediate inclination does not favor the action, in this case going to class. The desire-based view is unable to explain this. Furthermore, to the extent that the commitment is not hers in the sense just described, i.e., when she is no longer self-determining with respect to her commitments, the desire-based view also undermines, as we shall see, the role of commitment in self-understanding and identity.

One might think this too hasty a conclusion. Borrowing from Harry Frankfurt's[17] discussion of first-order and second-order desires, one might argue that a desire-based view of commitment might adequately explain its filtering role in the absence of evaluation by adding to the first-order desires, second-order ones, i.e., desires directed toward first-order desires. The picture I described above was essentially that of a wanton, an agent who lacked the capacity to form second-order volitions, i.e., the ability to want certain first-order desires and not others to be effective (Frankfurt, "Freedom of the Will," p. 86), and followed only her first-order, immediate inclina-

---

[16] Note that the agent cannot believe, for example, that one ought to finish one's projects, or that it would be in one's best long-term self-interest to carry through the commitment, since these fall under the category of believing the commitment worthwhile, which has already been excluded.

[17] H. Frankfurt, "Freedom of the Will and the Concept of a Person," in Gary Watson (ed.), *Free Will* (Oxford: Oxford University Press, 1982).

tions. If we suppose, though, that she has the capacity to form second-order volitions we might be able to recapture the filtering role of the commitment as well as relocate it in the possession of the agent herself. The filtering role of commitment could then be attributed to the second-order volition: she does not act solely on the basis of her first-order desires, but constrains them according to her second-order volitions which will provide the stability of the commitment in the face of changing inclinations. More importantly, with this model one avoids having to appeal to any sense of evaluation, or so it seems. For as Frankfurt states, "second-order volitions express evaluations only in the sense that they are preferences. There is no essential restriction on the kind of basis, if any, upon which they are formed" (*ibid.*, p. 89 n. 6). So far, so good. We seem to have recaptured the filtering role of commitments, as well as their stability, through the aid of second-order volitions which direct us toward certain first-order desires. As a result, we are apparently able to bypass an agent's evaluation of the desires themselves. The question is, though, at what price.

The above sentence quoted from Frankfurt is preceded by a more worrying qualification on the constraints on second-order volitions. He adds: "[A] person may be capricious and irresponsible in forming his second-order volitions and give no serious consideration to what is at stake" (*ibid.*). If this is so, then we can pose the same challenge to the second-order volitions as we posed to the first-order ones, namely, in what sense are they the agent's? If the second-order volitions are simply higher-order desires that are formed arbitrarily, then they too can be revised or abandoned arbitrarily just like the first-order desires described above. I say "arbitrarily" since their revision is neither initiated by the agent nor is it the consequence of a reasoning process. Yet if this is the case, and if we keep to Frankfurt's weak sense of evaluation as simply expressing a preference, the second-order volitions seem as detached from the agent as the first-order ones. Why she has them, why she retains them, and why they take the objects they do is not explained by the mere fact of her having them. On one occasion she may have them and on another not, and why this is so is simply because she ceased to desire that certain of her first-order desires be effective. The problem with the wanton was that her desires were not hers – she merely responded to whatever desires had the most conative or affective force. The capacity for forming second-order volitions was supposed to return control of the desires to the agent, changing the wanton into a person. But if these, too, are capriciously formed and expressive of nothing more than preference, it seems that the agent is once again reduced to the field of play for her desires, whether they be first- or second-order ones. The appeal to second-order desires does not solve the problems of the simpler desire model, but only reverts them to a higher level.

In an interesting discussion on integrity, Cheshire Calhoun[18] notes that second-order desires amount to an endorsement of first-order desires, yet adds an important qualification, which he attributes to Gabriele Taylor,[19] that "*how* one comes to endorse a first-order desire matters" (Calhoun, "Standing for Something," 237). That is, if the first-order desires are endorsed by whim – capriciously and irresponsibly – then wantonness infects the second-order desires as noted above. In order to avoid wantonness at this level, the agent's endorsements must be "determined by her own practical reasoning" (*ibid.*). This seems right: endorsing one's desires for reasons which are the agent's own captures the distinction between an agent and a wanton. As Gabriele Taylor states, "a non-wanton is in control of his desires. He will engage in some form of reasoning. If he does not just act on whatever inclination happens to be the strongest he must have some reason for wanting one desire rather than another to be effective" (G. Taylor, *Pride, Shame, and Guilt*, p. 113). Now this reasoning will involve discriminations among various first-order desires based ultimately on comparative evaluations between them, since the criterion for ranking them and deciding which one should be acted upon is not tied to the conative strength of the desire – otherwise the second-order desires would be superfluous. And the reasons which figure in the endorsement will themselves reflect certain evaluative beliefs. The attempt to explain the commitment in terms of desire ultimately turns back to the beliefs regarding value formulated in condition (2).

Self-understanding This claim gains more support when we look at the roles of commitment in identity and self-understanding. According to David Velleman, we have an intellectual desire for self-understanding: a desire to understand the motives and reasons behind our actions (Velleman, *Practical Reflection*, pp. 27 ff.). When we are unable to

---

[18] Calhoun, "Standing for Something."   [19] Taylor, *Pride, Shame, and Guilt*.

understand the "why" of our actions and as a result enter what he calls "reflective puzzlement," we typically stop doing whatever it is we are doing. Return to the example of learning a new language and the explanation of this commitment in terms of the evaluation-free desire model proposed above. This model encountered problems when faced with the filtering role of the commitment and its stability. We tried to solve this problem by introducing second-order volitions. The agent's desire to go to class on Saturdays might not be the strongest one, especially when faced with more attractive prospects, but she remains "committed" to going to class as a result of her second-order desire that this desire be acted upon. In the absence of any evaluative beliefs that would serve as reasons in her endorsement of the first-order desire, we must explain how the agent herself arrives at an understanding of her own actions and how she recognizes the motives of her actions as belonging to her or as being her own.

In this case I think we can say that her understanding of her action would, to a considerable degree, remain opaque to her. One way for her to understand her own action, or to explain it to herself, would be to think of reasons or situations in which she would reconsider her commitment. Keep in mind that she does not believe that learning a language is valuable, either in terms of the skills one acquires in doing so or as meeting her ideal of being well educated. Moreover, she is often faced with the option of doing other more enjoyable activities on Saturday afternoons, like going to the beach or watching a movie. If this is so, it is unclear under what circumstances she would ever revise her "commitment" or what would count as a reason for reconsidering it. But without any criteria for revision or reconsideration, her going to class more closely resembles a compulsion than a commitment. Her determination or "commitment" to learning a new language seems not at all under her control, and to the extent it escapes her control she is, we might say, detached from the "commitment." If she were suddenly to lose this determination and we asked her why, the only answer we could expect would be that she simply lost the determination; but this is more of a description than an explanation. Once again, it seems that when one removes the evaluative beliefs from the commitment, the agent becomes the passive spectator of her own actions. It is difficult to see in what terms the agent could understand what it is she is doing since she cannot claim any of the motives as her own.

Gary Watson[20] suggests something along these lines in his criticism of Frankfurt's notion of the "sense in which some wants may be said to be more truly the agent's own than others" (Watson, "Free Agency," p. 107). For Frankfurt, to identify with one's first-order desire is to make a "decisive commitment" to it which simply means not questioning the "pertinence" of higher-order desires or volitions which endorse this desire (Frankfurt, "Freedom of the Will," p. 91). But Watson notes that the decisive commitment does not answer the question, "What gives these volitions any special relation to 'oneself'?" (Watson, "Free Agency," p. 108). "It does not tell us," he says, "why or how a particular want can have, among all of a person's 'desires,' the special property of being peculiarly his 'own'" (*ibid.*). To the extent this decisive commitment is arbitrary, the agent is no less wanton with respect to his second-order volitions than to his first-order desires. Rather, we must situate second-order volitions within practical judgments (p. 109). Importantly, for Watson, such judgments (at least for free agents) will involve a "valuation system," that is, a "set of considerations which, when combined with his factual beliefs . . . yields judgments of the form: the thing for me to do in these circumstances, all things considered, is *a*" (p. 105). And among these considerations are values which reflect one's "more or less long-term aims and normative principles that we are willing to defend" (*ibid.*).

There is, however, another response one could give according to which commitment could still play a role in self-understanding as well as identity without having recourse to evaluative beliefs. One might simply say that the agent understands his actions because he is doing what his second-order desires recommend: he likes doing what he wants to do. Moreover, to the extent that identity is understood as a "psychological phenomenon" in which we "understand who we are in terms of our deepest impulses and what feels natural or unforced" (Calhoun, "Standing for Something," 243), it would appear as though such evaluation-free commitments also play a role in identity since they depend, once again, on these second-order desires. Following this line, we could also say that the agent in fact is not the detached spectator of his actions since he comes to identify with the desire itself. Frankfurt, in response to Watson's criticism, says that identification with a desire through decisive commitment is not in fact arbitrary

---

[20] Watson, "Free Agency" in *Free Will*.

but "means that the person who makes it does so in the belief that no further accurate inquiry would require him to change his mind."[21] Thus, when a person makes a decisive commitment to a desire, he "no longer holds himself at all apart from the desire," and "in making a decision by which he identifies with a desire, *constitutes himself*" (Frankfurt, "Identification and Wholeheartedness," p. 181; original emphasis). Consequently, this desire will no longer seem alien to him, will in fact be an integral part of him, and so will provide an understandable motive for his actions. There are, however, two things to notice here.

First, according to Frankfurt, it is through a decision that a person identifies with a desire (*ibid.*, p. 172), so that the question which characterized the quest for self-understanding – why act on this desire? – is now replaced by the question, why decide on this desire? Yet he is in no better position than before for reaching self-understanding, since if he did not have an answer to the first question, he will not have an answer to the second question. As we saw earlier, Frankfurt's model simply moves the problems one level higher. We would now have to unravel what is involved in the decision to identify wholeheartedly, without reservation, with one's desire. Although Frankfurt acknowledges that "[i]t is very difficult to articulate what the act of deciding consists in" (p. 183), he does not offer any insights by which we could understand how such a decision is made and why it is identity-constituting.

Second, there is more than one sense in which we can understand the notions of "identity" and "identifying with." In addition to the characterization of identity as a "psychological phenomenon" (call this "trait-identity"), Calhoun also defines a "deliberative" notion of identity according to which we "understand who we are in terms of our considered judgments about what is of value, what principles ought to be endorsed, and how they should be hierarchically ranked" (Calhoun, "Standing for Something," 244) – what one might label "deliberative-identity."[22] The notion of identity that will be operative in this book is deliberative- (or *ipse*) identity since the term "identity"

---

[21] H. Frankfurt, "Identification and Wholeheartedness," in John Martin Fischer and Mark Ravizza, (eds.) *Perspectives on Moral Responsibility* (Ithaca: Cornell University Press, 1993), p. 180.

[22] These roughly approximate to the two kinds of identity Paul Ricoeur describes as *idem* and *ipse*, respectively.

used in the context of persons refers to more than their distinguishing traits, features, or habits – those aspects *by* which one is identified. Although this latter notion of trait- (or *idem*) identity is important, it fails to capture the equally important element of identity, namely, its connection to endorsement, reflection, and the things *with* which one identifies. Now, as Calhoun notes, and as experience sometimes painfully teaches us, what feels natural or unforced – what constitutes trait-identity – is not always what is reflectively endorsed. (Calhoun gives the example of the homosexual who accepts the view that homosexuality is a form of neurosis. In the literature in psychology this is termed "ego-dystonia."[23]) The point here is that identity is not reducible to one or the other formulation, but combines both senses. Although Frankfurt, too, seems interested in deliberative-identity – "Since it is most conspicuously by making a decision that a person identifies with some element of his psychic life, deciding plays an important role in the formation and *maintenance of the self* "[24] – he does not clarify how one constitutes identity through, for example, taking responsibility for one's desires and characteristics (Frankfurt, "Identification and Wholeheartedness," p. 182), or willfully incorporating desires into oneself (*ibid.*, p. 183). So long as these processes are left unexplained, Frankfurt's thesis remains open to the earlier charges of arbitrariness: it leaves open the pressing question of in what sense and why these desires are more the agent's own than others and, in doing so, it opens a space for introducing evaluative beliefs into the structure. Finally, Frankfurt's analysis, as I tried to extend it to this topic, confuses the two notions of identity: do the desires constitute one's identity because they are now more deeply embedded traits of

---

[23] See, for example, Harold I. Lief and Helen S. Kaplan, "Ego-Dystonic Homosexuality," *Journal of Sex and Marital Therapy* 12 (1986): 259–66. The DSM-III, they say, provides two criteria for ego-dystonic homosexuality:

> (a) the individual complains that heterosexual arousal is persistently absent or weak and significantly interferes with initiating or maintaining wanted heterosexual relationships; and (b) there is a sustained pattern of homosexual arousal that the individual explicitly states has been unwanted and is a persistent source of distress (*ibid.*, 259).

This will be discussed more in the context of Velleman's noncognitivist theory of self-conception in chapter 5.

[24] Frankfurt, "Identification and Wholeheartedness," p. 183; emphasis added. Compare this with Ricoeur's notion of self-constancy in *Oneself as Another*.

the agent, or because they are endorsed and maintained by the agent?

The Frankfurt-type model of evaluative-free commitments I have tried to construct tells us that desire-based commitments play a role in identity because one identifies with one's desires. Clearly, this fails as an explanation. If commitment is to play a role in identity, we must explain the process of endorsement involved in both the second-order volitions and deliberative-identity – mere identification with what feels natural is not sufficient for explaining the role of commitment in the constitution of identity. In order to do this, it looks as though, in light of the earlier discussion, evaluative beliefs will have to be introduced.

Planning As a final proof of the truth of condition (2) – *S* is committed to *A* only if *S* believes *A* is valuable or doing *A* is worthwhile – I turn briefly now to the role of commitment in planning. Commitments help agents plan and are elements in plans because of their stability: given one's commitments, one can more easily plan what one will do in the future. Again though, if we assume that the agent does not value a commitment,[25] then this undermines its role as a filter, as we have just seen, which further destabilizes the commitment. Whether or not the agent will be committed to her project in the future depends on how she feels – something she very likely cannot predict or at the very least guarantee. But if this is so, there is little reason why she should include this commitment as an element in her plans. If she does not believe the commitment is valuable or worthwhile, she cannot as strongly guarantee her continued commitment, and so is hampered in forming plans which depend in part on this commitment.[26]

Given that condition (2) is true, i.e., that the belief that the commitment is valuable or worthwhile is functionally required, we

---

[25] There is clearly a difference between valuing *X* and believing *X* is valuable. While the former entails the latter, the reverse is not true. Although I am interested in the belief associated with commitments, namely, the belief that the commitment is valuable, I will sometimes use the simpler locution valuing *X*.

[26] A similar argument is made with respect to belief constraints on intention. If intending to *A* does not involve the belief that one will *A*, why should such an intention figure in plans that depend upon one's *A*-ing? See Robert Audi, "Intention, Cognitive Commitment, and Planning." This objection is, I think, part of the rational explanation I have been using. The objection says that the "noncognitive" account of intention does not make sense of, or render intelligible, other actions connected to intention such as planning.

can also see (a) why commitments face coherence and consistency constraints, (b) why we reason about and try to justify them when challenged, and (c) how the possibility of being wrong is related to them (see section 4.1.2). As rational agents, not only do we aim at consistency and coherence in our beliefs, but also in our evaluative rankings. Thus, if evaluative beliefs are part of commitments, they will be doubly bound by the requirements for consistency and coherence, not only by other "factual" beliefs regarding, for example, the appropriate means to the given ends, but also by the agent's other evaluations. A commitment to learning a new language is constrained, on the one side, by consistency requirements as to how best to go about that, e.g., spending one's Saturdays in class or at the beach, and also by evaluative beliefs regarding what it is to be well educated or a person of culture, or the importance of communicating with different people.

As for (b), when our commitments are challenged or called into question by others, we defend them by offering reasons for believing that our commitments are worthwhile or valuable. Moreover, these reasons are presented as more than personal quirks or idiosyncrasies, but are expressed as being reasons that others, though they might not accept them, could at least find intelligible or reasonable or see as reasons they themselves might give were they similarly committed. The commitment is not just something one happens to have, like a preference for vanilla over chocolate ice-cream, but is instead based on a belief which in turn is supported by reasons that one would expect others to at least recognize as being understandable and reasonable. What I want to suggest at this time is that there seems to be some independent validity to one's commitments in the sense that our justifications of them appeal to something more than the fact that we have them: a kind of validity which can only be explained in terms of belief (this will be developed in section 4.2 of this chapter). In the challenge and defense of commitments there is a demand for agent-independent reasons why one should or should not believe certain commitments are worthwhile or valuable.

This, too, helps us understand (c) the connection to the possibility of error. In giving publicly acceptable reasons for my beliefs, I am also open to their refutation, i.e., I remain open to the possibility that my belief regarding the value of the commitment might be wrong, or that somehow my commitments might be misguided. This will be an important point when I argue that the beliefs amount to realist beliefs about value and reassess Rorty's and Gibbard's analysis of commitment within the context of their broader theories. Once we take away the possibility of error, and remove any criteria for what would count as being wrong, as Rorty does, it remains to be seen how the agents understand their commitments.

4.1.8 Conclusion

By considering the various roles of commitment in self-understanding, identity, and planning, and some of its features, e.g., its stability and revisability, and asking how commitment fulfills these or how we can explain them in the absence of any evaluative beliefs, we have been able to show that certain beliefs are in fact functionally required. When we have tried to formulate explanations in which desires played the roles of beliefs, we encountered considerable problems.

The main obstacle for alternative, "noncognitive" explanations was accounting for commitment's role in identity and self-understanding. What the first part of this chapter has shown is that evaluative beliefs are functionally required for commitment. What needs to be developed now is the connection between these evaluative beliefs and self-understanding and identity. Yet one must not lose sight of the fact that the overall goal is to build an argument for moral realism. Fortunately, these two goals eventually coincide. The intermediate steps, however, still need to be filled in. In what follows, I argue that the role commitment plays in self-understanding and identity depends on "objective" beliefs about value. The key link is found in the notion of "self-conception."

4.2 VALUES AND SELF-CONCEPTION

4.2.1 Introduction

If the discussion of section 4.1 above is correct, then at least for the intention-like commitments the belief that the commitment is valuable or worthwhile is functionally required. At this point, one could turn to the substantive commitments and carry out the same analysis. The result would be the same, but not as informative since we are left with the rather vague notion of "believing a commitment is valuable or worthwhile." The problem now is to find out what this means and I want to address this before moving on to the beliefs involved in substantive commitments. In doing so, we will need to take a closer look at the notion of self-conception and how it is constituted.

In the previous chapter I left the question about value fairly open, saying only that what we value in the intention-like commitments is either (a) the skills we acquire or qualities we develop in having and fulfilling the commitment, or (b) certain ideals associated with the commitment. The problem is to specify what this valuing itself consists in. (Again, I switch between the belief that X is valuable and valuing X. In the case of commitment, I think that not only does one believe it is valuable, but in having the commitment one also values it.) This will lead us to a distinction between personal and impersonal values. Before doing so, however, I want to take a brief look at current discussions on integrity and caring, since the problem of value arises in a similar context.

In the recent discussions on integrity and caring the question often arises as to what may be the objects of our care[27] and whether there are "no constraints on the content of the principles or commitments a person of integrity may hold."[28] The answers are as one would expect: the things we care about we usually value and the principles and commitments a person of integrity holds are usually thought to be important. The problem here is the same as the one in the case of commitment; namely, what does it mean to value something or think it is important?

Blustein tells us that "in order to regard something as of *value*, rather than merely as fun to do and the like, one must reflect on it from a point of view independent of one's desires" (Blustein, *Care and Commitment*, p. 239, n. 5). Gabriele Taylor also suggests that "to value something is to see it as either a (human) good or as the means toward achieving such a good" (G. Taylor, *Pride, Shame, and Guilt*, p. 26). In either case, to value something seems to imply that the object of value must be seen to some extent as being independent of the agent's desires. Thus, G. Taylor says that:

[t]o value something is to regard that thing as of value, where this value does not consist in just being the satisfaction of some desire of the agent

---

[27] Jeffrey Blustein, *Care and Commitment: Taking the Personal Point of View* (New York: Oxford University Press, 1991), p. 45, *passim.*   [28] Lynne McFall, "Integrity," p. 9.

in question. She must see that in virtue of which she values it as being other than and independent of its capacity to satisfy some desire of hers. She cannot think of it as being a good just for herself, and the reasons which in her view justify her to act in this way rather than any other way will not refer to just her own maximum desire-satisfaction. She cannot explain the point of what she wants and does by referring merely to what *she* likes or dislikes, what *she* finds fun to do or finds unpleasant. The point of her thinking one course of action more worthwhile than another must be that it is directed toward something which it is at least possible to conceive of as a (human) good" (*ibid.*, p. 117).

To value something is to see it either as a good or as a *human* good. But even when one sees it as good in a less global sense, one must see it as something more than mere satisfaction of one's desires – as something more than "being a good just for herself." Thus, when one values, say, learning a new language, though it is unlikely that one conceives of it as a human good, one must still see it as something more than desire-satisfying or being fun, but as somehow desire-independent. For lack of a better description, it must be seen to have some measure of objective merit, according to G. Taylor and Blustein.

If they are correct about what valuing something entails, then the argument I have been developing regarding the requirements of commitment would be greatly advanced. I argued that the intention-like commitments, and *a fortiori* substantive commitments, involve evaluative beliefs. But if valuing something entails conceiving it as objectively valuable, even in G. Taylor's qualified sense, then this clearly helps my argument: it is a (relatively) short step from the objectivity of value to a modest realism, the belief in which is a condition for the possibility of commitment. Unfortunately, I cannot so easily use G. Taylor's and Blustein's arguments.

G. Taylor rests her argument for the objectivity of value in part on David Wiggins' own discussion of value and his rejection of non-cognitivism.[29] Like other critics of noncognitivism (and existentialism, in particular),[30] Wiggins argues that it fails to make sense of what he calls the "inner view" of the will which "picks and chooses,

---

[29] D. Wiggins, "Truth, Invention, and the Meaning of Life," in *Needs, Values, Truth* (Oxford: Basil Blackwell, 1987).

[30] See Charles Taylor, "What is Human Agency?" in *Human Agency and Language: Philosophical Papers*, vol. I (Cambridge: Cambridge University Press, 1985), p. 29.

deliberates, weighs, and tests its own concerns [and] craves objective reasons" (Wiggins, "Truth, Invention, and the Meaning of Life," p. 99). Without preexisting objective values "in the world," the argument goes, the picking, choosing, deliberating, and weighing make no sense. The problem with noncognitivism, according to Wiggins, is that it renders life meaningless since it levels the value of all our pursuits: for noncognitivism, pushpin is as good as poetry, and we "know" this is not so. The objection to noncognitivism and the argument for the objectivity of value turn on what is (thought to be) required for a *meaningful* life. This is a standard move, particularly among those writing on the topics of integrity, care, and commitment.

Thus Jeffrey Blustein asserts that "if commitment to something is to give my life meaning, then I must believe that my commitment is impersonally recommended and that the value of what I commit myself to does not emanate simply from myself" (Blustein, *Care and Commitment*, p. 48). Loren Lomasky,[31] who also argues that commitment must rest on a "foundation" of objective value states that "unless there is value in the world that is ours to grasp, all our planning, and scheming, and dreaming seem to be in vain," i.e., are meaningless (Lomasky, *Persons, Rights, and the Moral Community*, p. 237). However, the question of meaning is, I think, a nonstarter, for it is always open to the existentialist and neopragmatist to respond that meaninglessness is precisely the point; life is absurd, and the challenge is to make commitments, and take stands, all in the face of radical contingency.[32] It is precisely this capacity that distinguishes Rorty's liberal ironist and is the hallmark of authenticity for Sartre. The need for objective values that are intended to make life meaningful is the kind of "terminal wistfulness"[33] of which neopragmatism is supposed to cure us. In short, the appeal to meaning is too tenuous a basis for the conclusion regarding the connection of commitment with objective value. The real question, indeed the question of the book, is whether we can meet the challenge described above, i.e., be liberal ironists and form commitments in the face of absurdity. Despite the intuitive pull of the quasi-phenomenological arguments that Wiggins, Blustein, and

[31] L. Lomasky, *Persons, Rights, and the Moral Community* (Oxford: Oxford University Press, 1987). [32] Cf. Rorty, *CIS* p. 189.
[33] See Jeffrey Stout, *Ethics After Babel* (Boston: Beacon Press, 1988).

Lomasky offer against noncognitivism and existentialism, they cannot silence the persistent dissenter who insists that such intuitions are only symptomatic of the failure to fully submit to the neopragmatist therapy. Although their arguments regarding the objectivity of value and what it is to value something are attractive, they are not fully warranted at this time.

4.2.2 *Personal and impersonal value*

Perhaps a better way of getting at the notion of what it is to value something is to make a distinction between two kinds of value: personal and impersonal. Again, though, one has to be careful not to build into these concepts too many normative constraints.

Personal value, Blustein says, "is value that we give to the objects of our care by caring about them," and so can be thought of as "value for a particular person, conferred by that individual on something in and through caring" (Blustein, *Care and Commitment*, pp. 43–4). Personal value is thus generated by our caring about something and contains an essential reference to the person who holds it. Impersonal value, however, "inheres in something apart from my caring about or wanting it. Its relation to *me* drops out of the picture in this way" (*ibid.*). It is important to note that even for something that has personal value, according to Blustein, it is not enough that it simply be fun or pleasing only for the individual who values it, but must instead be regarded from a point of view independent of her desires (*ibid.*, ch. 3, n. 5), and so to this extent might be thought to have a measure of objectivity.

Although from Blustein it is not immediately clear why this last claim should be true, we could, as suggested by G. Taylor's earlier passage, attribute this to an intelligibility requirement on what one values and the actions arising from one's values; that is, it must be possible for others to at least be able to conceive of it as a possible object of value in order for it to count as a value instead of some kind of personal or psychological quirk. It might be helpful to think of this in terms of Elisabeth Anscombe's analysis of "wanting."[34] Just as the notion of "wanting" needs a desirability characterization answering the question "What for?" in order for us to understand it as "wanting" and not something else, so too, Blustein might say, in order to understand

---

[34] E. Anscombe, *Intention* (Oxford: Blackwell, 1957).

something as a value, even a personal one, it needs to be characterized in a way that makes it understandable to us. And this means that it needs to be characterized from a point of view independent of the agent's desires in a way that answers the question "Why do you value this?" without restating the fact that one happens to desire it. Just as we do not understand what a person wants a pin for (using Anscombe's example) by being told that it will satisfy her want, neither do we understand why a person values something by being told it satisfies a desire. There are many things we desire but do not value. In this way, it might then be possible to insinuate objectivity into value.

Now if indeed care generates personal value, and personal value is "objective" in the sense just described, then it might be possible to connect objective value to even the intention-like commitments through care. The connection is simply that we care about our commitments. However, this path from commitment to objective value is blocked by the following obstacles.

4.2.3 Care, value, and commitment

To care about something, says Blustein, is to be invested in it. This personal investment, I argued in chapter 3, is what distinguished commitments from policies. However, care and commitment differ in important respects. In the first place, while being committed to something (or someone) entails caring about it (or them), the converse is not true. As Blustein correctly notes, "not everything or everyone people care about is an object of their commitment" (Blustein, *Care and Commitment*, p. 38). The things I am committed to are not coextensive with the things I care about. Second, Blustein points out that caring does not have the same "deliberative priority" as commitment (*ibid.*). In forming plans, in deciding what to do, in filtering possible courses of action, care does not figure as prominently as commitment in our practical deliberations. And third, while one can care about something without placing value on it (according to Blustein at least),[35] from what I have argued in the preceding sections, the same is not true of commitment.

With these distinctions in mind, we might say that to be committed

---

[35] Blustein says that if I care about something, it must be important to me; but placing importance on something and valuing it are not equivalent (pp. 38, 42).

to *A* involves caring about *A* which, by Blustein's account, generates the personal value we place on *A*, a value which, though particular to the individual, is still regarded from a desire-independent standpoint. There is, however, a bootstrapping problem with this formulation. Simply put, if the commitment generates its own value which is, I have said, necessary for the maintenance of the commitment, how was the commitment formed in the first place? Without our antecedently valuing the object of the commitment, the commitment must somehow pull itself up by the bootstraps.

One way around this is to say that the personal value in fact rests upon a prior *impersonal* value, which in turn supports the commitment. This is Lomasky's line of argument. He states: "The value to me of *this* project is consequent upon my commitment to it and not to some other end, but the personal value that accrues to me as I pursue the project that is *mine* presupposed the impersonal value of project pursuit" (Lomasky, *Persons, Rights and the Moral Community*, p. 243). The impersonal value underlying one's commitment is not in the particular project, but resides in the "construction of a coherent and connected life" (*ibid.*, p. 242). This answer, however, does not really solve the bootstrapping problem: although we now have a reason to form commitments generally, we have no reason to form any particular commitment since its value to me is still subsequent to the commitment itself. A second problem is that it implies that all commitments must somehow be related to impersonal value. But do we want to make this claim? Are there no differences between our commitment to learning a new language which has only personal value, and a commitment to treating people fairly, or avoiding cruelty as the worst thing one can do, which have, one might suppose, impersonal value? Blustein, in the context of caring, makes a similar point:

> It seems extravagant to require that the personal value generated by all caring, no matter how serious or trivial this caring might be, point beyond itself to impersonal value . . . The person who cares about [a hobby] and gives it personal value through caring need not believe that it is also valuable from an impersonal, non-egocentric point of view (Blustein, *Care and Commitment*, p. 46).

In order to avoid the bootstrapping problem and the "extravagance" problem, it must be the case that the value attaching to commitment is not generated by the commitment, but rather is a reason for forming it in the first place.

4.2.4 Personal value and the intention-like commitments

The personal–impersonal distinction between values is useful since it is relatively normatively neutral. It is a better characterization of valuing than the one given by G. Taylor in terms of the good, since it is less dependent upon any conditions of meaningfulness. Blustein's formulation, though leading in the right direction, needs to be refined, not only because personal value, as he defines it, is generated by care and so also by commitment, but because the notion of objectivity he seems to appeal to is vague.

The distinction between these two types of value and their relation to an objective basis receives considerable attention from Thomas Nagel in both *The Possibility of Altruism*[36] and *The View from Nowhere*.[37] For Nagel, personal value, impersonal value, and objectivity are all interrelated. In his earlier work, *PA*, Nagel defines the personal standpoint, from which personal judgments are made and personal values are formed, as the vantage point which has "token reflexives" (*PA*, p. 101); that is, the vantage point which contains references to the subject and of which the subject is the locus (*ibid.*). The impersonal standpoint, which he identifies with the objective point of view, abstracts from any particular relations to the subject (*PA*, p. 102) and detaches from the individual perspective (*VN*, p. 140). Personal values, what he later calls, following Derek Parfit, agent-relative values, provide reasons for someone "to want and pursue [something] if it is related to him in the right way" (*VN*. p. 153), while impersonal values (or agent-neutral values) provide anyone with a reason to want the objective value to be realized since they are independent of any personal perspective (*ibid.*). The central difference between them is whether or not they contain an essential reference to the person who has them.

Now the interesting theses Nagel proposes in *PA* are that "[w]henever one acts for a reason . . . it must be possible to regard

---

[36] T. Nagel, *The Possibility of Altruism* (Oxford: Clarendon Press, 1970), henceforth, *PA*.

[37] T. Nagel, *The View from Nowhere* (Oxford: Oxford University Press, 1986), henceforth, *VN*.

oneself as acting for an objective reason, and promoting an objectively valuable end" (pp. 96–7) and that "the requirement of objectivity can be regarded as a condition on *whatever* values one holds" (p. 97). I have argued that commitment involves having beliefs about the value of the commitment which figure as reasons for both forming the commitment and acting on it, and I have tried to isolate the content and status of these evaluative beliefs. According to Nagel, the evaluative beliefs, as reasons, must be seen as objective reasons and the values they embody as objectively valuable. For Nagel, what is objective is perspectiveless, and what can be formulated from the objective standpoint holds validly for all individuals. Thus what people have reason to do, objectively, is true or false independent of our beliefs and inclinations (*VN*, p. 144). Nagel's position is, in short, that "there are reasons for action, [and] that we must *discover* them instead of deriving them from preexisting motives" (*VN*, p. 139, emphasis added). Clearly, this is in tune with the modest form of realism I defined in chapter 1 and for which I hope to argue. Thus, if it is true that objectivity is a condition on whatever one values, i.e., is a condition for one's values being warranted, and if realism[38] underwrites the possibility of objectivity,[39] then since values and their warrant are conditions of commitment, one could conclude, *pace* Rorty and Gibbard, that realism is a condition of the possibility of commitment.

The obvious question to ask first is why objectivity should be a condition on the values one holds. Nagel's answer to this in *VN* is that the pursuit of objectivity and objective knowledge is an undeniable part of who or what we are. The need to shed our subjective perspective in order to "view the world from nowhere within it" (*VN*, p. 67) is part of our "natural realism [that] makes it impossible for us to be content with a purely subjective view" (p. 74). According to Nagel, there is no "denying the objective pretensions of our dominant aims in life" (p. 218). Once again, however, I want to avoid, or at least delay

---

[38] Nagel argues for what he calls normative realism, namely, the view that "propositions about what gives us reasons for action are true or false independently of how things appear to us" (*VN* p.139).

[39] In saying that realism "underwrites" objectivity, I mean that objectivity as we typically understand it only makes sense within a framework in which statements, judgments, propositions, etc., can be right or wrong independently of our attitudes toward, or knowledge of, them.

as long as possible, this line of argument. For it is easy to imagine what a neopragmatist like Rorty, or even a modest pragmatist like Jeffrey Stout, would say about Nagel's project. Realism, they would say, with its reliance on our ineluctable drive toward the objective, when combined with our unavoidable engagement in the subjective, is itself the source of the painful moral dilemmas we face and in fact engenders a sense of absurdity toward our life and our projects. The ineliminable conflict between the subjective and objective standpoints introduces an element of tragedy many of us would be glad to do without. Modest pragmatism, however, by releasing us from the pursuit of objectivity and refusing to see anything extraordinarily deep in the truth of our propositions, avoids the "giddiness" accompanying the act of viewing our practices and beliefs from nowhere. Leaving our feet firmly planted on the ground, it annuls the absurdity that follows upon our probe into the depths of meaning or our ascendance into the heavens for Truth. The pragmatist's "Buddhist-like" detachment[40] is a welcome relief from the realist's neurotic preoccupation with objectivity. Once the pragmatic therapy sinks in, the neopragmatists might argue, the realist longings characteristic of Nagel's work will become an itch we no longer want to scratch. In light of this objection, the appeal to a "natural realism" must be carefully formulated. This said, I think the seeds for a better argument for objectivity can be found in Nagel's earlier work, *PA*.

4.2.5 Self-conception: a first step

In *PA*, objectivity figures as an important part of an argument for altruism and against solipsism. Although Nagel later reconsiders this argument (*VN*, p. 158), in part because of criticisms from Nicholas Sturgeon,[41] there are important ideas to be gleaned from his account which are independent of the altruism argument which itself derives from a more general principle regarding the rational constraints on action (*PA*, p. 88). It is from this general principle that I want to draw support for the objectivity of value as it figures in commitment.

As quoted earlier, Nagel asserts that:

---

[40] Stout, *Ethics after Babel*, p. 253.

[41] N. Sturgeon, "Altruism, Solipsism and the Objectivity of Reasons," *Philosophical Review* 83 (1974): 374–402.

the only acceptable reasons are objective ones; even if one operates successfully with a subjective principle, one must be able to back it up with an objective principle yielding those same reasons as well as (presumably) others. Whenever one acts for a reason . . . it must be *possible* to regard oneself as acting for an objective reason, and promoting an objectively valuable end (*PA*, pp. 96–7).

What underlies this is a certain kind of self-conception common to all (rational) agents; that is, "a conception of oneself as simply a person among others all of whom are included in a single world . . . a conception of oneself as identical with a particular, impersonally specifiable inhabitant of the world, among others of a similar nature . . . a conception of oneself not merely as *I*, but as someone" (*PA*, p. 100). This self-conception places a constraint on reasons for action and hence also on values in so far as they figure in deliberation as practical judgments. This self-conception involves, as part of the view of oneself as *someone* and not just as *I*, a view of oneself as someone who acts on reasons and whose practical judgments could be understood and recognized from, using Nagel's term, the objective standpoint.

Nagel's mistake, as he himself recognizes in *VN*, was to claim that not only must these judgments be impersonally valid, but their "motivational content . . . be present in their impersonal as well as personal versions," and that this was the "basis for an interpretation of objective reasons" (*PA*, p. 109). Surely, it is overstated to require that the practical judgments I make regarding, for example, what is worth doing, or the reasons I might offer supporting the things I value, need to provide the same kind of *motivation* for others as they do for me in order to be objective reasons. Rather, what this self-conception of myself as not only just one person among others, but also, I would add, as one who is interested in acting for reasons, requires is that the reasons I cite in either my judgments or actions be *recognizable* by others as possible reasons, and not that they necessarily accept them. The intelligibility requirement noted above in the discussion of Blustein and G. Taylor stems from this self-conception. One's reasons and the practical judgments one makes from the subjective standpoint must also be thought to be valid, though again not motivating, when viewed from the objective standpoint, precisely because one sees oneself not just as this particular person with this particular perspective, but as one person among similar other persons.

It is important not to read this constraint in overly Kantian terms. This is not a reformulation of the categorical imperative, nor is it another version of the kingdom of ends. Moreover, this constraint is not a condition on what count as moral reasons or judgments. Rather, the constraint says that even our relative reasons must be thought to be general and not exclusively subjective: a constraint derived from our conception of ourselves as individuals inhabiting two standpoints, the subjective and objective, i.e., who I happen to be and the person I am. This self-conception is fairly common.[42] It is what motivates, as Nagel suggests, the search for and weighing of reasons, deliberation over what is valuable and worth doing, and the care taken in making choices: these practices are, in part, responses to the demands of objectivity, to answering to the objective point of view. It is the attempt to discern the objective merit of what we value, rather than a search for meaning as Wiggins, Blustein, and Lomasky state, that drives the will to pick and choose, deliberate, weigh, and test its own concerns.

However, this so-called attempt to discern the objective merit must also not be understood as Nagel sometimes seems to understand it, namely, as an ineluctable drive to shed the subjective perspective and see the Truth. Such a characterization makes it vulnerable to the pragmatist criticisms already noted. Rather, it is as a consequence of the conception of ourselves as one person among others, and as ones who act for reasons, that we try to act for objectively valid reasons.

Personal value, we will finally say, is value for a particular person, conferred by that person upon the object. The value placed on the object is not, however, due exclusively to the fact that one cares about it, or that it is desire-satisfying. The objects of value are still constrained by an intelligibility requirement that others be able to recognize the value as such, because of our self-conception; that is, the value must be thought to have some objective merit.[43] The notion of objectivity for personal values is clearly limited, since the requirement is not that all rational beings recognize it, but that reasonable people

---

[42] One could argue that Rorty's call to expand the notion of "we" is in fact premised on such a self-conception.

[43] Objective validity is more than intersubjective agreement, although our best measure of objectivity might at times be intersubjective convergence. It is important to separate the epistemological problem of how we know something is objectively true from the alethiological problem of whether anything is objectively true.

do so, where the notion of "reasonable," as an obviously normative concept, will be regionally defined. Thus, when Blustein says that even personal values have to be viewed from a standpoint independent of one's desires, we can now see why they must be seen as something more than a psychological quirk. It must be possible for others to conceive of it as a possible value themselves, or to understand how it could be of value to someone.[44] This is also a better formulation of objective values than the one given by G. Taylor since it does not rest on conditions of meaningful existence, but instead is derived from a simpler notion of self-conception. Personal value, however, will still depend on certain facts about who *I* am, that I am a certain way, and enjoy certain things. The self-conception that is operative, I claim, for all agents, places very broad constraints on personal value, and only renders them intelligible. Though more than purely subjective preference, personal values are *not* fully objective in the sense I shall need. For the kind of objectivity required of moral realism, we need to turn to impersonal values.

Whereas personal value is defined against a very minimalist conception of oneself as inhabiting, at least in part, the objective standpoint, which is to say, as being simply one person among others, impersonal values are derived from a more robust self-conception. From this objective point of view, our self-conception is not limited to viewing ourselves as simply one person among others, but instead incorporates certain fundamental *beliefs* about what constitutes a person and what are basic human needs. That is to say, impersonal value derives from a self-conception involving beliefs about the human good. Such values, clearly, are independent of any contingent personal characteristics or preferences I might have. They are objective values in the sense that they purport to capture certain facts about human nature or the human good, and as a result can be said to be a value for anyone who is not influenced by personal prejudice or the short-sightedness of refusing to step beyond the personal point of view. While personal values are, to some extent, parochially (or regionally) defined, impersonal values are not, precisely because they

---

[44] The fact that something gives one pleasure is not by itself enough to render a personal value objective even in the limited sense. Despite the fact that everyone could understand valuing pleasure, others must also understand in what sense, in what respect, or in virtue of what, that specific activity or object gives one pleasure.

reflect a conception of ourselves as persons with a certain nature for whom there exist certain human goods. What is important to note here, beyond the definition of impersonal value, is the claim that our self-conception has an essential cognitive component, i.e., "factualist" or "realist" beliefs about what constitutes the human good, or what human needs are, or what it is to be a person.

Although I will defend below this "cognitivist" theory of self-conception, some support for this claim is given, once again, by the fact that even for the personal values involved in, for example, the commitment to learning a new language, we seek and offer justifications and reasons for why we value it, not necessarily to convince others to value the same thing, but to understand why one could. The belief that the object of one's commitment is valuable, or that the commitment is worthwhile, involves the belief that it possesses certain features that other reasonable people could recognize as meriting concern, care, or attention. To this extent we believe the value is "objective."

What I have formulated is a minimal notion of self-conception in which objective beliefs – objective in the sense defined above – occupy an important role. Once again, because we at least minimally conceive of ourselves as one person among others, as simply someone, we try to act for reasons that others could understand and accept and that are not exclusively the result of our own peculiar constitution. The constraint of objectivity on the things we value is not a consequence of our "natural realism," but rather of our self-conception. The things we value, even in the case of personal values, are seen by us, that is are believed, to have a certain degree of objective merit. This kind of belief is an essential part of our self-conception, which is to say that our self-conception has a cognitive component. Before defending this "objectivist" self-conception, I want to show how beliefs regarding the objective value of our intention-like commitments more adequately explain the various roles of these commitments. If we allow this kind of self-conception, which forms the basis for the beliefs in objective value, we are in a position to get a clearer picture of how commitment fulfills its roles in filtering and self-understanding, as well as its source of stability. In chapter 5 I will offer a full defense of the objectivist self-conception.

One can now define two senses of "objective": a weak and a strong sense. Weak objectivity is the kind of objectivity associated with personal values and hence with the intention-like commitments, as I argue in the following section. In keeping with our conception of ourselves as one person among others, and not simply the particular person who I happen to be, weak objectivity imposes an intelligibility constraint on the things I value, that is, a requirement that they be recognizable by, though not necessarily motivating for, others as possible objects of value. Strong objectivity, which I shall argue is associated with substantive commitments, does not only require that one's reasons or values be intelligible to others, but also that they hold for other persons generally. Strongly objective values are formed from the point of view which, though abstracted from our own particular individual desires and beliefs, is informed by beliefs regarding what it is to be a person, and what the conditions for its fulfillment are. It is in this sense that they are said to have a standpoint-independent truth.

4.3 OBJECTIVE BELIEFS AND INTENTION-LIKE COMMITMENTS

4.3.1 Introduction

Returning to the role of beliefs in commitment, I claim that in being committed one not only believes that

(B1) the commitment is valuable,

but also that

(B2) the value is objective

in the weak sense defined above. I showed in section 4.1 how B1 is functionally required for the intention-like commitments. I now want to show how B2 reinforces and explains the roles of the intention-like commitments. However, in order to show that B2 beliefs figure in the substantive commitments, I will not only need to defend the objectivist self-conception, but will also have to introduce a new criterion of explanation – one derived from the limitations of standard action explanations. I shall call this criterion the Indispensability Thesis (IT).

4.3.2 Filtering, stability, and self-understanding

So far, I have argued that the conception of ourselves as being one person among others, or inhabiting the objective standpoint, leads us

129

to try to form objective reasons for the things we do and the things we value. I will now show how B2 – the belief in the objective value of our commitments – is functionally required for the intention-like commitments. With the addition of B2 beliefs, we reach a better understanding of how commitment is able to fulfill its roles of stability, guidance of action, and enhanced self-understanding.

4.3.3 Filtering

The noncognitivist, or desire-based, view of commitment, was unable to explain the filtering of commitment while retaining at the same time a place for the agent. This remained true even with the addition of Frankfurt's notion of second-order volitions. I concluded there that what was needed was some notion of endorsement which explained both how the commitment was retained in the face of desirable alternatives, and in what sense it was the agent's own. As G. Taylor has suggested, an agent must have some reason for wanting one desire rather than another to be effective, if she is not just to act on whatever inclination happens to be the strongest. Moreover, her reasoning will involve discriminations between various first-order desires based ultimately on evaluations between them, since the criterion for ranking them and deciding which one should be acted upon is not tied to the conative strength of the desire.

Now the kind of objective belief I have proposed above occupies exactly this place, i.e., it provides the requisite reason for wanting one desire over another to be effective. The belief in the objective merit or value of the commitment amounts to an endorsement of the relevant desires. In the case of maintaining a commitment when confronted with desirable alternatives, the objective belief will weigh in favor of the commitment because of its accordance with one's self-conception. This is roughly Velleman's argument in *Practical Reflection*, according to which we have an "intellectual" desire for self-understanding which favors those actions that fit our conceptions of ourselves – a conception of ourselves, I now claim, as occupying in part the objective standpoint. In this way the belief plays an essential role in the filtering of options and the stability of commitment. More importantly, we overcome the alienation problem of the desire-model, since such a belief accords with our self-conceptions. I will discuss this last point in greater detail in the following section.

Finally, though, we have a much simpler theory to explain the role of commitment in filtering options. Rather than having to posit a hierarchy of ever-higher-order desires whose efficacy in action depends on an obscure "decisive commitment," we have instead a simpler model involving only beliefs, self-conception, and standard desires. Although the dynamics between them is somewhat complex, the structure itself is fairly simple.

4.3.4 Stability and self-understanding

One of the distinctive features of commitment, recall, was its role in self-understanding. Since in this section I am interested in the intention-like commitments, I will restrict the notion of self-understanding to Velleman's formulation of it as simply the knowledge of one's motives and reasons for action. As I move to the role of (B2) beliefs in the substantive commitments, I will offer a richer, "broader" (to use Velleman's term) notion of self-understanding. But by way of underlining once again the continuity between the various types of commitment, from the intention-like to the more substantive, I shall begin with the former.

If we have a commitment, returning to our example, to learning a new language, and we believe this has objective merit in the weak sense, then this enhances our self-understanding since it provides us with a reason that accords with our objectivist self-conception. Moreover, to the extent this belief supports our self-conception, it will also add to the stability of the commitment since, as Velleman argues, we are inclined to do those things that are intelligible to us, and prefer to act on reasons that will make sense of the action. This belief thus prevents us from falling into the state of reflective puzzlement in which we would refrain from acting. The belief in the objective merit of the value of the commitment helps explain its stability and shows in what way it improves self-understanding.

Part of the problem with the noncognitivist theory of commitment was that it alienated the agent from her actions. In the absence of any kind of evaluative belief, let alone objective belief, why the agent had the desire to fulfill the commitment, why she continued to act on it, and under what conditions she would revise it, the commitment was inexplicable to her from her own standpoint; that is, she was in a sense alienated from her desires and actions based upon them. This was highlighted by the case of ego-dystonia, an extreme form of self-alienation. However, when we introduce a belief in the objective value of the commitment, in conjunction once again with one's self-conception, these problems are avoided. Through this kind of belief the agent reappropriates, by way of endorsing, the desires and actions as belonging to her, if you will. Such a belief results from a process of deliberation and assessment on the part of the agent, a process which she initiates and which provides (or could provide) a coherent account of why she has this commitment. She is now in a position to consider situations in which she would reconsider her commitment and potentially formulate criteria, drawn from the reasons supporting the objective belief, for revision. Now the revision criteria also enhance self-understanding in Velleman's (thin) sense of the term. Given our desire to know the motives of our actions, the "why" behind what we are doing, we will be in a better position to gain an understanding of the motives if we know under what conditions, and for what reasons, we would cease doing whatever it is we are doing.

Note also that through this belief and its connection to revision criteria, we are also able to make sense of the way in which the possibility of error, as discussed by Robert Adams in section 4.1 of this chapter, is connected to commitment. We may be mistaken regarding the objective value of the commitment because the reasons we adduce in favor of the commitment and on the basis of which we form the belief may be wrong. The possibility of error is connected to these reasons which inform the belief. On a purely desire-based view, it is difficult to formulate in what sense commitments could be in error, or how one could be mistaken. Mistake in that case would be possible only if the commitment failed to meet a given desire; but if desire is the driving force behind commitment, so that when I no longer have the desire I also let go of the commitment, when could commitment not meet the desire, i.e., be mistaken? Does that mean that commitment must instead maximally fulfill certain desires, so that one might be in error with respect to a commitment that fails to do so? Yet our experience clearly indicates that commitments are not like this. Once again, the objectivist belief model provides a clearer, explanatorily stronger picture.

4.3.5 Conclusion

On the basis of the objectivist self-conception, I showed not only that (B1) beliefs that a commitment is valuable are functionally required for the intention-like commitments but, more importantly, that (B2) beliefs that the value supporting the commitment is objective, are so required as well. That is, I showed the truth of condition

(2*) S is committed to A only if S believes A is (objectively) valuable or doing A is (objectively) worthwhile,

where the degree of objectivity – whether it is weakly or strongly objective – varies according to whether the value involved is a personal one (as in the case of most intention-like commitments), or an impersonal one (those involved in the substantive commitments). What remains to be shown is, clearly, that condition (2*) applies to the substantive commitments as well. And in order to do that, I will need to return once again to the objectivist self-conception.

In the course of the proof of the truth of condition (2*), I have marked a methodological shift in the argument away from Mele's strictly causal explanation and toward a form of rational explanation in which self-understanding plays a central role. One of the constraints on this type of explanation was to explain the action by asking how the agent performing the action understands it herself: that is, to explain it from a first-person perspective. As we move on to the substantive commitments in which self-understanding plays an even greater role, the move away from causal explanations will become more pronounced. In what follows I will argue for a new type of explanation, one similar to rational explanations, but for which the notion of *interpretation* is key. The justification for this type of explanation will be defined in terms of the limits of causal (and third-person) accounts of human action. Once the interpretive model is established, I will return to the bifurcation problem discussed in chapter 2: a problem which Rorty and Gibbard crucially ignore.

5

Self-conception and substantive commitments

5.1 DAVID VELLEMAN ON SELF-CONCEPTION

5.1.1 Introduction

The kind of self-conception I defined in the previous chapter and its relation to objective value and beliefs are by no means uncontested. The strongest challenge to my position comes from Velleman with his "noncognitivist" theory of the self.

As I noted in chapter 2, self-understanding and the "intellectual desire" to make sense of oneself to oneself play important roles in Velleman's work. Recall that he distinguishes between self-awareness – knowing the "what" of one's actions – and self-understanding – knowing the "why" of one's actions (Velleman, *Practical Reflection*, pp. 15–16). More importantly, I remarked that Velleman viewed self-understanding as an "interpretive or explanatory" description of one's behavior. With this definition of self-understanding in mind, we can examine in what way it is related to one's self-conception.

In developing his theory of self-conception, Velleman begins with traits of character and shows that these, along with desires and beliefs, can also figure as reasons for action. One identifies a trait of character as a rationale of one's action because it is "the aspect of [one's] self-image under which [one] comprehend[s] the action" (*ibid.*, p. 249). That is, one's character, or collection of traits of character, provides a context in which one's actions can be understood. In light of the general desire for self-understanding, then, an action which accords with one's character will provide a greater reason for action since by the very fact of accordance it will enhance self-understanding. All things considered, one is more inclined to perform those actions which are in keeping with one's self-image.

However, one's concern for self-understanding and the influence of this intellectual desire extend beyond one's immediate actions; that is, one not only cares about one's current self-knowledge, but also about one's future self-knowledge (p. 271). As a result, says Velleman, an agent

> will be moved to compile a lasting self-conception that is likely to serve his future needs for reflective description and explanation. He will not be content with continually identifying his motives at the last minute, as they become relevant to his next decision . . . A standing conception of what he tends to want in typical situations will tell him, whenever those situations arise, which intentions he would fulfill and which ones would make sense for him to form (*ibid*).

A standing self-conception will thus enhance one's self-knowledge by providing stable motives that will help agents understand, and to some extent predict, the actions they will undertake, since the agent knows in advance what motives he will always, or most likely, have. It is in this way that self-understanding and self-conception are related. One's self-conception provides a context in which self-understanding can be attained. This sounds reasonable. However, the problem with Velleman's account is that it defines self-conception exclusively in terms of one's "intrinsic desires" (p. 278).

5.1.2 Intrinsic-desire view of self-conception

In all fairness to Velleman, I should point out that he begins his analysis of self-understanding with the recognition that although "a person's motives comprise both desires and beliefs, [he] shall discuss only [the person's] efforts to understand his desires." Thus, despite the fact that "a person's efforts to understand his beliefs would make a suitable topic for an entire book, [it is] a different book from the one [he is] writing" (p. 241). It is not that beliefs have no role to play in self-understanding, and for that matter in one's self-conception, it is just that this is not the role that interests Velleman. Yet the conclusions he eventually reaches regarding, for example, the role of values in one's self-conception and his reduction of it to a set of intrinsic desires, ignore, and in fact contradict, his initial hypothesis that beliefs have a place in self-understanding.

Velleman states that "one self-conception may be more perspicuous, more coherent, or more elegant than the other and may therefore offer a better understanding of its object than the other conception"

(p. 272). Consequently, we can "prefer to hold and satisfy some self-conceptions rather than others on the grounds that they would afford us a better understanding than the others of the person we'd be if we satisfied them" (*ibid.*). According to Velleman, "the self-conception by which an agent understands himself amounts to a theory – an unscientific theory, to be sure, but one that shares much, in structure and function, with its scientific counterparts" (p. 272). Drawing from the philosophy of science, Velleman states that our criteria of theory-choice are generality, precision, accuracy, and simplicity (p. 273). That is, the ideals that a theory aspires to are often times something other than, or beyond, just truth. In light of our intellectual desire for self-understanding, we will be driven, says Velleman, toward "seeking" selves, or forming self-conceptions, that are more intelligible, by which he means self-conceptions that better combine these theoretic virtues than others. Some sources of intelligibility will be, obviously, regularity as well as order since these will easily satisfy the demands of generality and simplicity. If self-understanding aims at knowing one's motives, and if one's self-conception provides the general context through which these motives are known, and given that desires are (clearly) among our motives, then the greatest self-understanding will be reached through those self-conceptions (or theories of the self) that incorporate the most general desires and that allow for the greatest predictability by providing the basis from which other desires are derived. That is, "[b]y specifying only his intrinsic desires, [an agent] can attain a self-conception that is simple and yet contains the first premise for every potential desire-based explanation and *prediction* about his *behavior*" (p. 278; emphasis added). "I shall therefore assume," says Velleman, "that an agent's standing self-conception contains information *only about his intrinsic desires*" (*ibid.*, emphasis added).

One immediate question we might ask is, what happened to beliefs? Nothing Velleman has said so far restricts one's self-conception *only* to intrinsic desires. Such desires which are stable and are the basis upon which we understand other desires would certainly be a part of one's self-conception. Granted. But it is entirely another question whether our self-conception consists of nothing more than these desires. As I will argue below, this model of self-conception becomes unstable unless it incorporates certain beliefs – specifically, what I have been calling realist beliefs. In fact, it suffers the same instability as the Frankfurt-type model discussed in chapter 4. Before broaching this topic, let me conclude the summary of Velleman's position.

The maximally self-understanding-enhancing desires, according to Velleman, are "timeless desires" since self-inquiry "leads a person to identify outcomes that make sense for him to want *at* all times, or to want *for* all times, or both; and then it leads him to establish these desires at the head of his motives" (pp. 281–2). These timeless desires Velleman identifies with one's values – "stable and broadly focused desires that are fundamental to the person's conduct and self-conception . . . The objects of a person's values . . . are the things that he knowingly and *willingly* desires at all times, for all times" (p. 282; emphasis added). Having identified values with timeless, intrinsic desires, Velleman addresses the objection that values differ from desires in that the former, while not the latter, have a cognitive component in addition to only a conative one. His response comes in the form of an instrumentalist theory of the good.

Again drawing from the philosophy of science, Velleman argues that value judgments, while false since they fail to represent any state of affairs, are still instrumentally useful in developing a coherent set of desires which in turn aids self-understanding. "Instrumentalism about a body of discourse," says Velleman, "is the view that the discourse is systematically false and yet defensible on other than epistemic grounds" (p. 291). Let me quote in full the main parts of Velleman's argument. He begins by asking us to perform a thought experiment:

> Take evaluative reasoning . . . and imagine replacing each of the desires with a judgment to the effect that the desire's object is good. The search for a stable, coherent, and simple set of desires will then appear in the guise of a search for a stable, coherent, and simple set of judgments about what's good. Thus disguised, it will look much like theoretical reasoning about a real property of things. The reason is that the intellectual satisfactions we demand from desires are the same as the ones we demand from beliefs. When the desires involved in evaluative reasoning are replaced by value judgments, our demand for a robust and unified set of desires becomes the demand for a robust and unified theory, and the resulting reasoning mimics theoretical reasoning about a phenomenon called value.

137

[O]ur search for intellectually satisfying desires has the same structure as a search for intellectually satisfying beliefs, and so we can switch back and forth between thinking about what to desire and thinking about what's good, with the assurance that a plausible set of judgments will correspond to a sensible set of desires, and vice versa (p. 292).

"Values," says Velleman, "are the desires in which we have managed to attain the coherence and stability that correspond to the structure of rational belief" (*ibid.*). We are only led to think that values represent reality because their coherence, stability, and simplicity reflect the qualities we seek in judgments about the world, when in fact these are the result of our efforts to construct an intelligible set of desires, i.e., a better self-understanding. Velleman goes on to say that:

evaluative reasoning is really a process of developing a stable and coherent set of desires for the sake of self-understanding, and judgments of goodness attain the structure of a plausible theory only because they serve as surrogates for, and hence come to mirror the structure of, the desires under development . . . [T]he plausibility of value judgments has nothing to do with whether those judgments are true" (*ibid.*).

What is more, although we recognize that value judgments are false, we continue using them since they are "a convenient proxy for the truth" (p. 294). That is to say, they are "convenient proxies for our desires in the procedure by which we pursue personal integration and self-understanding" (*ibid.*). Velleman concludes that "our motive for thinking about what's valuable is quite independent of the assumption that anything really is. Our motive for thinking about what's valuable is our drive for a stable and coherent conception of ourselves – a drive that is an ineradicable element of our natures as agents, whether value exists or not" (p. 296).

5.1.3 Criticisms: the cognitive model of self-conception defended

My criticisms of Velleman come in two parts. The first focus on the argument itself and can be thought of as internal to his work. The second, however, raise questions regarding his method and general background assumptions, and will draw on sources which, although external to his argument, are highly relevant, not only to his project, but to the kind of explanation and argument I will offer.

5.1.4 Internal criticisms

The first question to ask is why intrinsic desires should offer a more stable self-conception and better self-understanding than any other desires. The fact that we desire something in itself and not as a means to satisfying another desire does not immediately facilitate our attempt to understand ourselves. This is similar to the problem encountered by the two-tier desire model of commitment in chapter 4. The challenge to Frankfurt was to explain in what sense a desire was more the agent's own by being a second-order rather than first-order desire. Using the example of ego-dystonia, I argued that what makes a higher-order desire constitutive of the agent, i.e., identity-conferring, is that it is endorsed by the agent in the sense that it is the object of an evaluative belief to the effect that it is good, or worthwhile, or perhaps even fitting. We can make a similar argument, I think, with respect to intrinsic desires.

One's self-conception, Velleman says, will consist exclusively of intrinsic desires, since these are the most general desires and are the basis upon which all other desires are derived. Although we can understand other desires in terms of the intrinsic ones, a natural question to ask is in terms of what do we understand these. We might be inclined to think that their intrinsic nature makes them self-explanatory, that we somehow naturally understand them, or that they possess an inherent intelligibility that other sorts of desires lack. Now sexual desire is a likely candidate for intrinsic desire, if anything is. Indeed, in certain strands of psychoanalysis it is the most basic desire and used (often indiscriminately) as an explanation for a wide range of actions. Libidinous desires might be successful in explaining one's interest, say, in red sports cars, one's concern for being physically fit, or ambition to be successful. And this would probably fit with one's self-conception of "just being human," with the standard sorts of drives and goals that "being human" entails. But intrinsic desires do not always have this nice fit.

Return to the case of ego-dystonia in which an individual sees his or her sexual desires as a form of neurosis or evil temptation. Again, these are intrinsic desires, but they are at odds with the individual's self-conception. What is more, these desires are timeless and stable in the sense defined by Velleman since they are, most likely, desires that one will have at all times, or for all times, or both. But far from enhancing the individual's self-understanding, they confound it, despite their stability and broad focus. Clearly, we could not identify these desires with that person's values, and the reason for this is in fact given by Velleman himself: namely, they are not "knowingly and *willingly* desire[d] at all times, for all times" (p. 282, emphasis added). This notion of "willingly" desiring something brings us full circle to the discussion of Frankfurt's distinction between first- and second-order desires in chapter 4. We saw there that the only way of making sense of the idea of a certain desire being more an agent's own than another, and why a higher-order desire should be more constitutive of a person than a lower-order one, was by introducing an evaluative belief. What I argued in that section was that the hierarchy itself had no identity-conferring power. Likewise, the intrinsic nature of a desire has no independent power to enhance self-understanding. The reason it contributes to self-understanding is that it is *willingly* desired, which is to say, as I said in chapter 4, that it is endorsed, i.e., is the object of some evaluative belief.

This argument finds support in the literature in psychology itself. In his article "Empathic Character Analysis," Lawrence Josephs[1] states: "In terms of Freud's structural model from which the term *ego-dystonic* derives, what is ego–dystonic reflects a superego *appraisal*. What is ego–dystonic is that of which the superego *disapproves* and what is ego–syntonic is that of which the superego approves" (Josephs, "Empathic Character Analysis," 45; emphasis added). One could argue that on Velleman's picture of self-conception, one based exclusively on intrinsic desires, there is no possibility for the phenomenon of ego–dystonia, since the conflict engendered by negative appraisals of one's desires would not be possible since such appraisals are only the product of the desires themselves. Joseph's description of ego–dystonia closely parallels the discussion on self-conception. He states,

> it may be clarifying to substitute the concept self for the concept ego and to begin speaking of self-syntonic and self-dystonic instead of ego–syntonic and ego–dystonic. Freud used the term *ego* in two different manners: (1) to refer to the part of the mind engaged in certain cognitive operations such as reality testing, judgment, defense, and impulse control and (2) to refer to the sense of self. Self-syntonic would refer to any self-experience congruent with one's sense of self and *self-dystonic*

---

[1] L. Josephs, "Empathic Character Analysis," *The American Journal of Psychoanalysis* 54 (1994): 41–54.

would refer to any self-experience incongruent with one's sense of self (ibid., 45, emphasis added).

In Joseph's new vocabulary, self-dystonic cases are those in which certain desires do not match up with one's self-conception, and these can include "intrinsic" desires – in the case of ego-dystonic homosexuality, sexual desires – which have the stability and broad focus required by Velleman. For self-dystonic cases to arise, it must be the case that there is a cognitive component – namely, the belief about the desire, the appraisal – which is more integrally a part of one's self-conception, "one's sense of self," than is the intrinsic desire. But if this is so, then Velleman's model cannot be correct.

One's self-conception certainly includes intrinsic desires, but clearly not all of them. At the same time, we do not simply choose which intrinsic desires do or do not define who we are – we do not form our self-conceptions *de novo*, and they do not develop spontaneously.[2] In order to understand why certain intrinsic desires are relevant to who we are and why others are not, we need to appeal to value, which is embedded in the very concept of "willingly desiring." *Far from being convenient proxies for desires, or dispensable surrogates, value and evaluative beliefs are an integral part of the formation of one's self-conception, and hence of one's self-understanding.* Moreover, we can ask how one reaches a unified set of desires independently of any evaluative beliefs and why the unification should enhance self-understanding; although one has an ordering of desires, why should that ordering be more intelligible than another? We can certainly reach a unified set of certain desires without any evaluative beliefs: a desire for sweet things, adventure, or an even tan could all be used in developing a coherent set of desires. But these are not the kinds of desires that are "fundamental to the person's conduct and self-conception" (Velleman, *Practical Reflectilon*, p. 282) since they are not, except in rare cases, intrinsic, much less timeless. The kind of unified theory of the self Velleman seeks, one based on a unified, coherent set of desires, is unattainable without a vocabulary of value, i.e., without beliefs regarding the value or the good of the desires according to which an *informative* ordering, one which enhances self-understanding, is developed. In light of the discussion of Nagel in chapter 4, I claim that

[2] That is to say, the development of one's self-conception is a process extended over time. One does not suddenly have a self-conception from one day to the next.

the desires which are endorsed by evaluative beliefs, which are seen as directed toward the "good," are more intelligible because they fit with what I take to be a more basic conception of ourselves as agents who act for objective reasons and who inhabit, as Nagel calls it, the objective standpoint. Since these evaluative beliefs and desires are objective in the sense that they could be reasons for others, in light of our objectivist self-conception they will be more intelligible.

One might object that Velleman's account is in fact capable of explaining or accommodating these cases of ego-dystonia.[3] In the attempt to reach self-understanding, we try to reach the most coherent set of intrinsic desires we could have, given the intrinsic desires we do in fact already have. In the case of ego-dystonia in which sexual desire is seen as a form of neurosis or evil temptation, despite the fact that it is an intrinsic desire, it confounds our self-understanding because when we try to integrate it into our *overall* set of intrinsic desires, we find that it is incompatible with them. Given other desires for chastity, or for "normal" sexual attraction, etc., and in light of certain means–ends beliefs regarding how these desires are best satisfied, the sexual desire will not make sense, even though it is, strictly speaking, an intrinsic desire.

It should be clear what the response to this objection is. If we grant that the agent *already* has a set of intrinsic desires which defines her self-understanding, then the objection might seem compelling. But if we ask, as we did in the discussion of Frankfurt, what makes these desires more the agent's own, or more definitive of who she is, than other desires, then Velleman's model encounters problems. Velleman's answer was that they were simply intrinsic desires. Yet if this is so, then in the case of such conflicts of intrinsic desires, it is difficult to understand why self-understanding should adhere to one cluster rather than another. One might suggest that the largest cluster trumps; that is, it is easier to retain a large set of coherent desires than to modify it to accommodate one other desire. However, I chose sexual desire precisely because it is such a powerful drive. In terms of conative strength, the desire for chastity, purity, or social acceptance, pale in comparison. In what sense is it then easier to retain the latter set of desires? Moreover, in terms of cardinality, the carnal pleasures far outnumber the desires for chastity, purity, plus whatever others one might add; after all, temptation is every-

---

[3] I thank one of the CUP readers for bringing this objection to my attention.

where. Perhaps one might argue that the intellectual desire for self-understanding weighs in favor of the largest set, which is what is meant by "easier to retain." However, this would mean that the desire for self-understanding, which was for Velleman simply a guiding desire, is now able to overcome such things as sexual desire. This seems highly improbable.

What is needed, instead, is an element of endorsement on the part of the agent. It is the evaluative belief that serves as the binding force between various intrinsic desires, and helps to define one set as constitutive of self-understanding over and above other possible sets. Left to themselves, the intrinsic desires are unable to form the basis of self-understanding. As Velleman himself says, and as Frankfurt also suggested, it is only when we willingly desire certain things that they become part of our self-understanding; yet to willingly desire something requires the introduction of a cognitive component.[4]

In short, Velleman misreads the place of values in the ordering of desires that constitute our self-conception. Values, and I would add evaluative beliefs, are not simply convenient proxies for desires in developing a coherent self-conception, but are, if my argument is correct, indispensable for the kind of self-understanding at issue. This claim reflects, and more importantly clarifies, a thesis Charles Taylor first formulated in "What is Human Agency?"[5] and later developed in *Sources of the Self* (*SS*). Taylor argues that our "self-understanding essentially incorporates our seeing ourselves against a background of "strong evaluations." . . . [that is,] a background of distinctions between things which are recognized as of categoric or unconditioned or higher importance or worth" (*HA*, p. 3).

5.1.5 External criticisms: redefining the terms of the debate

Now agreement with Taylor certainly does not count as proof of my argument, but it is worth exploring the parallels between not only the

---

[4] As a last attempt to avoid evaluative beliefs and stay with the noncognitive model, one might try to argue that the desires which define our self-understanding are those desires we would have from the objective point of view. First, it is unclear what desires one would have from that perspective, except to say perhaps certain "basic" human desires. In the absence of a Rousseauian view of human nature, this does not seem like a promising approach. The only alternative would be to introduce enlightened desires, but then one needs a conception, i.e. belief, regarding the good.

[5] Taylor, in *Human Agency and Language* (henceforth, *HA*).

present discussion and Taylor's project but also Taylor and Velleman. Taylor would certainly take issue with Velleman's assertion regarding the purely instrumental value of value. For, according to Taylor, the connection between strong evaluations and self-understanding "is not just a contingent fact about human agents, but is essential to what we would understand and recognize as full, normal human agency" (*ibid.*). Taylor thus argues in *SS* that without such a "background," or "framework," or "horizon," individuals break down, are at sea and suffer a crisis of identity (*SS*, p. 27), and those who live without them can only be described as "pathological" (*ibid.*, p. 31). Again, think of Meursault in *The Stranger*. For Taylor, there is a very urgent sense in which value and evaluative beliefs are indispensable, not just to one's self-conception and self-understanding, but to the very possibility of agency itself. This is, clearly, a much stronger argument than the one I want to make, and, fortunately, it is not one I need to make. However, some of the ideas Taylor brings out in defense of his thesis will be very useful in expanding the notion of self-understanding from the some-what limited sense used by Velleman, and in introducing a kind of explanation that extends the narrow causal explanation heretofore dominant by focusing on "interpretation." This is not to say that the explanation I will be using is alien to the action theorists so far studied, in particular David Velleman, but rather that this explanation is implicit in some of their arguments and in need only of being more explicitly stated.

In many ways, the projects of Taylor and Velleman overlap. Their aim is to "make sense" of our actions[6] and to connect our attempts at making sense to some account of self-understanding. One will immediately object, however, that despite their shared vocabulary their projects are fundamentally different in both scope and method. While Velleman is interested in how we make our way down the street, Taylor wants to know how we orient ourselves in a moral space;

---

[6] See Velleman, *Practical Reflection*, p. 8: "your efforts to understand your conduct are aided by your reciprocal efforts to make it intelligible. You don't just try to make sense *of* yourself, you also try to make sense *to* yourself. Hence your practical self-understanding is the product of a collaboration that you carry on with yourself." And *SS*, pp. 48, 50: "making sense of my present action . . . requires a narrative understanding of my life," and since "self-understanding necessarily has temporal depth and incorporates narrative," the attempt at making sense is intimately tied to self-understanding.

whereas the one appeals to desires and beliefs, the other makes use of horizons of meaning. There are, I suggest, important affinities between them, and rather than seeing them as diametrically opposed to one another in both substance and form, I think it is possible to put them at different places on a continuum of ideas and topics which would begin with Velleman and develop into Taylor. Velleman acknowledges early on that there are different kinds of self-understanding and that his examples do not "exhaust the possibilities" (Velleman, *Practical Reflection*, p. 40). He states:

> Among those who want self-understanding, some won't feel that they can explain an action unless they have a Freudian diagnosis of it, complete with cross references to the master's own cases; others will find an action intelligible so long as it resembles the behavior of a fiction character with whom they identify; and yet others will go by their horoscopes. I have chosen as my example an agent with more mundane intellectual tastes – an agent who favors commonsense explanations couched in terms of familiar motives (*ibid.*).

His explanation, in other words, does not necessarily cover the full range of actions, although it does cover the most standard cases, like walking down the street or planning a trip. But there are other actions, like fulfilling a commitment, which are also commonplace and, though not necessarily the objects of Freudian psychoanalysis or astrology, might require somewhat different tools of analysis. Thus Taylor states that making sense of my present action, when we are not dealing with such trivial questions as where I shall go in the next five minutes but with the issue of my place relative to the good, requires a narrative understanding of my life, a sense of what I have become which can only be given in a story (*SS*, p. 48). In a sense Taylor begins his discussion where Velleman apparently leaves off. But as we saw above in the discussion of self-conception and intrinsic desires, although Velleman is initially careful to draw the limits of his hypotheses, he soon overextends their boundaries.

Velleman moves in Taylor's direction when he says such things as:

> I am confident that if the reader will only reflect on the *whole of his practical life*, rather than on that portion in which the pursuit of goals is most salient, he will find himself evaluating options in light of all of his core dispositions . . . You evaluate the alternatives by the standard of what

makes the most sense for you, for all of you, in light of your entire way of life (p. 302, emphasis added).

And again, when speaking about agents who act on values, he extends the notion of self-understanding he had originally limited to the mundane. "These agents," he says, "understand what they're doing in the *broadest possible way*: they know what they're all about. And the reason is that they have fundamental values in light of which their conduct can be *broadly understood*" (p. 283, emphasis added). Why is this important? For two reasons: first, it shows that self-understanding is more than knowledge of one's desires and motives for one's immediate actions, that self-understanding is a much broader concept; and, second, it opens the way for a form of explanation as interpretation that is more appropriate to this kind of self-understanding and the role it plays in commitment, particularly the substantive commitments. Let me explain.

5.1.6 Interpretation and action

Velleman, as we have already seen, defined the attempt to know what one is doing as an "interpretive" description of one's conduct (p. 15), and is generally interested in the project of "making sense" of one's actions and oneself, where the object of examination is no longer one's immediate action, like walking down the street, but can extend to an entire way of life, as we saw in the preceding section. Now the connections between "interpretation," "explanation," and "making sense" have been explored by Charles Taylor, who greatly influenced G. H. von Wright, who in turn played an important role in the development of Paul Ricoeur's thoughts.

In "Interpretation and the Sciences of Man,"[7] Taylor argues that the human sciences are an appropriate object for a science of interpretation, where by interpretation he means the "attempt to make clear, *to make sense* of an object of study" (*PHS*, p. 15, emphasis added). Because we view human behavior "as the action of agents who desire and are moved, who have goals and aspirations, [this] necessarily offers a purchase for descriptions in terms of meaning. The norm of explanation which it posits is one which 'makes sense' of the behavior,

---

[7] C. Taylor, in *Philosophy and the Human Sciences: Philosophical Papers*, vol. II (Cambridge: Cambridge University Press, 1985) (henceforth, *PHS*).

which shows a coherence of meaning" (*PHS*, p. 27). Once again, we see that the notion of interpretation occupies a central role in the examination of human actions. Now "making sense" of something just is, according to Taylor, "the proffering of an interpretation" (*ibid.*): these two activities – making sense and interpreting – are the same. For Taylor, making sense of an action has the same meaning as it does for Velleman: to understand why it was engaged in. "We make sense of an action," says Taylor, "when there is a coherence between the actions of the agent and the meaning the situation has *for him*. We find the action *puzzling* until we find such a coherence" (*PHS*, p. 24, emphasis added; cf. Velleman on reflective puzzlement). Clearly, this is in keeping with Velleman's general project. Yet Velleman, and action theorists generally, do not fully appreciate the implications of this interpretive activity.

There is a real question, then, regarding the nature of explanation in analytic action theory, as well as action theory's relation to the natural and human sciences. We saw a first indication of this problem in the discussion of Alfred Mele's analysis of intention in chapter 4, and his use of causal as opposed to rational explanations of action. Now the division of the natural and human sciences and the categorization of their methods has been a topic of interest since Aristotle and Plato, through the Middle Ages with Thomas Aquinas,[8] and for countless philosophers of the modern (and postmodern) eras.[9] However, within the context of the current discussion, namely, the explanation of human action and its relation to self-understanding, we can draw some informative insights from the literature. We can set aside the question of the alleged dichotomy between the natural and human sciences, between explanation and understanding, and instead restrict the discussion to the role of explanation in action theory and, in particular, to the criteria of explanation used by Velleman. In doing so, I will at times need to draw on sources outside the standard purview of the analytic philosophy of action; but these sources are not so much foreign to action theory – and so of potentially questionable relevance – as they are simply unacknowledged elements of its method.

[8] Aristotle, *Metaphysics* XI; Plato, *The Republic*; Boethius, *De Trinitate* 2; Aquinas, *The Division and Methods of the Sciences*.
[9] See G. H. von Wright, *Explanation and Understanding* (Ithaca: Cornell University Press, 1971).

Within the philosophy of action one has the sense that there is a tension between its explanatory goals and its self-descriptions. While many action theorists aspire to models of explanation befitting the natural sciences (for example, Myles Brand and Alvin Goldman), they find themselves unable to avoid explanations couched in terms of intentions, desires, and beliefs – notions notoriously difficult to reduce to purely causal terms – and repeatedly describe their tasks, as we have seen, as "making sense," "rendering intelligible," or "seeking to understand" human *action* as opposed to simply *behavior*.[10] Despite the naturalizing tendency of many action theorists toward mechanistic models of action, the discourse of explanation such theorists offer does not fit the classical covering-law model characteristic of scientific explanations, nor does it meet the criteria for nomological subsumption. There is a real question regarding the nature of explanation in analytic philosophy of action, and reason to think, according to its own self-descriptions as we saw earlier, that interpretation occupies a central role. This confusion is, I think, particularly acute in Velleman, who argues forcefully against value realism, and in favor of a "noncognitive" basis for one's self-conception.

In arguing for the claim that one's self-conception incorporates only intrinsic desires, Velleman states, as quoted earlier, that "[b]y specifying only his intrinsic desires, [an agent] can attain a self-conception that is simple and yet contains the first premise for every potential desire-based explanation and *prediction about his behavior*" (Velleman, *Practical Reflection*, p. 287, emphasis added). The criterion that a theory of the self (i.e., one's self-conception) must meet is predictability, and the object of such a theory is *behavior*, not action. The scientific model insinuates itself in Velleman's theory through the demand for predictability and the focus on behavior: what is sought is not understanding, but explanation; and what is to be explained is not a meaningful action, but an event in the world. In light of this scientific model, Velleman offers an account of value that "explains" its role in a theory of the self, without having to posit anything to which values attach, or which they purport to represent. Since

[10] Action is a subcategory of behavior. While behavior can be understood generally as any bodily event, or as Jaegwon Kim says, as "whatever people, organisms, or mechanical systems do that is publicly observable," action instead has meaning that depends on context; that is, unlike behavior, it is not "naturally" identified. See Jaegwon Kim, *Philosophy of Mind* (Boulder: Westview Press, 1996), p. 28.

Velleman is interested, at least at this point in his discussion, in explanation-as-prediction, and given the law-like regularity of "behaviors" arising from intrinsic desires, as well as the latter's relatively easy assimilation into generalized formulae, it is no wonder that a theory of the self should be restricted to intrinsic desires, and that values should be defined in terms of them.

There are, however, two important things to notice: first, if Velleman is endorsing a scientific model for the analysis of human action, then he needs to answer serious objections to such an approach; and, second, it is not at all clear that this is what Velleman is endorsing. But if he in fact does not follow such a model, yet makes his claims regarding self-conception and values with its aid, what are we to conclude regarding them? Specifically, while Velleman speaks here of explanation as prediction, and focuses on behavior generally, he elsewhere defines explanation in terms of the broader categories of understanding and interpretation (*ibid.*, p. 15), and shifts from mere behavior – an event in the world – to intentional action, i.e., *meaningful action*. In so far as explanation extends beyond prediction, and the object of the analysis is meaningful action, we can question whether the model he uses in order to establish his noncognitivist thesis is in fact tenable. There are good reasons to think not.

Here again the discussion risks getting lost in debates which are, though highly interesting, potentially irresolvable. For example, what does a science of intentional action amount to? Can intention and other mental states be reduced or eliminated through computational models of the mind? What is the place for a folk psychology, which uses such terms as intention, belief, and desire, among the natural sciences? What I want to do is to turn very briefly to some of these debates to raise questions with Velleman's method (and action theory's generally) by way of introducing and justifying an alternative approach. My argument, though, will not rely exclusively on an admittedly cursory review of some very important topics, but should open enough of a space through which a more "hermeneutical" style of explanation can enter. Indeed, I think that it is this kind of explanation, as opposed to his self-professed scientific one, that underlies much of Velleman's discussion.

Before proceeding, two qualifications should be made. The argument that follows is not meant as an argument against the reasons-as-causes view popularized by Donald Davidson. I do not intend to defend an anticausalist theory of action. Rather, the argument aims to show: first, that interpretation plays an important role in the explanation of action, not that it necessarily excludes or preempts causal accounts; and, second, that the ambiguous notion of "cause" in action theory, and the ambiguous use of scientific criteria in action explanation, have led to distorted conclusions regarding, for example, the causal role of values.

The second qualification is that I am not embracing a hermeneutics of action, despite my emphasis on the interpretive aspect of action explanation. Paul Ricoeur[11] has perhaps done the most work in formalizing a hermeneutic theory of action, and I should say why I refrain from following his lead.

Part of the task of Ricoeur's work is to show that the alleged dichotomy between understanding and explanation, which is supposed to reflect the division between the human and natural sciences, is a false one. Understanding and explanation, says Ricoeur, both belong to the human sciences and, rather than being opposed to one another, are involved in a complex relation which makes possible the move from a naive to a critical interpretation of a text or action. Along what Ricoeur calls this "hermeneutical arc" of interpretation (*TA*, pp. 121, 164), of which understanding and explanation are two stages, structural analysis plays a crucial role, and it is the place of structural analysis in Ricoeur's theory of interpretation that causes me to hesitate in turning to it at this point.

It is the "objectivity" of the text and of action, defined by the four-fold process of distanciation – the fixation of action, the autonomy of the action's meaning from the intentions of the agent, the action's transcending of the original situation and conditions of production and, finally, its being addressed to an infinite number of "readers" (*TA*, pp. 150 ff.) – that makes explanation possible in the human sciences (*TA*, p. 157). Yet by explanation is to be understood not the causal explanations of the natural sciences (nor even causal explanation in the Humean sense), but a kind of explanation appropriate to the human sciences themselves, namely, structural explanation; that is, an

---

[11] P. Ricoeur, *From Text to Action: Essays in Hermeneutics*, vol. II trans. Kathleen Blamey and John B. Thompson. (Evanston: Northwestern University Press, 1991), (henceforth, *TA*). For an earlier formulation of his views on this topic see *Sémantique de l'Action*, lecture notes (Louvain-la-Neuve: Université Catholique de Louvain, 1970–71).

explanation "based on stable correlations between discrete units rather than on regular sequences between events, stages or phases of a process" (*TA*, p. 128). The prime examples of this kind of analysis and explanation Ricoeur invokes are, of course, the works of Claude Lévy-Strauss on primitive myths and Roland Barthès on folklore. By using this noncausal form of explanation, Ricoeur expects that "interpretation will no longer be confronted by a model external to the human sciences, [but rather, that] it will be confronted by a model of intelligibility that belongs, from birth so to speak, to the domain of human sciences, and indeed to a leading science in this domain: linguistics" (*TA*, p. 117). Instead of clarifying and refining a sequence of events by placing them in the appropriate causal order, explanation will now aim at bringing out the structure of its object, i.e., "the internal relations of dependence that constitute [its] statics" (*TA*, p. 122). Explanation then is a form of structural analysis.

But why is such an analysis necessary? All interpretation, according to Ricoeur, has as its starting point the inscription of an exteriorized intention. Since this inscription is carried out according to the codes of its relevant discourse, and since these codes govern "reading" (whether it be of texts or actions) in a manner similar to the way in which grammatical codes guide the understanding of sentences, in order then to pass from a superficial to a deeper understanding of a text or action, it will be necessary to appeal to structural analysis which brings these codes to light (*TA*, p. 130). Yet a structural analysis assumes, or rather requires, that its object have a general semiological character, i.e., that it can be considered as a *system* of relations between signs, or as a *pattern* of relations between the units of its codes. As a result, Ricoeur recognizes that the generalization of the structural model of explanation is limited by the extent to which "*social phenomena*" possess this semiological character (*TA*, p. 165, emphasis added). As a limit on the scope of structural explanation, the "semiotic requirement" is at the same time a limit on the scope of hermeneutics, since the "hermeneutic arc" from explanation to understanding is completed only through structural analysis.

Ricoeur claims that action undergoes an intentional exteriorization similar to that of discourse since it can be identified and reidentified according to its sense content which is determined by the propositional content and illocutionary force of the action itself. While discourse is easily inscribed as writing, the questions of "how is what is done inscribed?" and "what corresponds to writing in the field of action?" (*TA*, p. 152) naturally arise since hermeneutics is limited to "written documents." Ricoeur's answer is that some actions are events that leave their mark on "social time" which he defines as the location of "durable effects" and "persisting *patterns*" (*TA*, p. 153, emphasis added). "An action leaves a 'trace,' it makes its 'mark,'" says Ricoeur, "when it contributes to the emergence of such patterns, which become the *documents* of human action" (*ibid.*). For an action to be inscribed, and hence for it to fit under the rubric of hermeneutics, it must leave patterned, systematic traces within the social sphere.

Clearly, then, Ricoeur has moved beyond the limits of the individual actions of agents, which he originally addressed in his discussion of Elizabeth Anscombe's book *Intention*. The focus of a hermeneutical analysis is the actions of individuals in so far as they take part in a larger, systematic activity; that is, it is the individual's action as an instance of a more general social action, one that has an identifiable pattern which can be correlated in a methodical manner with other social actions, for example, the practice of certain rituals or religious rites, that is the target of hermeneutics. Indeed, it is the very possibility for action to assume "a fixed form in *habitual patterns*"[12] that allows its meaning to become detached from the event, and hence is a condition for the third step of distanciation – the separation of meaning from intention. For what allows the actions to be identified and reidentified as the same, and as having a certain sense content which in turn helps to establish their meaning, is their patterned form; and since this form is not determined by the agent but by the social or cultural "structure" to which she belongs, one can say that the meaning of the action transcends the agent's intentions. Other commentators have also stressed that, for Ricoeur, "action is seen as a delineated *pattern* confronting the observer as an object to be understood"[13] and that "the problem of analysing meaningful action is the problem of the relation between action and the *social structure*."[14] When Ricoeur states that the

---

[12] Josef Bleicher, *Contemporary Hermeneutics: Hermeneutics as Method, Philosophy and Critique* (London: Routledge, 1980), p. 231.

[13] John B. Thompson, *Critical Hermeneutics* (Cambridge: Cambridge University Press, 1981), p. 124.

[14] Henrietta Moore, "Paul Ricoeur: Action, Meaning and Text," in Christopher Tilley (ed.), *Reading Material Culture* (London: Blackwell, 1990), p. 111.

"autonomization of human action" (*TA*, p. 153) constitutes its *social* dimension and that, as quoted above, "an action is a social phenomenon not only because it is done by several agents in such a way that the role of each of them cannot be distinguished from the role of the others, but also because our deeds escape us and have effects we did not intend" (*ibid.*), he is speaking of general categories, or types, of action that are realized by substitutable agents.

The emphasis on the social dimension of action is inextricably tied to the role of structural analysis. Indeed, the appeal to structural analysis becomes clearer once we understand that hermeneutics is concerned with action in this larger sense. For it is only in this larger sense that we can speak of the inscription of action according to codes, of the "internal relations of dependence" (*TA*, p. 122) for which it is the task of explanation to reveal, and of the use of linguistics as a model for a science of interpretation. As we saw above, structural analysis can be extended to social phenomena provided they can be characterized semiotically, i.e., as a system of signs. Ricoeur's repeated use of Lévy-Strauss's examination of myths suggests that the kind of action Ricoeur has in mind when he seeks a comparison between a theory of action and a theory of texts, is action at the level of the myth, i.e., actions such as ritual practices or religious rites. Consequently, it would seem that if action is to be an appropriate object for this kind of strictly hermeneutic analysis, it too must exhibit this systematic character, which is to say that it must be a form of social as opposed to individual action; hence, my disinclination to pursue a formal hermeneutics of action, despite my use of standard hermeneutic terms such as "interpretation."

5.1.7 Scientific models of explanation in action theory: limitations

Now the analysis of commitment from an action-theoretic perspective soon leads one to a number of problems concerning action theory itself, or at least to the kinds of conclusion action theorists draw based on the model of explanation they assume: namely, the causalist model. Once given the green light by Donald Davidson, in his seminal article "Action, Reasons, and Causes,"[15] to explain actions in a "causalist" way, they soon forgot some of the key restrictions

---

[15] In D. Davidson, *Essays on Actions and Events* (Oxford: Clarendon Press, 1980) pp. 3–20.

Davidson placed on such explanations – restrictions which are now leading several philosophers to read Davidson as an interpretationist with respect to the explanation of action.[16] These restrictions are, of course, his theories of the anomalism of the mental, holism, and the constitutive role of rationality (a highly normative concept) in the ascription of propositional attitudes.

Some action theorists who have taken an interest in ethics, and those philosophers in ethics who have engaged in a form of action theory, once again as concerns such phenomena as commitment, notably Gibbard and Velleman, have forgotten another important tenet of Davidson whom they often cite: namely that theories of action are reflexive. That is, the standards or norms which guide an interpreter apply equally to the interpreted. In light of this reflexivity, one can ask to what extent an explanation of an action, or more broadly a normative practice, must be self-transparent, which in turn means questioning the validity of error theories, like those proposed by Velleman, Gibbard, and most famously J. L. Mackie.[17] Recall that it was exactly this reflexivity that characterizes explanation in economics and which rational expectation theory tries to accommodate. As we saw in the discussion of Chiappori, economic models are subject to the constraint of self-transparency. If this is true of explanation in economics, it would seem *a fortiori* to be the case of action explanation.

[16] See, for example, Simon Evnine, *Donald Davidson* (Stanford: Stanford University Press, 1991).

[17] There are a number of interesting parallels to be developed here between action theory and problems in sociological explanation. Nicolas Dodier, for example, provides three constraints on interpretation for sociological explanations, the most interesting of which states that sociological interpretation of actions must draw on the same world of objects as those constituted by the persons in their discourse of action and, more importantly, cannot contradict the existing representations. See N. Dodier, "Représenter ses Actions," in *Les Formes de l'Action* (Paris: Ecole des Hautes Etudes en Sciences Sociales, 1990) pp, 115–48. The Touraine school of sociology also imposes a criterion of homogeneity. A similar debate takes place between Claude Lévy-Strauss and Marcel Mauss regarding the reduction of an explanation in intentional idioms, those used by the subjects themselves, to a naturalistic (and also causalist) account, which admittedly would violate Dodier's criterion. See Claude Lévy-Strauss, "Introduction à l'Oeuvre de Marcel Mauss," in Marcel Mauss, *Sociologie et Anthropologie* (Paris: Presses Universitaires de France, 1950) pp. ix–lii. See also Vincent Descombes, *Les Institutions du Sens* (Paris: Les Editions de Minuit, 1996), ch. 18.

Taken in its strictest sense, a causal theory of action would require that we be able to provide covering-law models demonstrating some sort of nomological connection between intentions and action. Drawing from the literature in cognitive science and psychology, Alan Gauld and John Shotter[18] argue against the possibility of scientific explanation – in the sense of providing covering-law models – of human action since such central notions as "intention" cannot be part of a mechanistic explanation or system. They argue that one cannot be said to act or to have intentions unless one possesses and exercises certain "conceptual capacities" (Gauld and Shotter, *Human Action*, p. 53), and the possession of these capacities cannot be represented in a machine-table form, an example of which would be a list of stimulus-response (S-R) classes. Clearly, for open-ended intentions such as the intention to do one's best, to treat others fairly, or to be polite, and for negative intentions (like the intention not to leave the house[19]), no S-R class can be specified in advance.[20] Yet if a system can be described in terms of causal laws, then it is possible, according to the authors, to provide a machine-table form (which in turn would mean it could be embodied in a computer). So, if a machine-table form is not available, it follows there is no causal description of the system. They conclude that "since the meaning of actions for the agents who execute them are given by those agents' intentions . . . beliefs, [and] desires . . . it is these everyday, yet systematically related psychological concepts that must constitute our initial, though not necessarily final, framework of thought"[21] (*ibid.*, p. 77). In short, because our explanations of human actions are inextricably tied to the notion of intention, and intention cannot be given a causal, "scientific" description since it resists reduction to an exhaustive machine-table list, it follows that the explanation of human action also resists so-called scientific description. The kind of description we must seek, according to Gauld and Shotter,

---

[18] A. Gauld and J. Shotter, *Human Action and its Psychological Investigation* (London: Routledge and Kegan Paul, 1977).   [19] See Gilbert Harman, *Change in View*, ch. 8.

[20] Recall the problem of vagueness with respect to commitment discussed in chapter 3.

[21] The emphasis on systematicity recurs later when they state: "it becomes possible to exhibit the different 'meanings' of different actions as having arisen through the operation of similar processes, and hence as *systematically* related in a non-arbitrary manner" (Gauld and Shotter, *Human Action*, p. 82, emphasis added). This is of potential interest for a hermeneutics of action in the style of Ricoeur's structuralism which requires precisely these kinds of systematic correlations.

155

will be defined by what they call a "hermeneutic psychology," and which might be known better today as folk psychology.

Besides the problem of having to provide an exhaustive machine-table list for open-ended intentions and other similar mental states, there is the further problem that even in the process of developing a machine-table form, one which would allow us "to *predict* for any input what output would be emitted"[22] by the system, the very specification of appropriate input–output correlations is already a highly interpretive task. In order to provide a machine-table description of a system (or, equivalently, for a system to realize a Turing machine), we need to know, as Jaegwon Kim indicates, "what is to *count* as input conditions and what is to *count* as output conditions." That is, causal explanations have interpretation built into them in the very process of selecting appropriate stimulus-response pairs, as well as in the determination of what even qualifies as a stimulus and what qualifies as a response. But in the case of human "systems," not all of our outputs (or responses), i.e., physical behavior, counts as action – the kind of "response" at issue. As Kim states, "the factors that determine exactly what it is that you are doing when you produce a physical gesture include the customs, habits, and conventions . . . as well as the particular features of a given situation" (Kim, *Philosophy of Mind*, p. 36). The consequence of this, according to Kim, and as Gauld and Shotter would likely agree, is the realization of "how futile it would be to look for interesting generalizations . . . connecting mental states" (*ibid.*) since no law-like regularities, as required by a science of action, are likely to be available. The role occupied by the social and psychological factors of customs, habits, and conventions is precisely the role of interpretation.

The obvious objection to this argument is that it has taken a much too narrow view of "causal explanation" and what would be required for law-like status of such explanations. Instead of providing covering-law models or requiring S-R classes defining intention, a broader notion of "cause" is more appropriate – one in which we only require that statements asserting a causal link be able to support counter-factuals and subjunctive claims. However, in order for these kinds of statements to do the kind of work expected of them, we have to add that they must be supported by their instances (or infirmed by their

---

[22] J. Kim, *Philosophy of Mind*, p. 88, emphasis added. See also pp. 93, 94.

counter-instances). In other words, we do not require an explicit causal law linking the action with its intentionally described antecedents. Clearly, this is the program that Donald Davidson initiated some thirty years ago.

Without reviewing the vast literature by and about Davidson, suffice it to point out a few of his key claims. It was Davidson who put respectability back into the view that reasons are causes for action. He defined a primary reason for an action, R, as a pair of mental states – a belief and pro-attitude – and argued that R is a primary reason why X did A only if X did A because X had a primary reason R: the "because" in this statement being best understood as expressing a causal explanatory relationship. The claim that R caused A entails only a weak sense of cause, that is, it entails only that there exists a causal law instantiated by some true descriptions of A and R. According to Davidson's physicalism, these true descriptions will be given in physical terms.

Davidson also held another central thesis, the anomalism of the mental, according to which there can be no psycho-physical laws: there can be no bridge laws connecting mental states to physical states. The argument for this, though long, concerns the holistic and normative nature of the mental: ascriptions of propositional attitudes depend on evaluations of rationality and rational coherence. Because the mental is constituted by the normative rules of rationality, whereas the physical is not, there can be no laws connecting them which would at the same time maintain their respective integrity. Yet some contemporary action theorists neglect this point.

The question is, given Davidson's anomalism and holism theses, can we still make sense of a causal theory of action: that is, can he still be quoted as a source of inspiration for causal theorists of action? Although it was Davidson's intention to set the basis of a causal theory of action, he is, interestingly, now the source of inspiration for interpretationist theories.

One consequence of Davidson's view is that the heteronomic generalizations or "laws" we ordinarily make linking mental states and actions are, strictly speaking, false, even though highly illuminating. It is only when the events are redescribed in a physical vocabulary that they do in fact instantiate true laws. But such laws, though true, would be highly unilluminating for our purposes. This disconcerting split has led some, like Dagfinn Føllesdal, to insist upon one set of regularities which are both informative and true. As Føllesdal states:

To say that A is a cause of B does not contribute to an *explanation* of the occurrence of B unless there is a law which is instantiated by A and B under *approximately* these descriptions. If the only law that connects A and B is instantiated by A and B only under descriptions that differ radically from "A" and "B," then the assertion that A is a cause of B will be more the pronouncement of an oracle than it will be an explanation.[23]

More importantly, Føllesdal concludes that: "This restriction on the kind of laws and vocabulary that are permissible in explanations makes the question of what is to *count as an explanation* relative to the person, or group of persons, for whom the explanation is intended" (*ibid.*). But deciding "what is to count as an explanation" is an importantly interpretive act. The question is what are the criteria of the interpretation in the explanation of action.

Other action theorists have also noted the "disconcerting" interpretationist implications of Davidson's causal theory of action. Kathleen Lennon states: "If Davidson's arguments are successful . . . [then] we must reject a causal explanatory account of the intentional."[24] She thus tries to rescue a casual account of action by showing how causal links depend on reason-giving ones. That is, while offering an antireductionist theory of intentionality, she at the same time wants to remain a materialist and explanatory physicalist.

It is worth looking at her arguments since they are typical of many such accounts in the literature, and show quite well the shortcomings of exclusively causal theories of action. Lennon tries to reconstruct a causal theory via conditional dependencies in which intentional states provide reasons, R, which *necessitate* in circumstances, C, the action, A; that is, Given C, if R then A. She argues that such intentional explanations are causal explanations and their supporting generalizations empirical causal laws (*contra* Davidson) since: (1) causal explanations support conditionals of just this kind; and (2) no other account of intentional explanation currently on offer provides an account of these conditionals. Thus everything hangs on the plausibility of such conditional formulations.

[23] D. Føllesdal, "Causation and Explanation: A Problem in Davidson's View on Action and Mind," in Ernest Lepore and Brian P. McLaughlin (eds.), *Actions and Events: Perspectives on the Philosophy of Donald Davidson*, (Oxford: Basil Blackwell, 1985), p. 315.
[24] K. Lennon, *Explaining Human Action* (La Salle: Open Court, 1990), p. 93.

However, a causal law need not only support counterfactuals, which such conditional statements do, they must also be supported or disconfirmed by their instances or counter-instances. Lennon's do not. Take her example of reaching for a glass of water: "(1') In the circumstances, if the agent's desire for a drink and belief that water will satisfy it are present, her reaching out to the glass of water occurs; (2') in the circumstance, if the agent's desire and belief are not present then her reaching out does not occur" (Lennon, *Explaining Human Action*, p. 53). Once we require, quoting Lennon, "the absence of defeating conditions" (*ibid.*, p. 43) this is true. But then it seems there are no disconfirming instances: any counter-instance can always be swept under the rug of "defeating conditions." Like many causalists in this domain, they indiscriminately throw in *ceteris-paribus* clauses. What we should say, rather, is that given the agent's beliefs and desires, her reaching out for a glass of water counts, or is interpretable as, a reaching-for-a-glass-of-water-to-quench-her-thirst. And in the absence of such mental states we can conclude, not that the reaching for a glass of water does not occur but that, if it does occur, then it cannot count or be interpretable as a reaching-for-a-glass-of-water-to-quench-her-thirst. Such strong conditional statements as hers cannot be supported.

One might object that the preceding arguments have misconstrued what explanations of action actually seek to explain, and that the role of interpretation can be reduced (or eliminated) if we focus only on the question of *why something happened*, which can only be explained in causal terms.[25] There are two things to say in response: first, the object of analysis for the philosophy of action is not simply an event, i.e., behavior generally, but human action with *discernible meaning*.[26]

---

[25] See Child, *Causality*, p. 92.

[26] Cf. Ricoeur, *Oneself as Another*. Although Ricoeur makes a similar criticism of analytic philosophy of action, based mostly on the early work of Donald Davidson, namely, it focuses on action as an event in the world and ignores its dimension as the performance of an agent, the conclusions he draws from this are mistaken. For he argues that because of this misunderstanding on the part of action theorists, they have not given (or even could not give) any attention to, for example, the future-directed component of intention. However, much of the recent work on intention, beginning with Michael Bratman's book *Intention, Plans and Practical Reasons*, sees this as one of the central aspects of intention.

We try to understand and explain actions in terms of the meaning they have for the agent performing them, which necessarily involves reconstituting the agent's understanding of her own actions, and the conditions in which such understanding is possible. The result is that the explanation of action is in part a task in which interpretation occupies an essential place. Second, in phrasing the constraint this way, as demanding *only* why something occurred, we come danger-ously close to robbing reasons and other intentional states of any explanatory power. Taken at face value, this "why" question puts us in another explanatory game, as Fred Dretske would say, for it asks us to give a triggering cause of why something happened now, as opposed to what Dretske calls a structuring cause (one that explains why this movement-process rather than another, what caused this causing), and as a result becomes a question for neurobiologists. Reasons would then have no role to play.[27]

With respect to the first response, many action theorists are inter-ested in examining how actions fit with one's other goals, as well as how we understand what we are doing in the "broadest possible way" (Velleman, *Practical Reflection*, p. 283). The aim of explanation is to make sense of the action, to put it in some sort of pattern or scheme, and to explain its meaning and significance (Child, *Causality*, pp. 92–3). To the extent we aim to explain these as well, action cannot be construed as merely something that happens, as just another event in the world.

The second response is related to the first-person criterion I intro-duced in chapter 2. Recall that the role of the self-consciousness of the agent had to be taken into account in the explanation of action as well as in the investigation of the psychological dynamics of agents. If, however, we were to give a *purely* causal account of action, we would fail to capture the idea that the action has meaning for, or in some way makes sense to, the agent performing it.[28] Instead, we have to take into account the personal, or first-person, point of view. As a result, the conception of action as just an event, as on par with physical behavior generally – a conception that is essential to purely causalist accounts – misses one of the central ideas of action explanation: namely, "the *idea*

---

[27] See Fred Dretske, *Explaining Behavior: Reasons in a World of Causes* (Cambridge, MA: MIT Press, 1988), pp. 36, 42, 52.   [28] Cf. Child, *Causality*, pp. 208–9.

of a person for whom the considerations we rehearse are reasons" (*ibid.*, p. 208, emphasis added).[29]

As a final attempt to make room for interpretation in the explanation of action in a manner that is congenial to the sciences, I want to return very briefly to cognitive science. Mark Johnson,[30] in examining the implications of recent findings in cognitive science for ethics, raises similar questions to those discussed by Gauld and Shotter. He states:

> The classical theory of categories and concepts that is still held by most people understands categories as picking out sets of properties possessed by objects that exist objectively in the world. Every concept or category is supposedly defined by a set of necessary and sufficient features a thing must possess if it is to fall under that concept.
>
> Psychologists, linguists, and anthropologists have discovered that most categories used by people are not actually definable by a list of features . . .

[29] A similar first-person constraint is used by Kim in his discussion of wide versus narrow content of mental states, and whether beliefs are supervenient on the internal states of the believer. Those who oppose the notion of wide content (i.e., the view that beliefs, for example, are individuated by conditions external to the agent) argue that the "wideness of wide-content states is not relevant to causal explanation of physical behavior," since causes generally must be local and proximate to their effects. Kim's response is that what we seek to explain is not physical behavior, but action: while "to explain physical behavior we need only to know what goes on in the head; to explain action we need to invoke wide-content states" (Kim, *Philosophy of Mind*, p. 206). But in the case of wide-content states, like belief, the place of the subject herself in the belief needs to be considered (*ibid.*, p. 203), since from a third-person perspective the content of the belief can often be misdescribed. In other words, we need to apply the first-person criterion.

As an aside, it is interesting to note that even in cases in which the "action" of the individual is probably best construed as mere physical behavior, as in the tics and jerks characteristic of Tourette's syndrome, Oliver Sacks suggests that a purely causalist, third-person account is inadequate to explain such behaviors. He states: "Neither a biological nor a psychological nor a moral-social viewpoint is adequate; we must see Tourette's not only simultaneously from all three perspectives, but from an *inner perspective*, an existential perspective, that of the affected person himself. *Inner and outer narratives here, as everywhere, must fuse.*" From *An Anthropologist on Mars* (New York: Vintage Books, 1995), pp. 78–9, emphasis added.

[30] M. Johnson, *Moral Imagination: Implications of Cognitive Science for Ethics* (Chicago: University of Chicago Press, 1993).

There is seldom any set of necessary and sufficient features possessed by all members of the category" (Johnson, *Moral Imagination*, pp. 8–9)

That is, most of our concepts have a "prototype" structure – one with a well-defined core but which becomes increasingly fuzzy toward the edges, thereby making it difficult to formulate general rules for the application of these concepts. While "the cognitive prototypes are important in defining our categories," Johnson argues, "they do not exhaust the structure of the category, *nor do they give us a list of necessary and sufficient conditions for category membership*" (*ibid.*, pp. 78–9, emphasis added). If this is the case, then it supports the point made above regarding the problem of providing purely scientific accounts of action.[31]

Human action is not "naturally" distinguished from human behavior, but depends for its categorization on the application of such concepts as intention, belief, or desire. Therefore, to the extent that intention serves as a key concept by means of which we separate human action from the larger category of behavior, then in light of Johnson's argument regarding such cognitive prototypes, there is no exhaustive list of necessary and sufficient conditions for what counts as intentional behavior, and hence as action. This is troubling for a proposed scientific account of action: if there is no list of necessary and sufficient conditions, then according to Gauld and Shotter's thesis, there is no machine-table form guiding the application of the concept, and hence no possible causal account. What this means is that a strictly scientific analysis of human action faces considerable problems – problems raised within its own discipline, in this case cognitive science.

Causalists have implicitly recognized such limitations in their accounts, but refuse to take an interpretationist approach. Kathleen Lennon responds to the concern that intentional kinds are not natural

---

[31] The problem of the uncodifiability of rationality ties in with Johnson's claim, and supports Gauld and Shotter's thesis. If it is in fact true that rationality cannot be codified by any set of laws, then it follows that "there is no system of strict laws on the basis of which actions and other mental phenomena could be exactly predicted and explained." Since we explain an agent's actions by ascribing to her certain beliefs and desires, and since this ascription depends on an assessment of what it would be rational for her to believe or desire, if rationality cannot be captured by any set of laws, then there can be no set of laws for the explanation of action, which would undermine the hope of providing purely causal accounts. See Child, *Causality*, p. 60.

kinds, and so cannot be part of causal explanatory systems, by introducing a new test for what constitutes a "real" object. She states:

> What more can we require of classifications which reflect the real struc-
> ture of reality, than that they allow the formulation of a body of explana-
> tory theory which is instantiated by parts of the world? . . . The key test
> of the naturalness of our kind terms, within a realist construal . . . [should
> be] whether the system of classification which they reflect allows the
> formulation of law-like generalisations which the world, *as thus classified*,
> satisfies (Lennon, *Explaining Human Action*, p. 72).

As we shall see shortly, this is very close to the interpretive-realist
thesis I develop. Although others might see this statement as a *reductio*,
because it allows such things as "injustice," or "cruelty," as natural-
kind terms, I see it rather as pointing in the right direction, and as the
natural consequence of the limits of purely causalist accounts of
action, even though Lennon tries to invoke it in their defense.

Finally, one might object that this argument excludes such commonplace explanations of actions as: "I went to the kitchen *because* I
wanted a drink," or "I went downstairs *because* I thought I heard a
noise." Aren't these causal explanations? There are two things to be
said in response. First, the fact that interpretation occupies an important place in explanation does not exclude the place of "causal"
explanations of action, but only makes us aware of the limitations of
such explanations. Second, the intention of the argument is not to
show that reasons cannot be causes of action – the two examples above
would indicate that they often are – but rather to show that the notion
of "cause" is fairly ambiguous, and to insist upon some degree of consistency in what we countenance as causes.[32]

[32] What exactly is supposed to follow from, or what the advantages are to, calling a
reason a "cause," is rarely very clear. We are told, rather uninformatively, that "a causal
theory of action is simply a theory which says that explaining actions by giving the
agents' reasons for doing them is a mode of causal explanation . . . S's -ing was an
action if and only if it was caused (*in the right sort of way*) by an intention, or by a belief
and desire (*of an appropriate sort*)" (Child, *Causality*, p. 99; emphasis added). Causes of
action must be causes "of the appropriate sort," but what that means is left unanswered.
The examples of "causal" explanations of action are even more mysterious. For
example: "You see a McDonald's sign across the street and you want to get a burger,
and the perception and desire apparently cause your limbs to move in such a way that
you now find your body at the doors of the McDonald's. Cases like this are among the
familiar facts of life, too boring to mention" (Kim, *Philosophy of Mind*, p. 8; emphasis

It should be clear then that some alternative approach to action explanation is needed. Gauld and Shotter, as I mentioned, propose a hermeneutic psychology. Mark Johnson, following Alisdair McIntyre and Paul Ricoeur, suggests that narrative is the appropriate mode of explanation for human action (Johnson, *Moral Imagination*, p. 168). What these two proposals have in common is the considerable role played by *interpretation*; but this should not be surprising given the high degree of indeterminacy uncovered by their analyses. Recall, though, that interpretation was already signaled by Velleman as an important component of his investigation, and heralded by Charles Taylor as the essential mode of analysis for the human sciences. We now see why. What remains to be seen is what the implications of this are.

To summarize, Velleman's noncognitivist theory of the self rests on a putative scientific account of action. What I have tried to show in the preceding discussion was that in so far as human action is concerned, explanation and interpretation are no longer so neatly separated, so that a "science" of action begins to lose its sense. Yet if this is the case, then the criteria for scientific explanation give way to those of interpretive plausibility and enhanced understanding. What we seek in a theory of the self, *contra* Velleman's thesis, is not exclusively (nor even usually) a high degree of *predictability* of *behavior*, nor necessarily the possibility of deriving highly generalized formulae for action – the hallmarks of scientific accounts. For as we saw, human action does not fit cleanly into the scientific categories. Yet it was on the basis of such categories and criteria that Velleman argued in favor of an instrumentalist theory of value, as well as the identification of one's self-conception with intrinsic desires. More importantly, however, Velleman, like many action theorists, is not always consistent with respect to the kind of explanation he offers. Once he establishes the noncognitivist theory of the self, he returns to the

added). I, myself, have never found my body at the doors of McDonald's, nor anywhere else for that matter. Cases like this would be far from boring. The point here is that reasons are not causes in the sense understood in other domains of science. This is even more evident when we look for law-like regularities in "causal" explanations of action, and can only find *ceteris-paribus* clauses, or rough-and-ready rules of thumb. But if we are still willing to treat these types of explanations as causes, then there is little reason not to treat explanations involving values as varieties of causal explanations as well. This is what is meant by the insistence on consistency.

vocabulary of "understanding" and "making sense," but in the contexts of "understanding what [one is] doing in the broadest possible way," (Velleman, *Practical Reflection*, p. 283) and of seeking "what makes the most sense for you, for all of you, in light of your entire way of life" (*ibid.*, p. 302). Although this might involve in part some sort of "causal" story, it will be at the same time a highly interpretive one.

In short, not only does interpretation occupy a central place in the examination of human action *tout court*, but it is especially relevant in the domains that interest Velleman, and especially in the study of commitment and its conditions.

It is essential to see Velleman's ambiguous position with respect to the role of "scientific" explanations in action theory. Velleman's defense of intention as a distinct mental state and his instrumentalist theory of value as a mere proxy for desire, reflect a much larger debate between folk psychology and the natural sciences. Since this debate is by now well documented in the literature, suffice it to say that what is at issue is whether our common-sense explanations of human behavior in terms of intentions, beliefs, and desires have any place as part of a legitimate theory of human behavior, or if they should instead be replaced by explanations expressed exclusively in the terms of the neurosciences. This debate has given rise to a number of, by now, famous (or infamous) positions, from eliminative materialism (the Churchlands), to instrumentalism (Daniel Dennett), functionalism (David Armstrong) and, finally, to unabashed realism about mental representations (Jerry Fodor). Now it might seem that in this foray into the philosophy of mind and folk psychology we are a long way from values and Velleman. But this is not the case.

Folk psychology (understood as "a body of causal-explanatory theoretical references to contentful psychological states employed by layfolk and scientific psychologists"[33]), when faced with criticisms from the neurosciences regarding its explanatory inadequacy, has typically responded by charging the advocates of neuroscience with employing an overly constrained, mechanistic notion of "explanation," by invoking criteria which broaden the scope of acceptable explanations beyond those used in the hard sciences, or by saying that our explanatory goals in the case of human behavior are somewhat

---

[33] John D. Greenwood, (ed.), *The Future of Folk Psychology: Intentionality and Cognitive Science* (Cambridge: Cambridge University Press, 1991), p. 5. (henceforth, *FFP*).

different than those in other scientific disciplines. In short, they argue, whether rightly or wrongly, that the standards employed in the neurosciences do not apply without qualification to our folk-psychological explanations, and in this way try to establish the autonomy of folk psychology, and the justifiability of positing the existence of such things as desires, beliefs, and intentions.

Velleman clearly falls into the camp of those who are realists about psychological states. They are, after all, the cornerstones of his overall noncognitivist theory of practical reasoning. Although he does not lay out the arguments himself, we can assume that he would oppose any attempted reduction of mental states, or any instrumentalist theory claiming that while such things as desires, beliefs, and intentions do not actually exist (given their ontological discontinuity, and lack of coherence with the rest of science) they often lead to useful predictions about behavior (Dennett's line), and to that extent are useful fictions. We can imagine him offering the kinds of defenses outlined above, which we can group into three broad categories:

1. *The Different Domain Defense (DDD):* Because the approaches of the cognitive and neurosciences are "contextless, ahistorical, completely extensional" (*FFP*, p. 14), they "cannot accommodate psychological phenomena located in the social space of a historically functioning culture" (*ibid.*). Or, similarly, the holistic natures of psychological phenomena make them resistant to any mechanistic reduction (cf. Gauld and Shotter). In short, because the domain of phenomena is essentially different, scientific criteria for explanation do not apply to them, hence a defense of instrumentalism based on such criteria is invalid.

2. *The Singular Causality Defense (SCD):* The typical user of folk psychology is interested in making "particular causal judgments about particular instances of human behavior, not in formulating new causal generalizations" (*FFP*, p. 153). Consequently, the charge that folk psychology is explanatorily inadequate since it does not permit of nomological, causal correlations, is misdirected since folk psychology, like history, considers only singular causal events.

3. *The Multiple Explanatory Dimensions Defense (MEDD):* Science does not exhaust all the dimensions of explanation, and to charge folk psychology with failing to restrict itself to those begs the question in favor of physicalist accounts. Intentional explanation highlights other important factors, for example, it "brings out patterns, provides groupings and

comparisons, that a [neuroscientific] explanation would miss"[34] (*FFP*, p. 179).

What these defenses all have in common is that they both recognize the place for scientific accounts, while showing how such accounts fail, in one way or another, to close off the possibility of folk psychological explanations; in short, neuroscience does not have the last word, and that when it comes to the realm of human behavior, and human *action*, there is much more to be said. While acknowledging the place of science, they also "distance" themselves from it. In order to find a rightful place for desires, beliefs, and intentions, they must lay claim to a certain autonomy from science or, rather, must in some ways go beyond it.

What is important to notice in this brief outline of the debate over folk psychology is the way it exactly mirrors the arguments Velleman uses against values. Recall that he argues for a reduction of value to desire along precisely the same lines that others argue for a reduction of psychological states: in terms of predictive power, ontological continuity, etc. In doing so he implicitly rejects the standards and criteria used in defending folk psychology – standards he himself would need in his own defense – in order to reject value realism. When it comes to the reality of psychological states, Velleman is (or would be) willing to allow a certain relaxation of the rigid scientific standards critics of folk psychology use against desires and beliefs. However, when the issue concerns the reality of values, the previously relaxed standards are now forcefully applied in order to do to values exactly what others try to do to beliefs; yet no reason is given for this fortuitous flexibility.

My arguments in favor of a cognitivist, realist theory of value have been (and will be) the same ones used by folk psychologists (such as Velleman) in favor of desires, beliefs, and intentions. The point of this digression is that the arguments I develop, contrary to first appearance, share considerable continuity with Velleman's own work and theoretical assumptions. Moreover, this is in keeping with the general strategy throughout this book: to remain as much as possible within the argumentative limits set out by the main protagonists. I want to underscore the point that I am not leveling a broad criticism against

---

[34] As an aside, it is interesting to note the structuralist overtones and similarities to Ricoeur's hermeneutics of action with the emphasis on patterns.

analytic action theory, nor relying on a cursory defense of, for example, folk psychology against the natural sciences, but rather that I am working within the confines of Velleman's argument (and method) in order both to show its limitations and elicit justifications for the development of my own arguments.

5.1.8 Interpretation, explanation, and the Indispensability Thesis

It should be clear that interpretation plays an important role – one that has largely gone unacknowledged by many action theorists – and that this role is defined by the limits of a science of action. In section 5.1.4 above we also saw the way in which interpretation and interpretive activities played a role in a good deal of Velleman's method and argument. I also drew out the parallels between Velleman and Taylor with respect to the investigation and explanation of action, and suggested that Taylor takes up where Velleman leaves off. While the notion of interpretation goes largely unthematized in Velleman, Taylor, on the other hand, emphasizes the interpretive dimension that any analysis of action must possess, especially in the examination of the connection between self-understanding and action, one with which Velleman is concerned, as well as the connection between commitment and self-understanding. In what follows, I discuss what the implications are for this increased role of interpretation. This will provide the tools needed to make the argument for the role of realist beliefs about value in commitment via their place in one's self-conception.

In *Sources of the Self*, Taylor offers what he calls the Best Account (BA) principle. In the attempt to "make sense" of our lives, says Taylor,

> [t]he terms we select have to make sense across the whole range of both explanatory and life uses. The terms *indispensable* for the latter are part of the story that makes best sense of us . . . The result of this search . . . yields the *best account we can give at any given time, and no epistemological or metaphysical considerations of a more general kind about science or nature can justify setting this aside*. The best account in this sense is trumps. Let me call this the BA principle (*SS*, p. 58, emphasis added).

Taken in isolation, this principle might sound like a call to irrationalism, or a return to an anachronistic nineteenth-century romanticism.

It is neither. And it should be clear, from the discussion in section 5.1.5, why this is so.[35]

The crucial term here is "making sense." As we have seen repeatedly, from Gibbard to Velleman, this is how they describe their central task: whether it be "making sense" of normative practices or human actions more generally. Taylor's argument, however, does not turn on a simple coincidence of idiomatic expressions. "Making sense" is an interpretive activity, and given the limits of a science of human action – limits defined by the cognitive sciences themselves – interpretation necessarily occupies a central place. But the criteria for interpretation do not exactly match those of the natural sciences. Thus, when Taylor asks, "What are the requirements of 'making sense' of our lives?" that is, criteria of interpretation, the answer is that "[t]hese requirements are not yet met if we have some theoretical language which purports to explain behaviour from the *observer's standpoint* but is of no use to the agent in making sense of his own thinking, feeling, and acting" (*SS*, p. 57; emphasis added).

The point here about the observer's standpoint is essential, and one that I have underscored repeatedly: an action is not simply an event in the world, but an instance of *meaningful* behavior. And it is precisely this meaning that we seek to elucidate and reconstitute in terms of the *agent's own understanding* of her actions. But this imposes severe restrictions on both the relevance and usefulness of scientific, third-person observer accounts of action *qua* behavior – restrictions that opened the way for interpretation. Now an interpretation of human action, when seen as part of the attempt of "making sense," must meet the test of "indispensability" (borrowing Taylor's term); that is:

> *Indispensability Thesis* (IT): The terms an interpretation uses and the objects it posits will be deemed valid or justifiable to the extent that they are indispensable for understanding oneself and one's actions across a broad range of instances and within a variety of contexts.

[35] There are some interesting similarities between Taylor's BA principle and Owen Flanagan's Principle of Minimal Psychological Realism (PMPR). Both place limits on any acceptable moral theory according to how well it captures our lives as they are actually lived. Thus PMPR could also be seen as trumps when it comes to other (non-naturalized) epistemological or metaphysical considerations. See Flanagan, *Varieties of Moral Personality*, p. 32.

There is an ineliminable interpretive dimension to human action. The "indispensability of a term," says Taylor, "in a non-explanatory context of life can't just be declared irrelevant to the project to do without that term in an explanatory reduction" (*SS*, p. 57). Once again, this bears striking similarities to the kind of arguments offered in defense of folk psychology, like MEDD above.

This in turn gives us a new measure by which to judge what is real and objective: no longer are we restricted only to those terms that figure in the best natural scientific explanation, but can now include "those terms which on critical reflection and after correction of the errors we can detect make the best sense of our lives" (*SS*, p. 57). Thus, what we cannot help but have recourse to in understanding our lives, in making sense of our actions from a critical, reflective standpoint – one from which this self-assessment concerns one's objectivist self-conception and the view of oneself as one person among others – is real: it is as objective a picture of human reality as we can have. It is on the basis of this indispensability test that the argument will be made for the realist evaluative beliefs and their place in commitment.

It should be clear that the Indispensability Thesis does not grow out of a hostility toward the natural sciences, but results from two conditions: first, the limitations of scientific accounts, in the strict sense, of human action and the place these limitations created for interpretation; and second, the self-avowed aspiration of rival noncognitivist theories – Gibbard and Velleman – borrowing heavily from the philosophy of action, of trying to make the "best sense" of our lives as we live them.[36] In fact, the Indispensability Thesis could have been drawn directly from them. Yet because of the confusion on the part of Velleman, for example, regarding what a "science" of action is capable of, and the attempt to import (methodologically foreign) criteria of explanation in order to bolster noncognitivist conclusions regarding the irrealism of value, without justifying the application of such criteria, it was necessary to support IT by way of a brief detour through cognitive science and the philosophy of mind, and to show why Taylor's appeal to it in fact had legitimate grounds beyond sympathetic tendencies to continental hermeneutics.

---

[36] IT differs from the BA principle in that the former places greater emphasis on interpretation and locates the source of interpretation in the limitations of a science of action.

Before moving on to the final argument, one objection needs to be addressed concerning IT. Given that the thesis is developed on the basis of the requirements or conditions of self-understanding, some may see this as some form of transcendental deduction,[37] and hence subject to the standard objection that such deductions typically encounter: namely, that what one must believe is not indicative of what is true.[38]

There are two things to be said in defense of this style of argument. The first is to say that the thesis is in fact only *quasi*-transcendental:[39] it claims that since one cannot maintain one's self-understanding as an individual with certain commitments without simultaneously conceding the conditions for the possibility of commitment itself, and since these conditions include realist evaluative beliefs which only make sense in the context of moral realism, then any adequate moral theory that seeks to explain and *retain* commitment cannot also deny moral realism. The conclusion of my argument, as I said at the outset, is not that moral realism is true – a conclusion that would follow from a strictly transcendental deduction – but, rather, that it is only on the assumption of moral realism (which underwrites the plausibility of realist evaluative beliefs) that commitment is possible.[40]

The second response is to point out that this form of argument is hardly as uncommon in current philosophical debates as the objection would lead one to believe. Indeed, it is found among a wide range of philosophers writing on action theory and the philosophy of mind. Donald Davidson, for example, can be read as undertaking a Kantian project in defining the conditions of interpretation and concluding

---

[37] L. W. Beck defines a transcendental deduction as the method of taking a body of alleged fact and showing (a) what it necessarily presupposes, and (b) the consequences of denying the presuppositions. Similarly, John Silber notes that a deduction establishes the concepts and relations that must be presupposed in order to give a rational account of (as concerns Kant in the *Critique of Practical Reason* and *Religion within the Limits of Reason Alone*) moral obligation. See L. W. Beck, *A Commentary on Kant's Critique of Practical Reason* (Chicago: University of Chicago Press, 1960), p. 170; and J. Silber, "The Ethical Significance of Kant's Critique," in *Religion within the Limits of Reason Alone*, trans. Theodore M. Greene and Hoyt H. Hudson (New York: Harper and Row, 1960), p. lxxxiii.

[38] To his credit, Kant was sensitive to this potential problem and attempted to answer one critic, Wizenmann, in a brief footnote. See, *The Critique of Practical Reason*, p. 151/Ak 144 fn.   [39] Eckart Förster's term.

[40] Recall that I did not set out to provide a *direct* proof of moral realism.

on the basis of what is required for understanding others that they cannot be radically different from us.

Jaegwon Kim highlights his own Kantian tendencies more explicitly. He states:

> The intentional psychological scheme – that is, the framework of belief, desire, and will – . . . is the framework that makes our normative and evaluative activities possible. No purely descriptive framework such as those of neurophysiology and physics, no matter how theoretically comprehensive and productively powerful, can replace it. As long as we think of ourselves as reflective agents capable of deliberation and evaluation – that is, as long as we regard ourselves as agents capable of acting in accordance with a norm – we shall not be able to dispense with the intentional framework.[41]

Jerry Fodor, too, invokes transcendental arguments in his defense of folk psychology and appeals to something akin to the Indispensability Thesis. He states:

> Even if psychology were dispensable *in principle*, that would be no argument for dispensing with it . . . What's relevant to whether common sense psychology is worth defending is its dispensability *in fact*. And here the situation is absolutely clear. We have no idea of how to explain ourselves to ourselves except in a vocabulary which is *saturated* with belief/desire psychology. One is tempted to transcendental argument: What Kant said to Hume about physical objects holds, *mutatis mutandis*, for the propositional attitudes; we can't give them up *because we do not know how*.[42]

And finally Daniel Dennett also embraces what I have called interpretive realism with respect to propositional attitudes and reveals his Kantian sympathies when he defends the optimality assumption in evolutionary-biological explanations on the basis of what is required of us as interpreters – something we simply cannot avoid being.[43]

---

[41] Lepore and McLaughlin (eds.), *Actions and Events* p. 386.

[42] J. Fodor, from *Psychosemantics*, reprinted in Scott Christensen and Dale Turner (eds.), *Folk Psychology and the Philosophy of Mind* (New Jersey: Lawrence Erlbaum Associates, 1993), p. 229, emphasis added.

[43] D. Dennett, *Intentional Stance* (Cambridge, MA: MIT Press, 1987), p. 278.

5.2 CONCLUSION: REALIST BELIEFS AND SUBSTANTIVE COMMITMENTS

5.2.1 *Summary: putting the pieces together*

Taking stock of the discussion so far, I have shown how the Indispensability Thesis is a legitimate form of argumentation, and have drawn grounds for its support from within folk psychology and cognitive science. Beyond the kind of functional analysis that I have used so far in the examination of commitment and its belief constraints, I now have at my disposal IT. What is more, IT is a continuation of the strategy employed by folk psychologists in defense of the irreducibility of mental states, and to that extent can be thought of as belonging to the same family of functionalist analyses. As a result, the shift from the functionalist approach in the examination of the intention-like commitments to the use of IT and the quasi-functionalist analysis in the discussion of substantive commitments that follows, is not, as should now be clear, a radical shift in argument.

If the preceding arguments are correct, then the conclusion that these chapters have been building up to should be fairly straightforward: what remains is to assemble all the pieces to fit a complete picture – a picture in which one should readily see the place of realist evaluative beliefs in commitment. All the necessary tools are available; it is just a matter now of knowing how to use them. What are these tools?

Objectivist self-conception

Drawing on Nagel's work in *The Possibility of Altruism* as well as *The View from Nowhere*, I have suggested that we view ourselves as inhabiting an objective standpoint, one in which we act for reasons which, though perhaps not motivating for others, could in principle – prejudices aside – be understood as possible reasons for action. It is from this standpoint, where we view ourselves not just as the particular persons we happen to be, but as one person among others, that we formulate what I called impersonal values; furthermore, this objectivist self-conception places a constraint on personal values that others be able to recognize them as something a (rational) person could value themselves. It is on the basis of this objectivist self-conception that we formulate and try to assess objective values: values which incorporate certain fundamental beliefs regarding what it is to be a person and, to some extent, what constitutes the human good, however roughly that might be defined. These objective values purport to capture certain facts about human nature or the human good, and consequently can be said to be values for anyone who is not influenced by personal prejudice or short-sightedness, or is limited by an unwillingness to step outside the personal point of view.

Objectivist cognitivist self-conception

Related to the objectivist self-conception, I have defended a "cognitivist" account of one's self-conception, arguing that evaluative beliefs occupy a central place in how one conceives of oneself. I have shown how Velleman's rival "non-cognitivist" theory of the self, in which intrinsic desires were the sole constituents of one's self-conception, failed to explain adequately the stability of certain desires, how certain desires were more "one's own" than others, and in what sense one "willingly" desired something. These arguments were supported by the literature in psychology on ego–dystonia. Velleman's account, I have argued, fails to explain the occurrences of such cases.

Expanded notion of self-understanding

Our desire to understand ourselves extends beyond the mere knowledge of the motives and reasons for our immediate actions but, as Velleman himself says, and as Taylor forcefully demonstrates, it extends to an understanding of a whole life in "the broadest possible sense," to an understanding of who one is and where one's place is, as Taylor would say, in relation to the good. Although this notion will be developed in the ensuing discussion, it should at least be clear that we are not limited to a fairly thin notion of self-understanding – one which is best, or only, suited to a causal explanation of immediate actions – but can appeal to a more robust notion that is more apt for the phenomenon of substantive commitment.

Indispensability Thesis

The explanation of human action, I have shown, is a highly interpretive task, especially when dealing with such phenomena as commitment. The causal explanations used by action theorists such as Alfred Mele, and ambiguously embraced by David Velleman, do not meet the standard criteria for causal explanation (except to say that the "causes" they postulate are "special" causes), nor do they meet the explanatory task at hand, namely, to "make sense" of the action or "render it intelligible." More importantly, the possibility of a strictly causal account of human action is put in doubt when we examine the presuppositions that would make such a project possible in the light of recent debates in cognitive science and the philosophy of mind. In short, there is an ineliminable interpretive dimension to the explanation of human action. What this means is that those terms which are essential to our understanding of human action, and which are indispensable to our own self-understanding, though they may not be part of our best natural scientific accounts, are still the best accounts we can offer and the best picture we can get of human reality. While Taylor called this the Best Account principle, I prefer to call it the Indispensability Thesis, in part to dissociate it somewhat from the former since the BA principle is often thought to be a (bad) hermeneutic ploy that refuses to acknowledge the place of natural scientific explanations.

The problem now is to put these pieces together.

5.2.2 Self-understanding, identity, and narrativity

Throughout, I have suggested that substantive commitments play an important role in our self-understanding and identity. How we understand what we do and who we are is to a considerable extent formulated in terms of our most fundamental commitments. They are the constancies around which we construct and, I would add, narrate our identities. These narrative constructs of our identities, and the narrative form of self-understanding, aim to *make sense* of our actions and of who we are. And this is done by forming a coherent story, so to speak, of our actions, the events in our lives, and the things that matter to us, that forms a narrative whole: one (largely) without gaps or radical discontinuities – a story which we can follow. But not every story is a good story, and not every tale is worth telling. In other words, this interpretive, narrative construction which I call the project of self-understanding, faces certain constraints: constraints imposed by our objectivist, cognitivist self-conception.[44]

---

[44] If there are any brute facts in this essay, this is one of them. Although I have tried to give the best grounds for it, in part by showing the shortcomings of rival positions, it is not a fact I can prove or derive from yet more basic facts. Another fact I will need concerns the unity of self-explanations: that is, the fact that we do not, or rather cannot, have explanations of our practices that conflict with explanations of "what's *really* going on."

Because we see ourselves as inhabiting the objective standpoint, the elements of our story which play a part in our identities must themselves be seen to be objectively valid, to have what I have called objective merit. The objectivist self-conception then acts as a filter on potential narratives by screening those that could not be supported from the objective standpoint. A second constraint comes from the demands of narrative itself and the need for a unified self-conception (recall, this was one of the virtues of a theory of the self Velleman spoke of). The story which forms a part of our self-understanding must not only be continuous, but also coherent, which means that we cannot have, as it were, two *different* stories running at the same time. What we seek, I suggest, is explanatory unity and transparency: we want a *single* story which offers the best account across the greatest number of explanatory dimensions. A unified story gives rise to a unified identity. Now if this is true, it speaks directly against the projects of Rorty and Gibbard, for as I showed in chapter 2, the tenability of their accounts depends crucially on a bifurcation between either public and private discourses, in Rorty's case, or between theory and practice, in Gibbard's case. It is only through a *unified* theory of the self, one that has wide explanatory power, that one reaches a stable, unified identity.

If this last claim is true, then the project is complete, for according to the Indispensability Thesis, we are allowed to postulate those items which figure in our best explanations of the self and human reality. And if realist evaluative beliefs are *indispensable* to our explanations of the self, the constitution of identity and the construction of self-understanding through narrative, then to that extent we must accommodate the possibility of realism about values. Moreover, in light of the demand for explanatory unity and transparency, it follows that any alternative explanation or story which excludes this possibility is false, since it would require its own self-effacement: we could not both accept the theory *and* be realists about value, which means we could not both accept the theory *and* retain the possibility of such things as commitment. But are realist evaluative beliefs indispensable terms in the narratives we construct and the explanations we offer, not only to others, but more importantly to ourselves?

The answer to this question brings us right back to the problem of commitment. Commitment, as we saw in the introduction and in the discussions of the various protagonists in this book, is an important part of everyday human reality. Therefore, if we can only understand how commitment works, or can only explain it by appealing to realist beliefs, then we can conclude that these "terms" are indispensable for the explanation of at least one aspect of human action. The alternative views I have considered – Rorty's neopragmatism, Gibbard's norm-expressivism, and Velleman's noncognitivism – have all failed in one way or another to explain commitment, to account for its roles in self-understanding and identity, and to make sense of its temporal stability.

The specific obligation I need to meet in responding to the challenges of these three should be defined more carefully; it is one thing to show that no alternative explanation is possible, and quite another to show that an explanation is the best one in the offing, given a certain set of assumptions. Proofs of the first type, though highly desirable, are rare to come by in philosophy. Although we can prove the incompleteness of any finite axiomatizable theory (thanks to Gödel), or the impossibility of squaring the circle (since we can show that pi is not a constructible number), to prove that *in principle* an alternative explanation of *human action* is impossible might just well be impossible. To say otherwise is to elevate the status of these kinds of explanations to a domain to which they have (as yet) no demonstrable right (recall the discussion on the scientistic aspirations of action theory). In keeping with the interpretive dimension of explanations of action, the best one can hope for is an explanation that does the job better than the others, and makes the most sense of the most data.

In chapter 4 I showed how the belief (B1) that the commitment is valuable and the belief (B2) that the value is objectively valid, or has objective merit, are functionally required for the intention-like commitments. For such commitments I argued that the associated value is typically, if not exclusively, a *personal* value – one which has an essential reference to the agent. I claim now that B2 beliefs also figure in substantive commitments, but that the value the B2 beliefs refer to is an *impersonal value*, and hence is objective in a more robust, realist sense; that is, it is objective in the sense that, whether the value is good or whether the commitment is right, does not depend upon the agent's specific desires, but instead depends on facts about the human good, human nature, and what we might call human flourishing – facts which are largely independent of our beliefs, desires, and cultural practices.

There are two ways one might go about proving this. The first is to assume the contrapositive: suppose the claim is not true, and examine what conclusions we then reach. This approach is in fact the substance of chapter 2–4. In the absence of these beliefs, we encountered any number of obstacles in trying to explain commitment and its functions. Although it is tempting to declare the argument won, since the contrapositive is false, a more direct approach is needed. Thus, I return to what I called earlier a quasi-functionalist analysis; that is, a functionalist analysis that respects the constraints of the Indispensability Thesis. The goal here is to show that in fact realist evaluative beliefs are indispensable terms for explanations of commitment's role in narrative self-understanding and identity.

What will be essential to the argument that follows are the tools I outlined above: an objectivist, cognitivist (OC) self-conception; an expanded notion of self-understanding; the Indispensability Thesis (IT); and the criterion of explanatory unity and transparency.

5.2.3 Identity, self-understanding, and stability

In light of the OC self-conception, it should be clear what role B2 beliefs play in substantive commitments. Recall the intellectual desire for self-understanding in which we prefer performing those actions of whose motives and reasons we are aware, and whose reasons fit best with our conception of ourselves. As we saw with Velleman, it is because of the desire for self-understanding that we are led to form a lasting self-conception. Now this self-conception, as I argued at length in chapter 4 and the first part of this chapter, involves our seeing ourselves as inhabiting in part the objective standpoint. Recall that, according to Velleman, reasons for action which do not accord with our self-conception we find puzzling, and with this puzzlement follows a disinclination to carry out the proposed action; in short, reflective puzzlement puts a halt to action and to that extent can be seen as destabilizing.

In the case of substantive commitments, there is at the very least the B1 belief that the commitment is valuable or worthwhile; this follows from the structural uniformity of commitments as a whole. Now the B2 belief further enhances stability because it is a reason for action that accords with, and in fact is demanded by, our OC self-conception: because we inhabit the objective standpoint, we will seek reasons for action which we take to be objectively valid, and so will be inclined to fulfill those substantive commitments which are believed to be objectively valuable. Given our objectivist self-conceptions, without the B2 beliefs we cannot explain one of the central features of substantive commitment, namely, its temporal stability.

The phenomenon of reflective puzzlement also highlights the role of B2 beliefs in self-understanding in a very easy and direct way since in the absence of these beliefs we do not understand what it is we are doing. Reflective puzzlement is just one indication of a lack of self-understanding. But I said that self-understanding extends beyond a knowledge of our immediate actions, that it is a more expansive notion and takes on a narrative dimension. Here, too, we see the explanatory advantages of a realist belief about values.

Our substantive commitments serve as fixed points around which we structure a continuous, coherent story about ourselves – a story which makes sense of ourselves in the broadest possible way, and not just of our immediate actions. Our self-conception provides the framework through which we arrive at a better self-understanding by retrospectively tracing, through our commitments, a continuity in our actions and even in our development. Yet this continuity is not necessarily provided by a single guiding principle which informs all of our commitments: for example, to "pursue justice," or to "maximize the most good for the greatest number." Rather, the continuity is based on, once again, what I take to be a fundamental conception of ourselves as being one person among others, as inhabiting the objective standpoint. Thus, our commitments, though they will vary from person to person, from one period in a life to another, will share at least this much: that they were (are) seen to be objectively valid. Equally important, however, with the addition of the B2 beliefs, we are in a better position to give an explanation and provide reasons regarding why we have the commitments we do – reasons which make essential reference to what it is to be a person, what is the human good, or the requirements of human development. And these are reasons which are open to public examination, criticism, defense, and acceptance: reasons which others may regard as good or bad, and about which they too can give reasons for accepting or rejecting. Because of the objective "pretense" of such reasons, we can also better understand the transitions between our commitments: the fixed points in our narrative constructions of our self-understanding and identity.

If our self-understanding amounts to a narrative reconstruction of our actions, and if our substantive commitments form fixed points around which we build such stories, then the transitions from one point to another will form an integral part of these stories. Once again, the B2 beliefs are essential to our understanding the transitions themselves, which is to say they are an essential part of the interpretive activity, which is to say, according to the Indispensability Thesis, that they are the best descriptions of (human) reality that we have. These transitions will be expressed in terms of "reaching a better understanding of," or "having a fuller realization about," or "seeing what was wrong with," the commitments one held. The coherent story we develop regarding the transition from one fixed point to another rests on the *reflective inquiry that takes place regarding our reasons for having certain commitments and how they fit, or failed to fit, with our OC self-conception*. What emerges from this process is a coherent narrative, a unified theory of the self, which makes possible a unified identity, for the agent now understands, despite the potentially dramatic changes in her life, the underlying thread that connects the transitions in a comprehensible manner. It is through realist evaluative beliefs, the only ones which accord with this self-conception, that a coherent story can be made, and a unified theory of the self, and hence also a more complete self-understanding, can be achieved.

It is in the process of constructing such a narrative that we reach (what Velleman calls) self-understanding in the broadest possible sense. It is not that we have simply an understanding of any given commitment but, rather, we understand both our particular commitments and where they fit in relation to one another: we understand why we came to have them, why we retain them, or why we abandoned them. We have what one might call a *diachronic* understanding of ourselves in terms of our commitments, and if what I have argued is correct, it is only by positing the realist evaluative B2 beliefs that we can make the connections between transition points and develop a coherent narrative.

Now identity and self-understanding are intimately, if not inextricably, related concepts. Recall that in the introduction I distinguished, following Paul Ricoeur, between two senses of identity – *idem* and *ipse* – and argued that human identity is irreducible to one or the other. It should now be clear that commitment constitutes identity in both senses: to the extent that a commitment remains constant through time, it can be thought of as an identifying mark or trait; and to the extent it is something taken up and maintained by the person herself, it is a source of identity in the *ipse* sense as well.

Because B2 beliefs add stability to substantive commitment by enhancing self-understanding and thereby decreasing the possibility of reflective puzzlement which, we saw, undermines commitment (or for that matter, any proposed course of action), B2 beliefs can be seen to play a role in *idem* identity since they make possible or facilitate the temporal stability of commitment. That is to say, they make possible the permanence through time, characteristic of commitment, which constitutes identity in the *idem* sense. But recall that we do not simply have commitments, but in fact maintain them, endorse them, in short, *accept them*, part of which involves having the B2 beliefs about them.

The acceptance of versus mere adherence to a norm or commitment was a topic raised by Gibbard, yet his analysis did not go much beyond making the distinction, though important, between the two. With the above tools at hand – especially the OC self-conception – we can now make out more clearly the distinction between them and see how accepting a norm is related to *ipse* identity. Drawing from the literature in applied psychology and organizational behavior, we have seen that commitment, as a kind of psychological attachment, results from "identification with attitudes, values or goals of the model; that is, some of the attributes, motives or characteristics of the model are accepted by the individual and become *incorporated into the cognitive response set of the individual*."[45] Recall also that the process of forming or accepting (organizational) commitments involved matching those requirements with one's "inner self" (Buchanan, "Building Organizational Commitments," 535). Now to "incorporate" something into one's "cognitive response set" or to match it to one's "inner self" just means, according to my view, to see that it fits with one's objectivist cognitivist self-conception. To pass from mere adherence to a norm or commitment to full acceptance and internalization requires that the norm or commitment fit with one's self-conception, which as we have seen is part of one's cognitive response set. Yet since one's self-conception is formed from the objective standpoint, in

---

[45] O'Reilly and Chatman, "Organizational Commitment and Psychological Attachment," pp. 492–9.

order for a norm or commitment to become part of one's cognitive response set, i.e., to fit with one's self-conception, it too must be seen to be objectively valid. Accepting a norm or commitment, then, essentially involves *believing* that it is objectively valid in the sense I have defined. And since *ipse* identity is defined in terms of the projects and commitments we maintain and endorse, these realist evaluative beliefs are crucially linked to identity, both in the *ipse* and *idem* senses. Once again we see that without the vocabulary of objective values, or the framework of realist beliefs, we undermine the possibility of internalizing norms or commitments, and so also the possibility of forming any stable identity.

6

Conclusion

6.1 RORTY AND GIBBARD REVISITED

The examination of commitment began with a dual challenge on the part of Rorty and Gibbard that realist or factualist accounts of commitment were either false or irrelevant: they both claimed to be able to explain such things as solidarity and normative governance without the benefit of realist evaluative beliefs – beliefs which aim at objectivity and purport to represent subject-independent facts. The arguments that followed were driven by the need to respond to their challenge: to limn the outline of commitment in order to reach a more informed position from which to assess their neopragmatist and norm-expressivist views.

6.1.1 Richard Rorty

The central question regarding Rorty's neopragmatist portrayal of the liberal ironist was whether it was in fact a human portrait or the portrait of some impossible hybrid Rorty calls the strong poet, a portrait more suited to the pages of fiction than an account of a possible human morality. We can now answer definitively that Rorty does not provide a plausible psychological picture of what it is to be a liberal ironist: one who believes that inflicting cruelty is the worst thing one can do, and at the same time has no beliefs regarding the human essence, the human good, or human nature.

Through the examination of the intention-like commitments and later the substantive commitments, of which solidarity forms a part, we saw how beliefs are functionally required for commitment to satisfy its roles in the guidance of action, self-understanding, and identity, and how these beliefs provided the stability of commitment and served as criteria for revision. This argument was further supported by the notable failure of desire-based theories of commitment.

183

More importantly, however, we have not only shown that there exist belief constraints on commitment, but also isolated to a considerable degree the *content* of these beliefs. Because these constraints were derived, and the content elicited, through what I have tried to show is a basic self-conception and through the process of self-understanding and identity construction, we have been able to develop a more psychologically plausible story of how commitment functions and the place of beliefs in it.

In short, neopragmatism does not meet the requirement of (using Flanagan's term) psychological realism. But it is important to remember that this was a requirement that Rorty himself was sensitive to and in fact tried to meet. Although ironic solidarity and commitment in the face of radical doubt might be possible for the strong poet, they are not possible for us, given what we now know about commitment and the requirements imposed by self-understanding and identity, the basic conception of ourselves as inhabiting, at least in part, the objective standpoint. Rorty's liberal utopia seemed feasible so long as we operated with a naive understanding of the requirements of commitment. Neopragmatism tells us a nice story, but it simply does not square with the facts – facts which it has been the task of the present work to draw out and defend.

6.1.2 Allan Gibbard

Gibbard's norm-expressivism was really the flip-side to Rorty's challenge to moral realism. While Rorty denied that realist beliefs could ever be true since they failed to represent anything, Gibbard denied that beliefs had any particular role to play in our acceptance of norms and in the governance by norms of our actions; rather, all this could be explained without any appeal to beliefs or facts. While Rorty represented the antirealist challenge, Gibbard represented the noncognitivist one. The question for Gibbard was not whether he presented us with a psychologically plausible story, but whether he offered a *unified* account of our normative practices: one that could explain (a) how we attach objectivity to norms in a manner consistent with the principles of norm-expressivism and (b) how norms play their roles and how we accept norms in light of the explanation of (a).

Now the justification for this demand for a unified account is based on both the standards of economy and simplicity regarding theory choice, as well as the limitations defined in chapter 5 regarding causal, would-be scientific accounts of human action. In so far as we seek to "make sense" of our actions or practices, then an essential criterion for the explanations we reach will be how well they enhance, or at least do not confound, our self-understanding. That is, when we seek to explain an action, we cannot take an exclusively third-person perspective toward the action – a stance that assumes the relevance of causal criteria, which in turn assumes the reducibility of action to an event and ignores an action's meaning component – but must instead try to reconstitute the agent's own understanding of her action. When we move away from third-person, event-centered, causal accounts, to first-person, agent-centered, "holistic" or unified explanations, we see in what ways Gibbard's account fails as an adequate explanation of our normative practices.

One of the main criticisms I have lodged against Gibbard was that he simply assumed some of the central "facts" that needed to be explained – for example, the fact of commitment and the fact of norm acceptance – and that it was only by assuming such facts that his norm-expressivist account could get started. Given that we already have certain commitments, or that we already accept certain norms as objective, then and only then is Gibbard able to tell a nonfactualist story of how these norms operate. Yet the real challenge is to explain these prior facts within a norm-expressivist framework, and under the "first-person" constraints of explanation. That is, we must ask how an agent understands her commitments, or the standpoint-independent validity she ascribes to certain norms, in light of the principles of norm-expressivism. That is not all. If Gibbard is in fact claiming to offer an adequate account of our normative practices, then he must also explain how this understanding fits with the roles norms are supposed to play in action and avowal. This is what a unified, self-transparent explanation requires. Under these requirements, however, Gibbard cannot explain the facts of commitment, let alone some of the key concepts in his story, most notably, conversational demands and sincere acceptance of norms.

To accept a norm (or commitment), rather than merely adhere to it, involves internalizing the norm, or some central features of it, which means in part that it be incorporated into one's "cognitive response set." Part of this set is constituted by an objectivist self-conception. Thus if one sincerely accepts a norm, one must successfully incorporate it into one's self-conception, which means that norm must be seen or believed to be objectively valid; that is, its endorsement or acceptance can be supported by reasons which hold for persons *generally* – reasons which are independent of that person's particular desires or perspective. (It is important to note that these are only *justifying reasons and not motivating reasons.*) Although Gibbard does not spell this out – indeed he actively avoids the question of what it is to be objective – this is in fact what standpoint-independent validity means.

Therefore, for an agent to make conversational demands on others essentially requires that she see these demands as objectively valid, which means that she represents them not only to others *but to herself* as supported by objectively valid reasons – reasons which in turn purport to reflect the way things are independently of her own idiosyncratic tendencies; that is, she represents or views these reasons as themselves representing a fact. Sincere conversational demands are possible only on the assumption of factualist (or what I have called realist) beliefs. And it is only through such factualist beliefs that an agent can reach some sort of self-understanding regarding the claims she is making on others: they answer the important questions of why she accepts the norms she does and why she makes certain demands on others. It is as a consequence of the objectivist self-conception, and of the need to explain the phenomenon of conversational demands from the perspective of the agent, that we are able to see the incompleteness of Gibbard's norm-expressivism.

Returning to the two-pronged challenge mentioned above (to explain (a) how we attach objectivity to norms in a manner consistent with the principles of norm-expressivism and (b) how norms play their roles and how we accept norms in light of the explanation of (a)), we see how Gibbard fails on both points. Given what we know about accepting a norm or having a commitment, norm-expressivism is wholly at odds with this, since it leaves no place for the factualist beliefs which are crucially involved in this process. Norm-expressivism does not have the tools at its disposal to explain how one gets to the point of norm acceptance, but can only tell a story (albeit incomplete) of what it is we do once we accept these norms: it does not have the tools needed to support the foundation on which the theory itself rests. As we saw in the previous chapters, these factualist-realist beliefs are needed for commitment, as well as norm acceptance, assuming they are alike, in order to fulfill its roles – in the language of action theory once again, they are functionally required. I showed how B2 beliefs regarding the objective basis of one's commitment were needed not only for self-understanding and identity, but for the very stability of the commitment (and again, acceptance of the norm) itself. A norm-expressivist story not only confounds self-understanding, since it requires us to accept and act on norms or commitments that potentially do not fit our objectivist self-conception – indeed, it leaves us with no criteria for determining how they might so fit – but in doing so it also undermines the stability of the norm or commitment and so also their role in what Gibbard called normative governance. If norm-expressivism is true, then norms cannot play the roles attributed to them, which were among the chief *explananda* of the theory: Gibbard has not explained our normative practices; rather, he has explained them away. But if the conservation of a practice is a measure of the adequacy of a theory, it should be clear that norm-expressivism is thoroughly inadequate. In short, the norm-expressivist picture falls apart in the face of the dynamics of commitment, the constraints on belief, and the conditions imposed by our self-conception and the requirements of self-understanding.

Finally, what of the fact of commitment? Recall that Gibbard provided us with two broad frameworks through which we were supposed to understand our normative practices generally; these were parochialism and relativism. Parochialism, I have shown, was incoherent. Relativism, for its part, relied on the fact of commitments – the view that commitments somehow mysteriously emerged through an almost organic process: we just had them. In being committed to a certain community, i.e., in having "communitarian commitments," some norms will apply validly for me that might not apply to others, and this, Gibbard says, is the basis of relativism. The norms that then emerge within the community can now be said to be held for a reason since they are norms that are part of the "ethos" to which the individuals are committed.

I said in chapter 2 that this sketch of relativism was incomplete since there was a crucial gap between the lower-order norms that emerged within the community and the acceptance of higher-order norms directing one to abide by the lower-order norms. Gibbard tried to fill in this gap with the fact of communitarian commitment which he likened to existential commitment, a kind of commitment that is possible only for individuals who accept voluntaristic norms – norms that "direct one to be governed by whatever norms one designates to oneself" (Gibbard, *Wise Choices*, p. 209). There is an increasingly *ad hoc* flavor to this story as Gibbard tries to patch the spreading holes in his account of relativism. For the central question that needs to be answered is importantly left unanswered by Gibbard, namely, what is it about a commitment to one's community and its grounds that lead one to accept certain norms? The fact of commitment needs an explanation and Gibbard does not, or cannot, provide one. Once we set aside the norm-expressivist and neopragmatist frameworks, we are quite able to explain this fact.

Quite simply, we accept the commitments we do because we believe them to be objectively valuable or worthwhile. This is the central constraint on substantive commitments, of which a communitarian commitment would certainly be one. The "deep rationale" supporting the higher-order norms is that they are "getting it right," "are true," or "hit on the facts." And when these statements are unpacked, what we will uncover are the reasons supporting the impersonal values which underwrite the commitment: reasons regarding what we take to be the human good, facts about human nature, or the requirements of human flourishing.[1] In so far as these factualist beliefs are indispensable to our explanation and understanding of these aspects of our normative practices, they are to an equal extent an ineliminable part of any adequate theory purporting to explain this segment of human reality. According to the Indispensability Thesis, Gibbard's norm-expressivism cannot be correct since it is incompatible with the possibility of such beliefs.

Gibbard's story does not decisively silence the proponents of factualism and realism. On the contrary, we see how factualist-realist accounts are crucial to the explanation of some of the central phenomena Gibbard set out to explain. The question of whether in the final analysis Gibbard's story cuts in any way against realism can be made even more prominent if we extend his norm-expressivism to other areas of human practice.

Gibbard's nonfactualist story of how our normative practices devel-

---

[1] These reasons can, and often will, be sensitive to local conditions so that, given my circumstances, the norms that I accept can still validly apply to me without applying to others in very different circumstances. Some *pluralism* is still possible.

oped could in fact be applied to almost any domain of human life.[2] That he can give a story of the "evolution" of our moral practices without referring to any moral facts loses its punch as an argument against realism in ethics when we consider that we can give similar nonfactualist accounts of the development of science, to take the most obvious example, without having to conclude that science does not describe any facts. Not only can this be done, it has been done. This is the externalist program in the history of science.

Consider Robert Merton's[3] famous thesis that the embodiment of the Puritan complex of values – utilitarianism, intramundane asceticism, empiricism, and antitraditionalism – in the culture of seventeenth century England was crucial to the development of modern science. Puritanism supported a system of values, or norms, that legitimized a new pattern of conduct which came to be known as organized scientific activity. Right away we see the parallels between Merton's thesis and Gibbard's norm-expressivism: proto-, or perhaps primordial, Puritan norms, e.g., those guiding feelings such as shame and guilt, legitimized a new pattern of conduct which came to be known as organized moral activity. Just as early hominids were subject to normative influence, so were seventeenth century proto-scientists. For according to Merton, "[t]he Puritan advocacy of experimental science was not . . . the result of a reasoned process [but] the inevitable outcome of an *emotionally consistent circle of sentiment* and beliefs locking into a chain of non-logic *various designated activities which satisfied these sentiments*" (Merton, *Science, Technology, and Society*, p. 115). Our new norm-expressivistic theory of science gains further grounding when we recall Gibbard's claim that the key to our moral life is cooperation, and that all of our normative practices can be explained in terms of the demands for coordination and harmony.

Now Steven Shapin and Simon Schaffer[4] have interestingly offered a similar story of the development of Robert Boyle's experimental program. They take Merton's externalist thesis one step further when they argue that the struggle between Hobbes and Boyle over the

---

[2] Indeed, as an account of normative governance and control, it is difficult to imagine to what domain of human life norm-expressivism would not apply.

[3] R. Merton, *Science, Technology, and Society in Seventeenth Century England* (New York: H. Fertig, 1970).

[4] S. Shapin and S. Schaffer, *Leviathan and the Air-Pump* (Princeton: Princeton University Press, 1985).

source of legitimate knowledge is best interpreted as reflecting a struggle over the means of protecting the *social order* in post-Restoration England. Whereas Boyle offered managed dissent, as exemplified in the rules of the experimental laboratory, as the best way of maintaining *civil harmony* among competing philosophical claims, Hobbes saw anything short of absolutely compelled assent from first principles as opening the way to civil war.

Nowhere in this externalist story of the history of science do we see any facts mentioned, just as Gibbard avoided reference to any normative facts in his story about the development of our normative practices. What are we to conclude? That there is no realm of facts that it is the task of science to describe? That science and its laws can be reduced to the language of sociology, economics, and political science? No. To do so is to overextend the very plausible claim that Puritanism had a role in legitimizing the *practice* of science, to conclusions regarding the *content* of science. Simply because we can give a nonfactualist account of the development of scientific or normative practices, this does not warrant us making any claims regarding the status of the putative facts of science or ethics. On the other hand, if we want to buy Gibbard's story regarding ethics, we have little reason not to buy the naive externalist account of science. If we follow Gibbard, the price of rejecting moral realism *for the reasons he gives* becomes extremely high.

6.1.3 Simon Blackburn and quasi-realism

Despite the foregoing discussion, one might think that the argument is not yet complete until it answers Simon Blackburn's quasi-realism.[5] Blackburn's quasi-realist is the person who, starting from an antirealist position, is able "to mimic the intellectual practices supposedly definitive of realism" (Blackburn, *Essays*, p. 15). Quasi-realism is essentially a sophisticated form of projectivism that is apparently able to avoid the standard objections to its more naive predecessors: objections to the effect that a projectivist account is not able to retain the phenomenological feel of obligation or duty that accompanies our various evaluative commitments, and must attribute systematic error to our evaluative practices.

[5] S. Blackburn, *Spreading the Word* (Oxford: Oxford University Press, 1984); and *Essays in Quasi-Realism* (Oxford: Oxford University Press, 1993).

According to the projectivist theory, "when we announce [our] A-commitments . . . we are neither reacting to a given distribution of A-properties, nor speculating about one," but simply "projecting" a certain attitude on the world (Blackburn, *Word*, p. 186). This raises the worry that "the projection is only explicable if we mistake the origins of our evaluative practices . . . [It seems that] were we aware of these origins we would give up some or all of our tendency to practice as if evaluative commitments had truth-conditions, and were not expressive in origin and in their essential nature" (*ibid.*, p. 171).

Blackburn suggests, however, that there is in fact no mistake: and the enterprise of showing "that even on antirealist grounds there is nothing improper, nothing "diseased" in projected predicates [is] the enterprise of *quasi-realism*" (*ibid.*). More importantly, Blackburn also claims that the quasi-realist is not guilty of two-level thinking, of an incoherence between his theory and practice. "Quasi-realist projectivism," says Blackburn,

> is *not* the position that one says realist-sounding things for public consumption, but denies them in his heart, so to speak. He affirms *all that could ever* properly *be meant* by saying that there are real obligations. When the context of discussion is that of first-order commitment, he is as solid as the most virtuous moralist. It is just that the explanation of why there are obligations and the rest is not quite that of untutored common sense. It deserves to be called anti-realist because it avoids the view that when we moralize we respond to, and describe, an independent aspect of reality (Blackburn, *Essays*, p. 157).

Given that Blackburn claims that we can retain our evaluative commitments and be quasi-realists without having to be theoretically akratic, the question arises: need we start all over again? Fortunately, the answer is no. The arguments Blackburn advances in favor of his projectivist theory are fairly complex, relating to topics in the philosophy of language and issues on supervenience. Yet in order to address the quasi-realist objections, it will not be necessary to enter into these new debates, since some of the key claims and arguments Blackburn makes can readily be answered once we see how they fit in with the earlier discussions.

The first thing to notice is that Blackburn is still caught in Mackie's metaphysical spell: moral properties and facts are some mysterious entities "out there," wherever that might be. Moral antirealism is defined by the view that we do not respond to or describe an "independent aspect of reality" (*ibid.*); that when we announce evaluative commitments, we are not reacting to evaluative "properties" (Blackburn, *Word*, p. 186); and that our explanations in ethics "make no irreducible or essential appeal to the existence of moral 'properties' or 'facts'; they demand no 'ontology' of morals" (Blackburn, *Essays*, p. 175). Indeed, for Blackburn, one of the advantages of antirealism is its ontological economy: it "asks no more from the world than what we know is there" (Blackburn, *Word*, p. 182). Yet when we speak of an "independent reality," we must ask ourselves, independent of whom? Surely facts about human beings are facts about the world, in so far as we are part of the metaphysical furniture of the universe. There is no special domain of facts to which moral realism appeals: it simply invokes facts about the world, human beings, and the effects the former have on the latter, and so remains well within the confines of the standard facts of which antirealists and noncognitivists are so fond. I readily agree that when we make evaluative commitments, we are not "responding" or reacting to various "wrongness" or "rightness" properties. Moral realism makes no extraordinary additions to our ontology, but just emphasizes the obvious but apparently forgotten point that we too are part of the world. This said, my main objection to Blackburn's quasi-realism will not concern the metaphysical or linguistic issues but, rather, the nature of commitment.

Quasi-realist projectivism, which, one must remember, is a form of emotivism, is able to accommodate commitment so nicely because, according to Blackburn, commitment is nothing more than an attitude (Blackburn, *Word*, p. 188; *Essays*, p. 168). He explicitly, and crucially, denies that it is a belief. There is a striking similarity on this point between Blackburn and Gibbard. Indeed, Blackburn in many respects outlines Gibbard's more detailed theory on normative acceptance and governance. Like Gibbard, Blackburn claims that the "state of mind" of commitment begins as a "stance, or conative state or pressure on choice and action . . . [whose] function is to mediate the move from features of a situation to a reaction" (Blackburn, *Essays*, p. 168). Blackburn gives considerable merit to the evolutionary accounts of the "emergence of cooperative and altruistic stances" and claims that commitments, like Gibbard's norms, result from a "pressure toward action [that] can be associated variously with pride, shame, or self-respect" (*ibid.*, pp. 168–9).

It should be clear why the discussion of Blackburn had to come at

192

the end. In answering Gibbard, we at the same time answered Blackburn; if the former is wrong, then so is the latter. The argument against Gibbard was an important step in showing that commitment is *not* simply an attitude, but is instead structured by beliefs. To the extent that commitment is essentially cognitive, the happy cohabitation of quasi-realism and ethical commitment is seriously jeopardized, for the quasi-realist is only able to avoid a "schizoid" stance (to use Blackburn's term, *Word*, p. 197) toward his moral commitments provided that commitment is just an attitude. By showing that commitment is in fact cognitive, we undermine one of the central claims of quasi-realism and its apparent advantage over other more naive forms of emotivism and noncognitivism.

There are two central theses in Blackburn's naturalist, quasi-realist account of ethics: "(1) the fundamental identification of the commitment in question as something other than a belief and (2) the existence of a neat, natural account of why the state that it is should exist" (Blackburn, *Essays* p. 169). According to Blackburn, (1) and (2) show that an "external explanatory story" of ethics is possible: "that nature and our theory of nature surround our ethical commitments in a way that gives us a *place* from which to theorize about them" (*ibid.*, p. 174). If I am correct, (1) no longer offers the appropriate support. Thus, without entering the debates on supervenience and linguistics, our analysis of commitment allows us to answer Blackburn's quasi-realism. In short, the potential challenge Blackburn posed was already addressed in the response to Gibbard, and in the establishment of the belief structure of commitment.[6]

6.2 REVIEW AND PROJECTION

The analysis of commitment has not only helped us define more clearly its structure and function, but has also shown its relation to issues in moral realism. Moreover, in the course of the analysis we have defended a new methodology in the explanation of human action.

The absence of any broad theory of commitment played well into the hands of any number of theorists – from liberals to communitar-

---

[6] Blackburn's appeal to an externalist, third-person account of ethics and to the possibility of finding a place outside our normative practices from which we can theorize about them, also violates the criteria of explanation discussed in chapter 2.

ians, and from neopragmatists to realists – who could safely make any claims regarding the ability or inability of certain theories to explain, retain, conserve, or threaten, the possibility of commitment without fear of challenge. Commitment was, for many of those involved in the debates, an opaque concept about which one could conjecture freely. This book instead provides an extended analysis of commitment.

Drawing on the literature from a number of disciplines as well as our own common-sense understanding of the term, I have defined three central features of commitment: its stability and potential revisability; its practical necessity (or action-guiding force); and its role in self-understanding and identity. It is on the basis of this generally accepted picture of commitment and its central features that we have been able to discern commitment's structure and develop the arguments regarding its belief constraints. In the course of these arguments, I introduced the one brute fact of the book – the objectivist self-conception. Readers will, perhaps, be most troubled by this fact since no direct proof of it is given. Rather, what I have tried to do is show how the objectivist picture fits better with the undeniably cognitive aspect of our self-conception (recall the arguments against Frankfurt-type models and Velleman's theory of intrinsic desires), and how it not only served to stabilize commitment and enhance self-understanding, but also informs, to a considerable extent, many of our normative practices. Indeed, we find appeals to it not only in real-life examples in the biography of Eugene Debs, but also in Richard Rorty's injunction to extend as widely as possible the notion "we," and in Allan Gibbard's discussion of standpoint-independent norms and conversational demands. Despite the absence of a direct proof for an objectivist self-conception, there is ample evidence supporting it. Such a self-conception was a key step in the argument for realist evaluative beliefs and their place in substantive commitments.

The context in which the analysis of commitment and its conditions has been pursued should not, of course, be forgotten. The aim has been to provide an indirect argument for moral realism. Breaking from the well-worn paths in which the debate over moral realism is cast as (merely) an extension of debates in the language of philosophy (what moral terms mean), or epistemology (how moral knowledge is possible), or the philosophy of science (where moral facts fit in causal explanations), I have instead opened up a new approach to the problem by taking seriously the question Nicholas Sturgeon once raised, namely, what difference does it make whether moral realism is true? Assuming that the most interesting difference would be a practical one, I have chosen to enter this debate from the point of view of the philosophy of action.

Now I say that I have sought, and have hopefully provided, an *indirect* proof of moral realism: a proof in which I do not show that moral realism itself is true, but that moral realism is the only theory capable of explaining certain key components of our moral experience, in this case commitment. If in fact realist evaluative beliefs are required for commitment, and since such beliefs make sense or are possible only within the context of a realist metaethical theory, then to that extent we can, indeed must, assume moral realism is true, provided of course that we want to retain such things as commitment. The truth of moral realism is what Kant might call a postulate of practical reason. Although it is still open to the proponents of irrealism in ethics to reject this conclusion, they can do so only at the price of rejecting at the same time the possibility of commitment. Thus, the goal has been in part to make the cost of rejecting moral realism prohibitively high. Yet since neopragmatists such as Rorty, and noncognitivists like Gibbard, want to retain such things as solidarity – a variant of commitment – and make critical use of such notions as communitarian commitments, and since these are possible only through realist evaluative beliefs, we see how deeply incoherent their systems are: an incoherence that was untroubling so long as no examination of commitment was forthcoming. We now see, however, that they cannot have it both ways – noncognitivist commitment is as untenable as ironic solidarity.

In order to reach the conclusion regarding the role of realist evaluative beliefs in substantive commitments, the final step in the indirect proof for moral realism, I have introduced a new method of analysis of human action.

The initial shift away from strictly causal explanations first took place in the discussion of Mele's work on intention, where I endorsed rational explanations of action. In the examination of substantive commitments, this shift became even greater as I focused on the highly interpretive dimension of human action. It was here that I argued for the Indispensability Thesis (similar to Charles Taylor's Best Account principle, but one grounded in the self-defined limits of cognitive science and folk psychology, rather than hermeneutics).

Although this interpretive or quasi-functionalist approach to the analysis of action seems, at first glance, to be thoroughly opposed to the standard methods of action theory, I hope to have shown how in fact it grows out of action theory's own self-descriptions and self-ascribed goals. Action theory, in many important ways, misunderstands its explanatory capacities and mistakenly aspires to be a subdiscipline of the natural sciences. But when we take seriously the criteria for adequate causal explanations in the natural sciences, we find that the explanations given by many philosophers of action fall exceedingly short of them. At best, they tell us that the causes they postulate are "special" causes and cause action in the "right" way.

The causal paradigm plays an important role in many of the non-cognitivist and antirealist arguments, for it allows them to focus on actions as events in the world, which in turn encourages explanations from the third-person observer perspective, both of which are crucial for their arguments against value realism. Yet when we reveal the inadequacy of purely causal accounts of human action, and bring to light the highly interpretive dimension of such explanation, as well as the importance of self-understanding from the first-person perspective in these explanations, the arguments against values and their (causal) explanatory irrelevance fall apart. Rather, we see that a realist theory of value is indispensable to the explanation of certain categories of human action, most notably, commitment.

I want to underscore the point that this is not a purely external critique of action theory. As I showed in the discussion of Velleman's theory of the self and his instrumentalism of values, action theorists often have an ambiguous attitude toward causal explanations, and it is this ambiguity which served as the basis for the development and defense of the quasi-functionalist, interpretive analysis. The ambiguity consists in their odd conversion from being "causalists" about such things as values and moral facts, to "interpretationists" about folk psychological explanations.[7] That is, the defense they give (or would give) of such things as "beliefs" and "intentions" against neuroscientific reductions do not apply to values and moral facts, even though the reduction of their cherished mental states follows exactly

---

[7] William Child also distinguishes between "causalism" and "interpretationism" as two schools in the philosophy of mind, the former holding that causation is central to psychological explanation; and the latter holding that thought is interpretable. See, Child, *Causality.*

the same logic as their reduction of values. If they are "interpretationists" about intention, they have no reason not to be "interpretationists" about values.

Thus, unlike other critics of "scientism" such as Thomas Nagel and Charles Taylor, I have offered a defense of noncausal explanations that finds its roots in action theory itself.

Antirealists and noncognitivists in ethics, when pressed with the question of whether their theories are conservative of the practices they describe, respond in one of two ways: either they reassure us that they are, with little or no argument saying why; or they distinguish between the logical and psychological possibility of their theory, claiming that the only criterion they need to meet is the former. This new approach presents a challenge to both responses.

The view that psychological plausibility does in fact serve as a constraint on theory-building is becoming more widely accepted with the increasing influence of cognitive science, especially in the field of ethics.[8] As we learn more about how the mind forms and applies concepts, about the processes involved in identity constitution, and the ways in which the self is formed and influenced, we are in a better position to assess various theories on the basis of the kind of psychological assumptions implicit to their system. It seems only natural that if a theory is in fact not possible for beings like us – not that it is hard, or difficult, or demanding, but runs contrary to what we understand to be the requirements of a stable identity, for example, or effective agency – then that theory is just wrong. This is not to say that discoveries in cognitive science or new findings in human psychology will provide answers to particular normative questions: it is unlikely that Paul Churchland will discover, or even that Amos Tversky could have discovered, the definitive answer to the question "Is abortion wrong?" by examining cortical fibers or the behavior of 18–20-year-old student volunteers.[9] That certainly is not what I am suggesting. The point is, rather, that our best knowledge of human psychology and of how the mind works will act as minimally necessary conditions that any theory regarding possible human conduct must meet. And

---

[8] See, for example, Larry May *et. al.* (eds.), *Mind and Morals: Essays on Cognitive Science and Ethics* (Cambridge, MA: MIT Press, 1996).

[9] For an extended critique of the relevance of cognitive science to normative ethics, see Virginia Held, "Whose Agenda? Ethics versus Cognitive Science," in May *et al.* (eds.), *Mind and Morals*, pp. 69–87.

since metaethical theories concern our normative practices – what it is we are doing when we say "stealing is bad," or when we make conversational demands on others, or are involved in expanding the scope of the term "we liberals" – they too must pass the test of psychological plausibility. Contrary to what many antirealists in ethics say, logical possibility is not the only condition a theory must meet. Practice does in fact constrain theory.

The arguments presented here have followed this constraint quite closely, and in doing so have repeatedly asked of each of the main figures in this essay – Richard Rorty, Allan Gibbard, and David Velleman – whether they do in fact offer a plausible psychological sketch of the human agent; if what they say accords with what we know (at this time) to be the internal working of a person. In each case, the answer we found was negative. Until this theory of commitment is challenged, moral realism remains the only framework capable of explaining and retaining this central aspect of our normative practice.

Bibliography

Adams, R. "Moral Faith," *The Journal of Philosophy* 92 (1995): 75–95.

Annas, J. "Doing Without Objective Values: Ancient And Modern strategies," in M. Schofield and G. Striker (eds.), *The Norms of Nature*, (Cambridge: Cambridge University Press, 1986), pp. 3–29.

Anscombe, E. *Intention* (Oxford: Blackwell, 1957).

Audi, R. "Intention, Cognitive Commitment, and Planning," *Synthese* 86 (1991): 361–78.

   The Structure of Justification (Cambridge: Cambridge University Press, 1993).

Ayer, A. J. *Language, Truth and Logic* (London: Camelot Press, 1953).

Bambrough, R. *Moral Scepticism and Moral Knowledge* (New Jersey: Humanities Press, 1979).

Bartley, W. W. *The Retreat to Commitment* (LaSalle: Open Court, 1984).

Beck, L. W. *A Commentary on Kant's Critique of Practical Reason* (Chicago: University of Chicago Press, 1960).

Becker, H. S. "Notes on the Concept of Commitment," *American Journal of Sociology* 64 (1960): 32–40.

Becker, T. E. "Foci and Bases of Commitment: Are they Distinctions Worth Making?" *Academy of Management Journal* 35 (1992): 232–44.

Benn, S. I. and Gaus, G. F. "Practical Rationality and Commitment," *American Philosophical Quarterly* 23 (1986): 255–66

Bernet, R. *et al. An Introduction to Husserlian Phenomenology* (Evanston: Northwestern University Press, 1993)

Blackburn, S. *Spreading the Word* (Oxford: Oxford University Press, 1984).

   Essays in Quasi-Realism (Oxford: Oxford University Press, 1993)

Bleicher, J. *Contemporary Hermeneutics: Hermeneutics as Method, Philosophy and Critique* (London: Routledge, 1980)

Blustein, J. *Care and Commitment: Taking the Personal Point of View* (New York: Oxford University Press, 1991).

Bratman, M. "Taking Plans Seriously," *The Review of Metaphysics* 9 (1983):271–87.

"Davidson's Theory of Intention," in B. Vermazen and M. B. Hintikka (eds.), *Essays on Davidson: Actions and Events* (Oxford: Clarendon Press, 1985), pp. 13–26.

Intention, Plans and Practical Reason [IPP] (Cambridge, MA: Harvard University Press, 1987).

"Intention and Personal Policies," in J. Tomberlin (ed.), *Philosophical Perspectives*, vol. III: *Philosophy of Mind and Action Theory* (Atascadero: Ridgeview, 1989).

Brink, D. *Moral Realism and the Foundations of Ethics* (New York: Cambridge University Press, 1989).

Brommel, B. J. *Eugene V. Debs: Spokesman for Labor and Socialism* (Chicago: Charles H. Kerr Publishing Co., 1978).

Bruzina, R. and Wilshire, B. (eds.). *Phenomenology: Dialogues and Bridges* (Albany: State University of New York Press, 1982).

Buchanan, A. "Assessing the Communitarian Critique of Liberalism," *Ethics* 99 (1989): 852–82.

Buchanan, B. II. "Building Organizational Commitments: The Socialization of Managers in Work Organizations," *Administrative Science Quarterly* (1974): 533–46.

Burnyeat, M. "Can the Sceptic Live his Scepticism?" in M. Schofield *et al.* (eds.), *Doubt and Dogmatism* (Oxford: Clarendon Press, 1980).

Calhoun, C. "Standing for Something," *The Journal of Philosophy* 92 (1995): 235–60.

Camus, A. *The Stranger*, trans. Matthew Ward (New York: Vintage International, 1988).

Chiappori, P. "Anticipations Rationelles et Conventions," in André Orléan (ed.), *Analyse Economique des Conventions* (Paris: Presses Universitaires de France, 1994), pp 61–78.

Child, W. *Causality, Interpretation, and the Mind* (Oxford: Oxford University Press, 1994).

Christensen, S. M. and Turner, D. R. (eds.). *Folk Psychology and the Philosophy of Mind* (New Jersey: Lawrence Erlbaum Associates, 1993).

Clark, D. A. "Depressive, Anxious and Intrusive Thoughts in Psychiatric Inpatients and Outpatients," *Behavioral Research and Therapy* 30 (1992): 93–102.

Connolly, J. and Keutner, T. (eds.). *Hermeneutics vs. Science?* (Notre Dame: University of Notre Dame Press, 1988).

Contat, M. and Rybalka, M. (eds.). *Les Ecrits de Sartre: Chronologie, Bibliographie Commentée* (Paris: Gallimard, 1970).

Cryle, P. M. *The Thematics of Commitment* (Princeton: Princeton University Press, 1985).

Davidson, D. *Essays on Actions and Events* (Oxford: Clarendon Press, 1980). *Inquiries into Truth and Interpretation* (Oxford: Clarendon Press, 1984).

Davis, W. "A Causal Theory of Intending," *American Philosophical Quarterly* 21 (1988): 43–54.

Dennett, D. C. *The Intentional Stance* (Cambridge, MA: MIT Press, 1987).

Descombes, V. *Les Institutions du Sens* (Paris: Les Editions de Minuit, 1996).

Dodier, N. "Représenter ses Actions," in P. Pharo and L. Quéré (eds.), *Les Formes de l'Action: Sémantique et Sociologie* (Paris: Ecole des Hautes Etudes en Sciences Sociales, 1990), pp. 115–48.

Downton, J. V. Jr. "The Determinants of Commitment," *Humanitas* 8 (1972): 55–78.

Dretske, F. *Explaining Behavior: Reasons in a World of Causes* (Cambridge, MA: MIT Press, 1988).

Dumouchel, P. "Social Systems and Cognition," unpublished paper (Paris: CREA, Ecole Polytechnique).

Empiricus, S. *Outlines of Pyrrhonism,* trans. Benson Mates (New York: Oxford University Press, 1996).

Evnine, S. *Donald Davidson* (Stanford: Stanford Univerity Press, 1991).

Farber, M. "The Ideal of a Presuppositionless Philosophy," in M. Farber (ed.), *Philosophical Essays in Memory of Edmund Husserl* (New York: Greenwood, 1968), pp. 44–64.

Ferrara, A. "The Unbearable Seriousness of Irony," *Philosophy and Social Criticism* 16 (1990): 81–107.

Fischer, J. M. and Ravizza, M. (eds.). *Perspectives on Moral Responsibility* (Ithaca: Cornell University Press, 1993).

Flanagan, O. *Varieties of Moral Personality: Ethics and Psychological Realism* (Cambridge, MA: Harvard University Press, 1991).

Flanagan, O. and Rorty, A. (eds.). *Identity, Character, and Morality: Essays in Moral Psychology* (Cambridge, MA: MIT Press, 1990).

Forrester, M. *Moral Language* (Madison: University of Wisconsin Press, 1982).

Frankfurt, H. "Freedom of the Will and the Concept of a Person," in Watson (ed.).
    The Importance of What We Care About (Cambridge: Cambridge University Press, 1988).

"Identification and Wholeheartedness," in Fischer and Ravizza (eds.), pp. 170–87.

Gauld, A. and Shotter, J. *Human Action and its Psychological Investigation* (London: Routledge and Kegan Paul, 1977).

Gibbard, A. *Wise Choices, Apt Feelings: A Theory of Normative Judgment* (Cambridge, MA: Harvard University Press, 1990).

Gillespie, N. (ed.). *Spindel Conference 1986: Moral Realism, Southern Journal of Philosophy, Supplement* 24 (1986).

Goldhagen, D. J. *Les Bourreaux Volontaires de Hitler: Les Allemands Ordinaires et L'Holocaust* (Paris: Editions de Seuil, 1997).

Greenwood, J. D. (ed.). *The Future of Folk Psychology: Intentionality and Cognitive Science* (Cambridge: Cambridge University Press, 1991).

Grice, H. P. "Intention and Uncertainty," *Proceedings of the British Academy* 57 (1971): 263–79.

Habermas, J. "A Review of Gadamer's *Truth and Method*," in F. R. Dallmary and T. McCarthy (eds.), *Understanding and Social Inquiry* (Notre Dame: University of Notre Dame Press, 1977).

"The Hermeneutic Claim to Universality," in Bleicher.

Hampshire, S. "Decision, Intention, and Certainty,: *Mind* 67 (1958): 1–12.

Innocence and Experience (Cambridge, MA: Harvard University Press, 1989).

Hare, R. M. *Freedom and Reason* (Oxford: Oxford University Press, 1963).

Harman, G. *The Nature of Morality* (New York: Oxford University Press, 1977).

Change in View (Cambridge, MA: MIT Press, 1986).

"Moral Explanations of Natural Facts," in Gillespie.

"Willing and Intending," in R. Grandy and R. Werner (eds.), *Philosophical Grounds of Rationality* (Oxford: Oxford University Press, 1986).

Honderich, T. (ed.). *Morality and Objectivity* (London: Routledge and Kegan Paul, 1985).

Hurley, S. *Natural Reasons* (Oxford: Oxford University Press, 1989).

Husserl, E. "Philosophy as Rigorous Science," trans. Q. Lauer, in P. McCormick and F. Elliston, *Husserl: Shorter Works* (Notre Dame: University of Notre Dame Press, 1981)

"Husserl's Inaugural Lecture at Freiburg im Breisgau (1917)," trans. R. W. Jordan, *ibid.*

"'Phenomenology,'" Edmund Husserl's article for the *Encyclopaedia Britannica* (1927), trans. R. Palmer, *ibid.*

"Author's Preface to the English Edition of *Ideas*," trans. W. R. B. Gibson, *ibid.*

Jackson, T. P. "The Theory and Practice of Discomfort: Richard Rorty and Pragmatism," *The Thomist* 51 (1987): 270–98.

"The Possibilities of Scepticisms: Philosophy and Theology without Apology," *Metaphilosophy* 21 (1990): 303–21.

James, W. "The Will to Believe," in J. McDermott (ed.), *The Writings of William James* (Chicago: University of Chicago Press, 1977).

Johnson, M. *Moral Imagination: Implications of Cognitive Science for Ethics* (Chicago: University of Chicago Press, 1993).

Josephs, L. "Empathic Character Analysis," *The American Journal of Psychoanalysis* 54 (1994): 41–54.

Jouard, S. M. "Some Notes on the Experience of Commitment," *Humanitas* 8 (1972): 5–8.

Kant, I. *Religion within the Limits of Reason Alone*, trans. T. M. Greene and Hoyt H. Hudson (New York: 1960).

Groundwork of the Metaphysics of Morals, trans. H. J. Paton (New York: Harper and Row, 1964).

The Critique of Practical Reason, trans. L. W. Beck (Chicago: University of Chicago Press, 1976).

Kavka, G. "The Toxin Puzzle," *Analysis* 43 (1983): 33–6.

Keke, J. "Constancy and Purity," *Mind* 92 (1983): 499–518.

Kemp, P. *Théorie de l'Engagement: Pathétique de l'Engagement* (Paris: Editions du Seuil, 1972).

Poétique de l'Engagment (Paris: Editions du Seuil, 1972).

Kim, J. *Philosophy of Mind* (Boulder: Westview Press, 1996).

Kolnai, A. *Ethics, Value and Reality* (London: Athlone Press, 1977).

Lennon, K. *Explaining Human Action* (La Salle: Open Court, 1990).

Lepore, E. and McLaughlin, B. (eds.). *Actions and Events: Perspectives on the Philosophy of Donald Davidson* (Oxford: Basil Blackwell, 1985).

Lévy-Strauss, C. "Introduction à l'œuvre de Marcel Mauss," in Marcel Mauss, *Sociologie et Anthropologie* (Paris: Presses Universitaires de France, 1950), pp. ix–lii.

Lief, H. I. and Kaplan, H. S. "Ego-Dystonic Homosexuality," *Journal of Sex and Marital Therapy* 12 (1986): 259–66.

Lomasky, L. *Persons, Rights, and the Moral Community* (Oxford: Oxford University Press, 1987).

Lovibond, S. *Imagination and Realism in Ethics* (Oxford: Basil Blackwell,1983).

Lyotard, J. *La Phénomenologie* (Paris: Presses Universitaires de France, 1954).

McCann, H. "Settled, Objective and Rational Constraints," *American Philosophical Quarterly* 28 (1991): 25–36.

McCarthy, T. *The Critical Theory of Jürgen Habermas* (Cambridge, MA: MIT Press, 1978).

McDowell, J. "Virtue and Reason," *Monist* 62 (1979): 331–50.

McFall, L. "Integrity," *Ethics* 98 (1987): 5–20.

McNaughton, D. *Moral Vision* (New York: Basil Blackwell, 1988).

MacIntyre, A. *After Virtue* (Notre Dame: University of Notre Dame Press, 1984).

Mackie, J. L. *Ethics: Inventing Right and Wrong* (New York: Penguin Books, 1977).

Marcel, G. *Etre et Avoir [EA]* (Paris: Aubier, 1935).
   Du Refus à l'Invocation [RI] (Paris: Gallimard, 1940).
   Homo Viator [HV] (Paris: Aubier, 1945).
   Présence et Immortalité [PI] (Paris: Flammarion, 1959).

May, L. *et. al.* (eds.). *Mind and Morals: Essays on Ethics and Cognitive Science* (Cambridge, MA: MIT Press, 1996).

Mele, A. *Springs of Action* (New York: Oxford University Press, 1992).

Merleau-Ponty, M. *Phenomenology of Perception,* trans. Colin Smith (London: Routledge and Kegan Paul, 1962).

Merton, R. K. *Science, Technology, and Society in Seventeenth Century England* (New York: H. Fertig, 1970).

Moore, H. "Paul Ricoeur: Action, Meaning and Text," in Christopher Tilley (ed.), *Reading Material Culture: Structuralism, Hermeneutics, and Post-structuralism* (Oxford: Blackwell, 1990).

Nagel, T. *The Possibility of Altruism* (Oxford: Clarendon Press, 1970).
   The View from Nowhere (Oxford: Oxford University Press, 1986).

Nielsen, K. "Morality and Commitment," *Idealistic Studies* 7 (1977): 94–107.

Novacek, J. and Lazarus, R. S. "The Structure of Personal Commitments," *Journal of Personality* 58 (1990): 692–715.

O'Reilly, C. III and Chatman, J. "Organizational Commitment and Psychological Attachment: The Effects of Compliance, Identification, and Internalization on Prosocial Behavior," *Journal of Applied Psychology* 71 (1986): 492–9.

Platts, M. *Ways of Meaning* (London: Routledge and Kegan Paul, 1979).

Plourde, S. *Vocabulaire Philosophique de Gabriel Marcel* (Paris: Editions du Cerf, 1985).

Putnam, H. *Realism with a Human Face* (Cambridge, MA: Harvard University Press, 1990).

Railton, P. "Moral Realism," *The Philosophical Review* 95 (1986): 163–207.

"Nonfactualism about Normative Discourse," *Philosophy and Phenomenological Research* 52 (1992): 961–8.

Rawls, J. *A Theory of Justice* (Cambridge, MA: Harvard University Press, 1971).

Ricoeur, P. *Sémantique de l'Action* (lecture notes) (Louvain-la-Neuve: Université Catholique de Louvain, 1970–71).

Soi-même Comme un Autre (Paris: Seuil, 1990).

From Text to Action: Essays in Hermeneutics, vol. II, trans. K. Blamey and J. B. Thompson (Evanston: Northwestern University Press, 1991).

Oneself as Another, trans. K. Blamey (Chicago: University of Chicago Press, 1992).

Robins, M. *Promising, Intending, and Moral Autonomy* (Cambridge: Cambridge University Press, 1984).

Rorty, R. *The Linguistic Turn* (Chicago: University of Chicago Press, 1967).

Consequences of Pragmatism (Minneapolis: University of Minnesota Press, 1982).

Contingency, Irony, and Solidarity [*CIS*] (Cambridge: Cambridge University Press, 1989).

Objectivity, Relativism, and Truth: Philosophical Papers, vol. I. [*ORT*] (Cambridge: Cambridge University Press, 1991).

Sacks, O. *An Anthropologist on Mars* (New York: Vintage Books, 1995).

Salvatore, N. *Eugene V. Debs: Citizen and Socialist* (Chicago: University of Illinois Press, 1982).

Sayre-McCord, G. *Essays on Moral Realism* (Ithaca: Cornell University Press, 1988).

Scheffler, S. "Ethics, Personal Identity, and Ideals of the Person," *Canadian Journal of Philosophy* 12 (1982): 229–46.

Schilpp, P. A. and Hahn, L. E. (eds.). *The Philosophy of Gabriel Marcel* (La Salle: Open Court, 1984).

Shapin, S. and Schaffer, S. *Leviathan and the Air-Pump* (Princeton: Princeton University Press, 1985).

Sheldon, M. "Investments and Involvements as Mechanisms Producing

Commitment to the Organization," *Administrative Science Quarterly* (1971): 143–50.

Shklar, J. *Ordinary Vices* (Cambridge, MA: Harvard University Press, 1984).

Silber, J. "The Ethical Significance of Kant's Critique," in *Religion within the Limits of Reason Alone*, trans. Theodore M. Greene and Hoyt H. Hudson (New York: Harper and Row, 1960).

Solomon, R. *Phenomenology and Existentialism* (New York: Harper and Row, 1972).

Stevenson, C. L. *Ethics and Language* (New Haven: Yale University Press, 1944).

Stoudemire, A. *Clinical Psychiatry for Medical Students* (Philadelphia: J. B. Lippincott, 1990).

Stout, J. *Ethics After Babel* (Boston: Beacon Press, 1988).

Striker, G. "Sceptical Strategies," in Schofield *et al.* (eds.), *Doubt and Dogmatism* (Oxford: Clarendon Press, 1980), pp. 54–83.

Sturgeon, N. "Altruism, Solipsism and the Objectivity of Reasons," *Philosophical Review* 83 (1974): 374–402.

"Gibbard on Moral Judgment and Norms," *Ethics* 96 (1985): 22–33.

"Harman on Moral Explanations of Natural Facts," in Gillespie.

"What Difference Does it Make Whether Moral Realism is True?" in Gillespie.

"Nonmoral Explanations," in J. Tomberlin (ed.), *Philosophical Perspectives*, vol. VI: *Ethics* (Atascadero: Ridgeview, 1992).

Taylor, C. *Human Agency and Language: Philosophical Papers*, vol. I [*HA*] (Cambridge: Cambridge University Press, 1985).

Philosophy and the Human Sciences: Philosophical Papers, vol. II [*PHS*] (Cambridge: Cambridge University Press, 1985).

Sources of the Self [*SS*] (Cambridge, MA: Harvard University Press, 1989).

The Ethics of Authenticity (Cambridge, MA: Harvard University Press, 1991).

Taylor, G. *Pride, Shame, and Guilt* (Oxford: Clarendon Press, 1985).

Thompson, J. B. *Critical Hermeneutics* (Cambridge: Cambridge University Press, 1981).

Trigg, R. *Reason and Commitment* (Cambridge: Cambridge University Press, 1973).

Urmson, J. O. *The Emotive Theory of Ethics* (London: Hutchinson, 1968).

Van Hooft, S. "Obligation, Character, and Commitment," *Philosophy* 63 (1988): 345–62.

Velleman, J. D. *Practical Reflection* (Princeton: Princeton University Press, 1989).

Vermazen, B. "Objects of Intention," *Philosophical Studies* 71 (1993): 223–65.

von Wright, G. H. *Explanation and Understanding* (Ithaca: Cornell University Press, 1971).

Watson, G. (ed.). *Free Will* (Oxford: Oxford University Press, 1982).

"Free Agency," in *Free Will*, pp. 205–20.

Wiggins, D. *Needs, Values, Truth* (London: Basil Blackwell, 1987).

Williams, B. *Morality: An Introduction to Ethics* (New York: Harper and Row, 1972).

"Deciding to Believe," in *Problems of the Self* (Cambridge: Cambridge University Press, 1973).

Moral Luck (Cambridge: Cambridge University Press, 1981).

Ethics and the Limits of Philosophy (Cambridge, MA: Harvard University Press, 1985).

Wittgenstein, L. *Philosophical Investigations*, trans. G. E. M. Anscombe (New York: Macmillan, 1958).

Index

action
  causal theory of, 155–6, 158–9,
    162–3, 196
  explanation of, 22, 95, 105, 133
  hermeneutics of, 150–3
  interpretation of, 144, 146–50,
    159–60, 168
Adams, Robert, 90
Audi, Robert, 14

Blackburn, Simon, 190–3
Blustein, Jeffrey, 116, 118, 121
Bratman, Michael, 60, 66, 84

Calhoun, Cheshire, 108, 112
care, 120, 121
Chiappori, Pierre-André, 23
Child, William, 21
commitment, 1–4, 62–3, 86
  and confidence conditions,
    96–8
  and intention, 63–6, 84–5
  and norms, 14
  and policy, 68–78, 84–5
  belief constraints on, 102–14
  cognitive component of, 88–91
  existential, 27
  fact of, 30, 36, 185
  features of, 5
  filtering, role in, 105–8, 130
  intention-like, 5
  phenomenological explanation
    of, 57
  planning, role in, 113
  promisory, 99
  revision of, 78–83
  substantive, 5, 179–81

Davidson, Donald, 153–4, 157–8
Debs, Eugene V., 8–12, 48–9, 52–3
depression, cognitive aspect of, 89
  n. 3
desire, orders of, 107–8, 110
Dumouchel, Paul, 24–5

ego-dystonia, 112, 140, 142
Empiricus, Sextus, 51 n. 41
error theories, 20–6, 33

Flanagan, Owen, 7 n. 5, 169 n. 35
Fodor, Jerry, 172
folk psychology, 165
  defenses of, 161–7, 170
Føllesdal, Dagfinn, 158
Frankfurt, Harry, 106–7, 111
functionalism, 73

Gauld, Alan and Shotter, John, 155
Gibbard, Allan, 6, 12–14, 18–20,
  26–38, 184–8

Harman, Gilbert, 1 n.1, 13

identity, 16–17, 111–12, 175–82
indispensability thesis, 129, 169,
    173, 174, 176
    and transcendental arguments,
    171–2
intention, 60–1
    act versus non-act, 64–5
    belief constraints on, 96, 102
    revision of, 78

Johnson, Mark, 161–2
Josephs, Lawrence, 140

Kemp, Peter, 5 n. 11, 13
Kim, Jaegwon, 172

Lennon, Kathleen, 158–9
liberal ironist, 6, 42, 45
Lomasky, Loren, 115

Mackie, J. L., 3
Marcel, Gabriel, 3
    on commitment, 91 n. 6
    on intention, 63 n. 9
Mele, Alfred, 61, 94–6, 104
Merton, Robert, 189
Meursault (character in *The
    Stranger*), 54–5

Nagel, Thomas, 122–6
norm expressivism, 12, 188
    about science, 189–90

objectivity
    about value, 123, 170
    normative, 26–34
    weak versus strong, 128–9

parochialism, 34–6, 187
perspective, first- and third-person,
    22, 28, 169, 185
policy, 66–8, 74–8
    defeasibility of, 69–70
    flexibility of, 70–2
    revision of, 81

quasi-realism, 190–3

realism, moral, 1, 2–3, 176, 192
    and evaluative beliefs, 170, 176
    and pragmatism, 124
    indirect argument for, 2, 194–5
relativism, 36–8, 187–8
Ricoeur, Paul, 16, 17 n. 14, 150–3,
    159 n. 26
Robins, Michael, 99–101
Rorty, Richard, 6, 39–47, 50–2,
    183–4

self-conception, 82–3, 125, 127–8,
    173–4, 186
    and intrinsic desires, 135–8
    cognitive component of,
    138–43
self-transparency, 20–6, 176
self-understanding, 14–16, 32,
    108–10, 131, 144–6, 174,
    175–82
Shapin, Stevin and Schaffer,
    Simon, 189–90
Sturgeon, Nicholas, 1 n. 2, 13 n. 9
systems, rational versus irrational,
    24

Taylor, Charles, 3, 143–7, 168
Taylor, Gabriele, 108, 116–17
two-level thinking, 6, 51

value
  and stable desires, 138, 140–1
  impersonal, 119, 121, 127, 177
  personal, 119, 126, 177
Velleman, David, 15, 47, 67–8,
    134–45, 148–9, 164

Vermazen, Bruce, 64–5

Watson, Gary, 110
Wiggins, David, 117–18